The Psychology of Effective Studying

This book provides a vital guide for students to key study skills that are instrumental in success at university, covering time management, academic reading and note-taking, academic integrity, preparation of written assignments, teamwork and giving presentations.

With each chapter consisting of sub-sections that are titled with a single piece of fundamental advice, this is the perfect 'hit the ground running' resource for students embarking on their undergraduate studies. The book uses evidence from psychology to account for the basic errors that students make when studying, illuminating how they can be addressed simply and effectively. Creating an 'insider's guide' to the core requisite skills of studying at degree level, and using a combination of research and practical examples, the author conveys where students often go fundamentally wrong in their studying practices and provides clear and concise advice on how they can improve.

Written in a humorous and irreverent tone, and including illustrations and examples from popular culture, this is the ideal alternative and accessible study skills resource for students at undergraduate level, as well as any reader interested in how to learn more effectively.

Dr Paul Penn is a senior lecturer in psychology at the University of East London, UK. He has led several introduction to psychology and study skills modules and teaches a variety of topics at undergraduate and postgraduate level. He is a Chartered Psychologist and member of the British Psychological Society's Division of Academic, Researchers and Teachers in Psychology. He is also a fellow of the Higher Education Academy. His research focuses on learning and teaching practices. He also offers consultancy on using psychological research to improve learning and presentation skills. Visit www.drpaulpenn.com for more information.

The Psychology of Effective Studying

How to Succeed in Your Degree

Paul Penn

LONDON AND NEW YORK

First published 2020
by Routledge
2 Park Square, Milton Park, Abingdon, Oxon OX14 4RN

and by Routledge
52 Vanderbilt Avenue, New York, NY 10017

Routledge is an imprint of the Taylor & Francis Group, an informa business

British Library Cataloguing-in-Publication Data
A catalogue record for this book is available from the British Library

Library of Congress Cataloging-in-Publication Data
A catalog record has been requested for this book

ISBN: 978-1-138-57090-0 (hbk)
ISBN: 978-1-138-57092-4 (pbk)
ISBN: 978-0-203-70311-3 (ebk)

Typeset in Sabon
by Wearset Ltd, Boldon, Tyne and Wear

For my wife Eliana, now and forever.

Contents

Preface

Take care to get what you like, or you will be forced to like what you get.

George Bernard Shaw

Well that's great. One quote into my first book and I've just realised that I'll never say anything as concise and eloquent about studying as a playwright from a period of history where you could walk into a chemist and buy arsenic pills as a tonic for a dwindling libido. I guess it's not like you could have complained if the pills you've bought for being dead from the waist down end up making you, well, just plain dead. Anyway, I digress. The point (yes, there is one) is that wanting to do something is one thing, knowing how to do it effectively is quite another. Indulge me by identifying what the following statements all have in common: "I study psychology"; "I study engineering"; "I study physics"; and "I study English literature". The answer is, of course, that the verb 'study' always comes before the subject being studied. Accordingly, developing effective study skills should always come before developing subject-specific knowledge; they are the tools that empower a student to succeed, whatever their choice of degree subject. Unfortunately, both research and bitter experience suggest that this is far from invariably the case.

I'd like to tell you about an experience I had as a junior academic that provided the impetus for the development of my lectures on the application of psychology to the development of study skills. It was this material that served as the catalyst for this book. This tale also nicely illustrates just how predisposed even students of psychology can be to using study practices that are as effective as an ejector seat in a helicopter, but slower and more painful! It was a Friday morning (never a popular slot). I was giving a lecture that I thought was being well received. The students who had the Amazon.com or Candy Crush applications installed on their smart devices were happily oblivious to my efforts. Those who had yet to download these apps were smiling politely. About 30 minutes into the lecture a student raised their hand and asked if I could possibly slow down a bit as she "couldn't keep up with" me. To be fair to the student, I have been known to lecture at speeds approaching a Busta Rhymes rap when I'm enthusiastic about something. Joking aside, the student's appeal had stopped me in my tracks somewhat. A bit of investigation confirmed my suspicion. The student in question was trying to make notes on the lecture by taking down what I was saying as close to verbatim as possible. This was a redundant exercise given that the lecture was being audio- and video-recorded. I was reluctant to point this out lest I came across as horribly condescending. I was also concerned that I might have got fixated at being on camera and used my trusty laser pointer to facilitate an impromptu audition for the next *Star Wars* movie.

The student's request aroused a concern that they might not be the only one using the verbatim copying approach. So, I asked the class a simple question: "how many of you are taking notes that are basically excerpts of what I am saying?" Most of them put their hands up. I followed up by asking them to keep their hands up if they could explain the part they'd learned about how memory works that had informed this note-taking approach. All hands were abruptly lowered. Amazon.com orders were put on hold. I think some of the people playing Candy Crush might have even paused their game! I suggested to the class that budding psychologists trying to take verbatim notes from a lecture is a bit like budding chemists looking for a gas leak with a lit match; they should really know better!

Here's the moral of the above tale. If even students who are studying psychology are prone to fundamentally bad study practices, then those who won't get exposition of topics like attention, memory and decision making as part of their degree are even more vulnerable. Happily, there is a simple solution. Acquiring just a bit of knowledge about the application of some well-established findings in psychological research can empower you to study much more effectively. In doing this you become the master, as opposed to victim, of your grades at degree level. That's my main motivation in writing this book. I want to help you learn to study more effectively by encouraging you to adopt effective practices that are informed by psychological research. My other motivation in writing this book is to provide me with an outlet for my references to internet culture and rather sad obsession with the 1980s.

Be honest, how much effort have you previously invested in learning to study more effectively? I wouldn't blame you if you were not well disposed towards study skills tuition. In all honesty, as an undergraduate student, I certainly wasn't! Because of this, for the first year or so of my degree, I blundered along committing exactly the kind of errors in my approach to studying that I'm going to try and prevent you from making with this book. Back then, had you asked me about my disinclination to engage with study skills material, I would have rehearsed the following argument. I had received sufficiently good A-level grades to get onto the degree. I was there to study psychology (not education). Also, to be frank, I did not want precious lecture or tutorial time occupied by someone telling me how to do something that I'd been working on in formal education since the age of five. Enough already! As we shall see in Chapter I, my reluctance to develop my methods of studying was in no small part due to some basic errors in my perception of my abilities. Studying psychology had yet to inoculate me against these errors. Well, either that or I skipped the relevant classes! There was, however, another reason for my reluctance to engage with any skills-based material. Can you guess where I'm going with this?

I got a study skills guide as part of my induction into university and can honestly say that it changed my life. By that, I mean that I used it to prop up the PC monitor on my desk at home. Not exactly the use that the author had intended for their efforts, I'm sure. I just didn't get on with it I'm afraid, but it's hard to tell if that was a reflection on the book, or just my attitude towards study skills tuition generally. I'd like this book to serve as something other than a monitor stand for you. So, before I put my fingers to the keyboard to produce the proposal for this text, I had another look at my old study skills book and examined some of its contemporaries. I didn't find one that made me think: "if I'd had this as a text when I was a student, I might have spent some time back then practising what I now preach". This got me thinking about what I could do to create the kind of text that I would have used. The remainder of this preface is devoted to me outlining what I've done differently to make this book a useful go-to resource for you. In doing this, I'm going to avoid being critical about other study skills texts. Instead, I'm going to tell you about the positive things I shall endeavour to do in this book. This approach has two advantages. First, it will be less of a turn off for you. Second, it negates the need for me to take Brazilian jiu-jitsu lessons on the off chance I bump into any authors of previously published study skills texts.

The most important part of the mission statement for this book is to ensure that, wherever possible, the advice offered is transparently informed by psychological research. The instruction I offer will not be based on well-intentioned pontificating around my anecdotal experience of being a student or lecturer. This is your assurance the guidance offered within these pages has a good chance of proving helpful if you implement it. I'm going to be using some key psychological research to illuminate effective study practice. However, this is not a psychology textbook. As such, I won't be filling each chapter with fully comprehensive reviews of the literature on particular topics. The research that I do cover will, by necessity, be limited, selective and used in an illustrative fashion. At various points I will indicate more comprehensive references for anyone that wishes to do further reading. This may sound like a convenient way to insulate myself from a barrage of comments from my peers to the effect of: "a-ha, but you didn't cover study x, y, z". That's because it is! Also, an author must leave something for the second edition *winks*.

On the subject of scope, this book is not a completely exhaustive skills resource. It doesn't contain any chapters dedicated to things like adapting to university life (hint: make finding out when happy hour is on at the student bar a priority). Instead, I've tried to distil things down to the most fundamental topics and keep the amount of advice on each of them manageable and easy to implement. You will note from the contents page that I'm covering the core requisite skills of studying at degree level in eight chapters. Each chapter concludes with a summary that reiterates the key advice that will make your studies more efficient, productive and enjoyable. You can use these chapter summaries as a quick reference once you've read the book. Yes, this does mean that you could just skip to the chapter summaries if you only want the abridged tips and tricks of the trade, as it were. However, you needn't worry about your already significant course reading load being compounded by a study skills text of a size equivalent to *War and Peace*. Sorry if this makes you feel a bit cheated, but I have a life (potentially) and so should you. The downside of its relative brevity is that this book won't make anywhere near as good a monitor stand height enhancer as would have otherwise been the case.

Third, and finally, I'll admit that the promise of some academically informed study skills advice doesn't sound like a barrel of laughs. Let's be honest, in the entertainment stakes it's unlikely that any skills text is going to compete with the latest *50 Shades of Grey* novel. If you're interested, Christian Grey and I do have one thing in common: we both have a pleasure room. Admittedly, mine is less S&M gear and more Hornby 00 railway, but the effect is the same: only a special lady could look inside that room without immediately running away. A study skills text may not be as intrinsically appealing as a racy novel. If you think it is, I'd suggest that you probably need therapy. However, it should at least be marginally more engaging than the assembly instructions for an Ikea wardrobe! Consequently, you won't find an abundance of bullet points, fact sheets, diagrams or checklists in this book. Instead, I've broken all of the chapters down into sub-sections, each of which is a manageable size and has its own specific message. I'll be using deliberately esoteric headings, questions, assorted quotations, various references to popular culture and irreverence to try and keep things stimulating and challenging. If I don't succeed then, unlike the Ikea wardrobe assembly manual, at least this book doesn't come with a bag of fittings for you to lose behind the sofa.

I have one request to make of you as you work through this book. You'll notice that I use key advice to delineate sub-sections within each chapter. When you see a piece of key advice, I'd like you to read the next sub-section of text with a view to answering the following simple question. "How is this key advice informed by the text that follows it?" Before you move on to the next piece of key advice and its associated section of text, I'd like you to think of an answer to that question. That's it! There are no right or wrong responses. The important thing is that you think of an answer that makes sense to you and that you can explain it! If you can find somewhere to write down your response, all the better! The rationale for me asking you to do this will become clear as the book progresses. For now, trust me on this one: it's worth the effort!

I hope you enjoy this book and, above all else, I hope it helps you to enjoy your studies. I wish you every success.

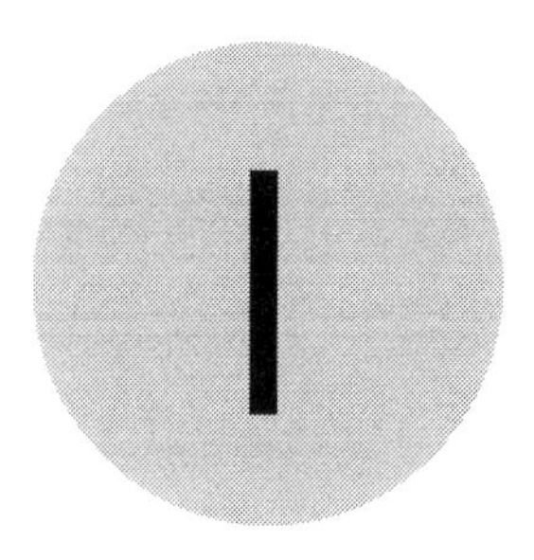

Introduction

Metacognition, the foundation of successful studying (or at least how to avoid being 'that person' on the TV talent show)

Nothing is so difficult as not deceiving oneself.
Ludwig Wittgenstein

1

Key advice: the least skilled are often the most deluded about their ability

You know that look, don't you? That one that Ant and Dec give the camera on *Britain's Got Talent* just before something painful happens. This act will usually have been preceded by several hopefuls that were entertaining, but probably less destined for Broadway, Hollywood than Butlins, Bognor Regis. "This is Doreen from Doncaster" smirks Ant. "She's going to give us a moving rendition of My Heart Will Go On from the feature film *Titanic*", exclaims Dec (who is visibly having trouble containing the giggles). As Doreen shuffles onto the stage living rooms across the nation think in unison: "This is going to be awful. Turn it up!" Of course, poor Doreen murders the song and throughout the country pet dogs howl and hearing aids feedback. Some people even contemplate shoving screwdrivers in their ears when they realise that their fingers aren't up to the job of muting the assault on their hearing. Then it ends and all falls silent for the verdicts from the judges. These are only marginally less painful than the performance. It's OK because this was clearly a joke, right? No one could be that bad and not realise it. Doreen just wanted five minutes of TV exposure to generate some infamy. Mission accomplished. Well played Doreen; many thanks for the car crash TV moment. Except she's not smiling. She looks surprised at the verdicts and her expression betrays indignation and hurt feelings. At this point, people on settees across the land look at each other and say: "It's like she's only just realising that she can't sing a note! How could she not have known this already?" In academic terms, the *Britain's Got Talent* moment often occurs in the examination room and is a more private, but no less dramatic, crisis. It was brutally (and beautifully) concisely summed up by a piece of graffiti etched into an exam desk I was seated at for my GCSE geography paper back in 1992. It read simply: "Oh Sh*t! There goes college, 1992." If you're currently smiling because you relate to that sentiment, then consider yourself busted. This means that, on at least one occasion, you did an academic version of Doreen on *Britain's Got Talent*. The question is: why?

You will probably have heard the old maxim that the first step on the road to recovery is acknowledging you're sick. In the same way, the first step on the road to improving your study skills is acknowledging that there is room for improvement. This means that you must be able to effectively monitor and evaluate your current level of attainment. In psychology, we refer to this as metacognitive ability. If your metacognition isn't veridical then your academic development is fundamentally handicapped right from the outset. Why would you spend time working on a skill if you think you are already good enough at it? Kruger and Dunning (1999) provided the seminal paper in our understanding of metacognitive ability. In their first experiment they asked psychology undergraduates to review a series of jokes that had been pre-rated for humour by a panel of professional comedians. They were asked to provide their own ratings for how funny they thought the jokes were without seeing the prior evaluations from the professionals. So, the performance measure for the participants was the extent to which their judgements of humour corresponded with that of the panel of professional comedians. After they had given their ratings, participants were then asked to predict how well they thought they could judge the quality of the jokes in relation to their peers. They did this by giving a percentile estimate of their position within the group of participants. For example, saying '50%' would mean that they thought their performance put them in the middle of their group. Overall, the results indicated that the students over-estimated their ability in relation to their peers. However, that was not the headline finding. A rather cruel twist emerged when the data was examined from the least competent at rating the quality of the jokes (i.e. the bottom 25% of the group). These individuals exhibited the biggest gap between their estimated and actual levels of ability relative to their peers. In other words, the more incompetent they were, the more deluded they were about their competence. Consider yourself forewarned. If you're at an open microphone night in a comedy club and a psychologist decides to share some of their material, hit the bar; you won't be missing much.

At this point you might question whether the results of a study examining the relationship between perceived and actual ability at rating humour translate to more academic contexts. Unfortunately, in the very same study, Kruger and Dunning found an identical pattern of results in tests of logical and grammatical ability. Over four experiments they reported that participants whose objective performance put them in the bottom 25% of a group gave subjective estimates of their ability that placed themselves near the top third of that group. OK, so that's not a great omen, but it was just one series of experiments, right? I'm afraid not. The Dunning–Kruger effect, as it has become known, has been very well replicated over two decades. It's the chief villain of the peace when it comes to metacognition. It doesn't just affect an individual's estimate of their performance relative to a group of peers. Researchers have also found that it applies when people are asked to predict their own attainment in isolation. So, it also shows up when you ask people to predict their score on a test. The least competent individuals exhibit the greatest discrepancies between their anticipated score and their actual score.

At this point I'm hoping it's obvious why any book that aspires to help you develop your study skills needs to start off with the Dunning–Kruger effect. It's the most fundamental metacognitive barrier you'll face on the road to improving your competence at studying. It can only be addressed with concerted effort to get the very kind of help and instruction that it lulls you into thinking you don't need. If, having read the above, you're concerned enough to keep reading, fantastic. If you're still convinced you don't need any help and have only read this far because your smart phone battery has died, then prepare for some discomfort.

Delusion comes in many forms, usually quite flattering

2

Key advice: having information available to you gives you an illusory impression about how much of it you've absorbed

We're over the first hurdle to this book being useful to you. You're still reading, which means you're receptive to the suggestion that you might benefit from some study skills instruction. Unfortunately, the Dunning–Kruger effect isn't the only metacognitive quirk that can condemn us to being perpetually dumber than we should be. With that in mind, we now run into a second issue, quite closely related to the first. Let me put it to you by asking a question. How good do you think people are at judging whether they will be able to recall a piece of information? Koriat and Bjork (2005) were interested in just this question. They also wanted to establish whether people could spot features about the way that information is presented that can determine their likelihood of being able to recall it. For example, let's say I present you with the following word pair: 'Fire' and 'Blaze'. Then, following a period of time, I show you one of those two words and ask you to recall the word it had been paired with. How confident (think of a percentage) would you be in recalling that word? Now, would that figure differ according to which of the two words I used as the cue and which served as the required answer? This scenario corresponds with the basic experimental set up of Koriat and Bjork. In their experiment, participants were asked to memorise a series of pairs of words. Following the presentation of each pair they were asked to indicate the probability that they would recall the second word when presented with the first. This is known as a judgement of learning. Here's where the clever experimental manipulation occurred. Think of the word pair I gave you above. How many words can you think of as being associated with the word 'fire'? Quite a few, I'd imagine: 'man', 'fighter', 'exit', 'axe', 'escape', 'engine', 'extinguisher', 'storm', 'fly'. Be honest, how far would the word 'blaze' have come down that list? The experimenters called this a backwards pairing, i.e. the target word was not likely to be elicited by the prompt word. In contrast, how many words can you think of as being associated with the word 'blaze'? Not that many, I'd guess. In fact, the word 'fire' would probably be the first, if not the only, word that came to mind. This was referred to as a forwards pairing, i.e. the target word was very likely to be elicited by the prompt word. Of course, the likelihood of remembering a target word under forwards pairing is much greater than backwards pairing. Do you think the participants in this experiment realised this and gave their judgements of learning accordingly? Did you? Overall, the participants gave judgements of learning that were equivalent for the forwards and backwards word pairing conditions. However, as you might now expect, their recall performance was significantly worse for the backwards pairings.

The illusory impression of learning evident in Koriat and Bjork's study was caused by the participants not anticipating the discrepancy between the conditions of learning and those of testing. They didn't realise that although the forwards and backwards word pairings appeared equally easy to remember when both words were present, only one of the words would be present upon testing. Therefore, they didn't take account of how readily each word in the pair generated the other word in making their judgement of learning estimates. An analogous judgement of learning error can easily occur when you are reading your source materials and considering the likelihood you will remember what you have read. Things that seem obvious or easy when you have the questions and the answers are not so easy when you're only left with the questions. Just like forward versus backward word pairings, answers generate questions more readily than questions generate answers. You might want to keep this in mind next time you're *sure* you'll remember something you've just read for that forthcoming test!

3

Key advice: being able to remember something is not an indication that you understand it

So, people aren't necessarily great at judging whether they have committed bits of information to memory. However, you might argue that this is a bit pedantic and that what matters more is how accurately people can judge whether they have understood the gist of something? OK, let's go with that line of thinking, but first it's worth pausing to consider how you might set up a parsimonious experiment to test comprehension. How do you ascertain whether someone understands a piece of information, as opposed to just whether they can recall it? Well, one approach is to see if they understand the meaning of the information by deliberately manipulating it so that it makes less sense. An easy way of doing this is to use contradiction. To spot contradictions you need to understand the information well enough to know that some of its constituent parts can't logically co-exist. For example, let's say you read a piece of text that claims that an individual was born on a particular date in one sentence, but then gives a different date in the following sentence. If you had understood that text, you would spot the contradiction because you know that it's not possible for someone to have two dates of birth. Therefore, spotting contradictions is a useful index of whether someone has understood a piece of information. Glenberg, Wilkinson and Epstein (1982) conducted an experiment that used contradictions in text to establish how well people made judgements about whether they had understood what they had just read. Participants were asked to read a passage at their own pace and as many times as they liked. They were told that they would be tested on the content and that the text could contain one or more contradictions that they should search for as they were reading. The participants were instructed to note down the numbers of any lines of text that contained contradictions and briefly indicate why they thought the information was contradictory. Having read the passage until they were content, the participants were then asked to judge how well they understood the text on a four-point scale and asked two true/false questions about the contents of the passage. They repeated this procedure for other passages of text, covering different topics. Each passage was either one or three paragraphs in length and, unbeknownst to the participants, there was contradictory information in every text. The contradictory information always appeared in the same place: the last two adjacent sentences right at the end of the piece. If a participant claimed to understand a passage of text and then correctly identified the contradictions present, then their perception of their understanding was accurate. However, if they claimed that they understood the text, but didn't spot the contradictions then they were exhibiting what psychologists refer to as an illusion of knowing. In other words, they thought they had understood the material when, actually, they hadn't! Remember, these were undergraduate psychology students who had been explicitly warned about contradictory information and told that they would be tested. They had to read short passages of text, where the contradictions were always in the same place and they got as long as they wanted to read and re-read each passage. Short of highlighting the offending text, the experimenters couldn't have done much more to tip the odds in favour of the students. So, what proportion of them do you think reported understanding the text, but missed the contradictions present? Go on, have a guess. Would you believe that up to 51% of them reported that they understood the text well, but missed glaring contradictions?

Having an inflated sense of the extent to which you understand something is not helpful at the best of times. Anyone who has previously handed in a piece of coursework and confidently expected it to be met with a Nobel prize only to be horrified when they get the academic equivalent of a Golden Raspberry will attest to this. However, when illusions of knowing compromise your benefit from study skills material designed to teach you how to get good grades, it's particularly damaging. For now, it suffices to say that all those times you binge read a 30-page book chapter and gave yourself a pat on the back for your Zen-like powers of comprehension might not have been entirely warranted. Still, hindsight is 20:20, right? Speaking of which…

4

Key advice: knowing something and implementing what you know are not the same thing

We now turn to the last major obstacle to you benefiting from this book that I'm going to cover in this introduction. I'll illustrate this in practice by using the TV game show *Who Wants to Be a Millionaire?* Here's the scenario: the contestant is up to, say, £64,000 and then gets a question that you are convinced you know the answer to. They, on the other hand, do not share your confidence. Your immediate reaction is probably to scoff and think: "Come on, this is an easy one." The contestant asks the audience, but they come back with a completely equivocal response. This makes you even more incredulous. Desperate, the contestant then phones a friend who turns out to be similarly stumped. At this point, you're shouting the answer at the TV (like they can hear you!). If you aren't watching the TV on your own, it's almost guaranteed that some smart ass in the room will say: "The question is only easy when you know the answer." At this point you'll dismissively say: "Well, duh!" Nonetheless, you'll remain quietly incredulous at the hapless contestant's plight. Are they really the one who is being clueless in this scenario? Or could it be the person who is incredulous that anyone might not be able to answer the question about the mechanisms of coastal erosion? I'll give you a hint: it's you! Sorry! Don't be too hard on yourself, you're just demonstrating another well-known metacognitive failing called the hindsight bias. As it turns out, we tend to view things that we know as being obvious/easy because we can't, or won't, take a perspective detached from our own knowledge. Fischhoff and Beyth (1975) demonstrated this in a classic experiment. They examined the difference between judgements of the probability of an outcome before an event (predictive judgement) and after the event (postdictive judgement). Their experiment revolved around an imminent visit to China by President Nixon. They postulated certain possible outcomes such as: "The USA will establish a permanent diplomatic mission in Peking, but not grant diplomatic recognition" (p. 6) and asked the participants to rate the probability of the outcome occurring. A couple of weeks following Nixon's visit, the participants returned and were asked to recall their predictive estimates of each of the outcomes occurring. They were also tested on their knowledge about whether each outcome had occurred. Knowing an outcome should not affect the recall of the predictive judgement of its probability. The outcome was not known at the time of making the predictive judgement. Therefore, there is no need to adjust that predictive judgement irrespective of whether it turned out to be accurate. Be that as it may, the experiment found that for outcomes that were believed to have occurred, postdictive judgements were higher than predictive judgements. Conversely, for outcomes that were not believed to have occurred postdictive judgements were lower than predictive judgements. The participants were systematically adjusting their recollection of the predictive estimates they had given to create the impression that they 'knew it all along'.

The hindsight bias can be a thorny issue with respect to study skills. As an example, whilst reading the last few pages, have you thought that any of the information being imparted was nothing new and/or obvious? However, what if I now asked you to explain each of the metacognitive issues covered thus far and, more importantly, suggest what might be done to alleviate them? Therein lies the problem: if we recall knowledge as being easier/obvious/more predictable than it was at the time of learning, then we tend to stop engaging with it at a superficial level. This tends to beget over-confidence and puts the brakes on further learning. Be honest, have you ever bunked off a study skills class or skipped over study skills course materials believing in earnest that there can't be much in there that you didn't already know? With any luck, you're starting to see that the Dunning–Kruger effect, the illusion of knowing and the hindsight bias are not disparate concepts. They are each part of an inter-related suite of metacognitive flaws that can handicap the development of your study skills right from the outset. So, what can you do about this?

The enemy within

5

Key advice: many students unknowingly use ineffectual study strategies that make them more vulnerable to metacognitive errors

To best understand what we might do to minimise the risk of falling foul of the metacognitive errors referred to previously, let's quickly revisit the Dunning–Kruger effect and consider what causes it. Think about the consequences of being incompetent (not exactly a pleasant thing to do, I know). The first is obvious: you won't perform well under conditions when the applicable ability is scrutinised. The second consequence is more insidious: you won't realise that you won't perform well, because you don't know what constitutes good performance or how to achieve it. As far as you're concerned your level of performance is already adequate! This is a gloriously cruel vicious circle: it's the same knowledge and skills that you need to be good at something that you also need to evaluate how good you are. So, what do you do to break the circle? Well, in answering this, let's put the spotlight on you for a moment. What I'd like you to do is get a scrap of paper and quickly note down what kind of strategies you use when studying. Then, you should rank order them from the most frequently used at the top of the list, to the least frequently used at the bottom of the list. Quickly do that before you read on. Now, be honest, did your list include re-reading as either the most, or one of the most, frequently used study strategies? If the answer is 'yes' then you're in good company. Karpicke, Butler and Roediger III (2009) asked a sample of undergraduates to do what I've just asked you to do. They found that 83% of students reported using re-reading and 54% of them identified it as their number one study method. Now, back to your list of preferred study methods. If you included practice testing on your list, was it below re-reading in terms of the frequency with which you use it? If the answer is 'yes' then, once again, you're in good company. Karpicke and his colleagues found that only 10% of students reported using practice testing (referred to as retrieval practice) and only 1% reported it as their top ranked study strategy. Even when given a forced choice response with practice tests as an option alongside re-reading and 'other study practice', only 18% indicated a willingness to use it. "So what?" I hear you say: if students prefer re-reading over practice testing as a study strategy then what's the problem? Well, which of these two strategies do you think would be more effective in combating errors in metacognition? If the penny hasn't dropped yet, think about the following question. What is the one thing that the studies we've reviewed on the Dunning–Kruger effect, illusion of knowing and hindsight bias had in common? They all involved some form of test. You may think you're great at something, but if that score on the test (i.e. the evidence) says otherwise then that's your metacognitive wake up call, so to speak.

6

Key advice: having a fixed view of intelligence promotes the use of ineffective study strategies and is not conducive with learning

There is nothing remotely novel about advocating the value of practice testing in learning. Literature indicating that repeated self-testing (i.e. retrieval practice) of material produces superior recall to an equivalent period spent re-studying has existed since the early part of the twentieth century. This well-established finding is called the testing effect. Look, I didn't name it, OK? There has been something of a resurgence of interest in the testing effect over the last decade and support for its use is pretty much unequivocal. So, if it's so great, why aren't more students using it? Well, one explanation is that students are simply unaware of its effectiveness. In the study by Karpicke and his colleagues only 8% of the students indicated that they thought it would be an effective learning aid. Karpicke and Roediger (2008) manipulated the approach used by students in studying material (re-reading versus retrieval practice). They demonstrated that predictions of subsequent performance on a delayed test from the students were similar between these learning conditions.

However, their actual performance was superior in the retrieval practice condition. In other words, even when students are instructed to use retrieval practice, its value is not necessarily self-evident.

Some of the reluctance to use self-testing might be due to ignorance. However, it might also be the case that our notions of learning and intelligence affect which study strategies we elect to engage with. Ehrlinger and Shain (2014) point to research that has examined student theories of intelligence. They distinguish between an incremental and an entity view of intelligence. In the incremental view, intelligence is seen as something that can be developed. In the entity view, intelligence is seen as fixed and something you're stuck with. Not surprisingly, the view of intelligence that a student takes affects their goals. Those who view intelligence as something that can be developed tend to adopt mastery goals and focus mainly on knowledge/skill acquisition. In contrast, those who think that intelligence is not something that they can cultivate tend to adopt performance goals, which focus more on avoiding failure and managing the impression of intelligence. These goals influence the study strategies that a student uses. Sure enough, it's the students who exhibit the fixed view of intelligence who tend to be the ones that are motivated by performance goals. These students are least inclined to use study strategies, such as retrieval practice, that entail feedback to the effect of: "You've not got this yet." No prizes for guessing what this does to their metacognition. You'll have heard the adage that "if you go looking for trouble, you find it". Well, in terms of academic success, it's not looking for trouble that tends to cause the biggest problems.

Summary

Preaching to the (hopefully now) converted

Let's summarise the main points covered in this chapter about metacognitive errors and how you can mitigate their impact when studying.

- Your perceived and actual levels of competence can be disparate. It's the least competent that usually hold the most exaggerated view of their ability (the Dunning–Kruger effect). This is a huge obstacle to your development. Therefore, you should formulate your impression of your learning based on what you can demonstrate you know, not on what you believe you know.

- You can get inflated impressions of the amount of information you have absorbed when the source of that information is in front of you. We often disregard the importance of the presence of sources in our judgements of how much we know. Therefore, it's wise to avoid having source material to hand when trying to assess the extent to which you have committed information to memory.
- You are liable to have an inflated sense of the degree to which you understand something that you have read. We often fail to spot signs that our comprehension isn't sound by, for example, missing glaring contradictions in a text. Therefore, you should not use your ability to recall information as a proxy for a measure of whether you understand it.
- It's easy for you to look back on knowledge you have gained as something you've known all along, or retrospectively rate the acquisition of that knowledge as being much easier than it was. Consequently, it's wise to reflect on more concrete metrics of ease of learning, such as the time required to acquire previous knowledge. Do not rely on your current impression of how obvious acquired knowledge seems when thinking about future learning.
- It's likely that you're not extensively using the strategy of retrieval practice (self-testing) when you study. This is the study strategy that research has shown to be most effective in promoting accurate metacognition. Start looking at self-testing as a tool of learning. Remember that the information you get from testing yourself is an integral part of learning, whether it's flattering or not! As we shall see in Chapters III and VIII, testing is your closest ally when studying, not your enemy.

Accurate metacognition is critical for successful studying. Unfortunately, we are all vulnerable to metacognitive errors that lull us into thinking that our approaches to learning are more effective than they really are. This makes us unreceptive to advice on how to study more effectively and reluctant to engage with sources of support. To this end, much of this chapter has served as a 'warning shot across the bows' so you are more receptive to the guidance offered on effective study practices contained within the following chapters. You also now have some preliminary advice on how to engage with this (or any text) that should help you avoid falling foul of the metacognitive errors we've referred to.

I'd like to end this chapter with some words of encouragement. As you progress through this book, you might get a dawning sense that your efforts to improve the way you learn are making you feel dumber rather than smarter. If so, don't be discouraged! This is what it feels like when metacognitive errors start losing their hold on you. Progress, more often than not, involves a degree of discomfort. In any case, by now you should be suspicious of anything that seems easy on reflection!

References

Ehrlinger, J. & Shain, E. A. (2014). How accuracy in students' self-perceptions relates to success in learning. In V. A. Benassi, C. E. Overson & C. M. Hakala (Eds.). *Applying science of learning in education: Infusing psychological science into the Curriculum*. Society for the Teaching of Psychology. Retrieved from http://teachpsych.org/ebooks/asle2014/index.php.

Fischhoff, B. & Beyth, R. (1975). I knew it would happen: Remembered probabilities of once–future things. *Organizational Behavior and Human Performance, 13*(1), 1–16.

Glenberg, A. M., Wilkinson, A. C. & Epstein, W. (1982). The illusion of knowing: Failure in the self-assessment of comprehension. *Memory & Cognition, 10*(6), 597–602.

Kruger, J. & Dunning, D. (1999). Unskilled and unaware of it: How difficulties in recognizing one's own incompetence lead to inflated self-assessments. *Journal of Personality and Social Psychology, 77*(6), 1121–1134.

Karpicke, J. D., Butler, A. C. & Roediger III, H. L. (2009). Metacognitive strategies in student learning: Do students practise retrieval when they study on their own? *Memory, 17*(4), 471–479.

Karpicke, J. D. & Roediger, H. L. (2008). The critical importance of retrieval for learning. *Science, 319*(5865), 966–968.

Koriat, A. & Bjork, R. A. (2005). Illusions of competence in monitoring one's knowledge during study. *Journal of Experimental Psychology: Learning, Memory, and Cognition, 31*(2), 187–194.

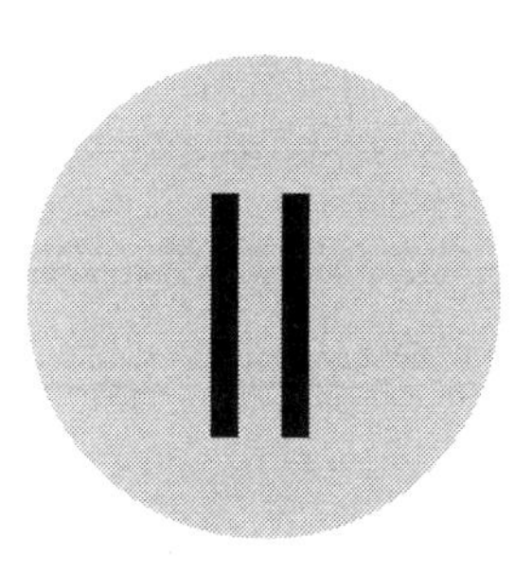

Conquering procrastination

Why it's so hard to DO IT. JUST DO IT!

In the universe great acts are made up of small deeds.
Lao Tzu

1

Key advice: understanding procrastination is the key to managing your time more effectively

If you recognise the Shia LaBeouf "DO IT" line in the title of this chapter, then you know the YouTube video I'm referring to. Be honest, when you first saw it should you have been getting on with work at the time? Me too! Oh, the irony: using a video intended to encourage you to stop putting things off to put off doing work! I'll be honest: this chapter was originally going to follow a very different format. I was going to compose a more conventional time management and organisation chapter. I was going to tell you about how important it was to understand and reflect on your usage of time, to identify your deadlines and be proactive in preparing for them. I was going to advise you to make contingency plans for when life just refused to play ball with your carefully constructed Gantt charts. I was going to … right up to the point where I looked at my own carefully created Gantt chart for the development of the draft of this book. Even though I had only just started writing Chapter II, I was already a month behind my intended schedule! What happened? Had anyone died? Not that I knew of. Had I won the lottery? Here's a hint: I continued writing this book! Had I been fired, made homeless, divorced, been stranded in a remote location and forced to live rough Bear Grylls style? Well, I did have to give a hotel I stayed at one weekend only three stars on Trip Advisor because the bed was hard and the food was bland. Other than those very first world problems I don't have any real excuses. Sure, a new term had started at university, which is always a bit chaotic. However, I had planned for this. I had even prepared for some lectures over my summer vacation to clear the decks so I could make progress with the book at the start of the new term. If I'm honest, this was anything other than the first time my best laid time management plans have gone to pot in my academic career. Tick the following examples off mentally as you recognise them. There were the notes I'd promised to make time to produce after my lectures, but didn't. That test I planned to revise for a good two weeks before the exam, but never quite got around to it. That essay that I'd scheduled to complete a full couple of days before the submission deadline, but ended up working on late into the night before it was due in. If none of the above examples resonate with you then I suggest that you, Sir/Madam, are: (a) fibbing, or (b) fibbing! Why do we do this to ourselves? Do we not learn from bitter experience? Maybe we are just a bunch of masochists that secretly enjoy making life infinitely more unpleasant for ourselves than it needs to be? Perhaps indolence is an integral part of the human condition? Alternatively, maybe it's because we don't really understand that most pernicious obstacle to seeing through our intentions and plans in a timely fashion: procrastination.

Rozental and Carlbring (2014) captured the essence of procrastination very concisely by defining it as: "One's voluntary delay of an intended course of action, despite being worse off as a result of that delay" (p. 1488). Procrastination is by no means an uncommon issue and students seem to be particularly vulnerable. It's not unusual to find reports that puts the prevalence of problematic procrastination in undergraduates as being 70% or above (e.g. Klassen, Krawchuk & Rajani, 2008). Meta-analysis of the research indicate that procrastination tends to be associated with negative academic outcomes (e.g. Kim & Seo, 2015) not to mention increased stress and anxiety (e.g. Krause & Freund, 2014).

Here's the issue with most advice on time management: it's all well and good knowing how to plan your time, but for a plan to work you must see it through. Procrastination is the enemy of seeing your plans through. Therefore, knowing how to recognise and deal with procrastination is a prerequisite for improving your time management. So, in this chapter I'm going to help you understand why we procrastinate and what you can do to avoid it. Procrastination is a rather more complex foe than you might have imagined. I could write an entire book on it, but probably wouldn't get around to it ... Boom, Boom!

Procrastination: first, know the enemy of time management

Appropriately enough, psychologists, economists, sociologists and philosophers have only really got around to making significant in-roads into understanding procrastination in the last 30 years or so. However, over that time several themes have emerged in research that addresses the likelihood and extent of procrastination occurring. It's worth having a quick look at these themes so you can see the components of what Pychyl (2013) referred to as the procrastination puzzle. If we understand how this puzzle works, we can solve it.

2

Key advice: you are more likely to procrastinate when you doubt your ability to get something done

You won't be surprised to learn that research has indicated that an individual's belief in their ability to get something done affects the likelihood that they will procrastinate. If you expect to be successful, you tend to crack on with things in a timely manner. On the other hand, if you harbour doubts that you will be able to complete a task successfully then the tendency to put it off will be that much greater. Psychologists refer to this as perceived self-efficacy and meta-analysis of the literature indicates that it is a reliable predictor of procrastination (e.g. van Eerde, 2003). The insidious thing about depleted perceived self-efficacy is that it tends to be self-reinforcing. If you don't feel up to completing a task, you won't engage with it optimally and this will have a deleterious effect on your performance. The consequence of your reduced performance is likely to be a negative (or at least a less positive) task outcome. You'll remember this negative outcome the next time you encounter a task that makes you doubt your self-efficacy. This memory further compromises your perceived self-efficacy and exerts an even greater toll on your engagement with, and performance, on the task at hand. Psychologists refer to this as a self-fulfilling prophecy. You might call it a vicious circle. I'd suggest that no one has ever described it more succinctly than Henry Ford when he said: "Whether you believe you can do a thing or not, you are right." This is fitting given that he is often credited as being the father of the moving assembly line where procrastination would have been most difficult and certainly not have gone unnoticed.

3

Key advice: boredom is an invitation to procrastinate

Newsflash: the likelihood that someone will procrastinate is affected by the characteristics of the task. Tasks that are deemed aversive are more likely to beget procrastination than tasks that are deemed less aversive. Hardly rocket science, granted. Has anyone in the history of humanity enjoyed putting out the recycling? However, task aversiveness is about more than just the intrinsic pleasantness of the task, it's also about the anticipated outcomes of the task, or incentives associated with that task. Doing the recycling doesn't seem quite so bad if it frees up the kitchen for having your mates over for beer, pizza and exchanges of liberal innuendo. Err, I mean a glass of wine, a cheeseboard and a robust discussion of metaphysics! As Lay (1992) argued, defining the aversiveness of a task must consider the interactions between individual and task characteristics that give rise to things like excitement, boredom or uncertainty. However, which of these person-task characteristics are most strongly associated with task aversiveness and conducive to procrastination? Also, are such characteristics as important at the beginning of a task as they are at its conclusion? These were the questions that Blunt and Pychyl (2000) were interested in. They asked participants to generate lists of personal projects and rate each of them in respect of task dimensions such as the control they had over the task, the uncertainty associated with the task and how much fun it was. Participants were also asked to rate tasks in terms of their aversiveness and indicate the extent to which they felt they had procrastinated in doing them. These ratings were taken for each task at the following stages: conception; planning; execution; and completion. Three task dimensions emerged as being most strongly predictive of reported levels of task aversiveness and procrastination. See if you can figure out what they were? Go on, take a wild guess! Ahem, drumroll please! In order of villainy, the task dimensions most strongly associated with viewing a task as aversive and conducive to slacking off were boredom, resentment and frustration. This was true of all stages of the task's lifespan; from inception to completion.

4

Key advice: your personality is not to blame for procrastination, but you might have certain traits that make you more vulnerable to it

You know, of course, that revising is going to pay off in the long run. However, in the here and now that re-run of season one of *Friends* seems to be a much more rewarding use of your time. Season one contains the episode where Joey flunks yet another audition because he was watching TV with Chandler when he should have been reading his lines. Silly Joey! Maybe Joey is just the kind of person who prefers to do things on a whim, be spontaneous, live for the moment? Maybe there is a procrastination-prone personality? That idea sounds plausible. Blaming your personality for procrastination would certainly be a most convenient way to rationalise it. However, meta-analyses (e.g. Steel, 2007) of research on procrastination suggests that there isn't a procrastination-prone personality per se. It's more accurate to say that there are components of certain personality traits more strongly associated with the tendency to procrastinate than others. A component of the personality trait of extraversion, i.e. impulsiveness, is a solid predictor of procrastination. Similarly, components of the personality trait of conscientiousness such as distractibility and self-control are reliably related to the likelihood of procrastination. Taken together, these components constitute an individual's sensitivity to delay. Individuals who have a high sensitivity to delay are impulsive, distractible and have low self-control. Individuals with a low sensitivity to delay are cautious, focused and self-disciplined. OK, so still no surprises thus far. However, my decision not to tackle time management advice by just advocating that you create a timetable is probably starting to make grim sense.

5

Key advice: we prefer doing things that don't make us wait for a reward

Ever noticed how the pleasure associated with procrastination tends to diminish the closer you get to the deadline for whatever it was that you should have been getting on with? Simultaneously, the benefits of doing (and consequences of not doing) what you should have been getting on with suddenly seem that much greater than when you first started slacking off. There is a technical name for this: hyperbolic discounting. It refers to a tendency to undervalue (and therefore put off) actions that contribute to distant goals with bigger rewards in favour of proximal goals with smaller rewards. Of course, as the deadline for that bigger goal gets closer, we start to value its reward much more and lament not having acted towards achieving it sooner. Most of us recognise the "Oh crap!" moment when it dawns on us that watching yet another series from our favourite box-set will do nothing to offset six weeks of neglected revision. Now we have some serious self-reprimanding to do! Oh, and we should probably start that revision for the exam that is taking place in LESS THAN TWO DAYS!! Hyperbolic discounting was clearly demonstrated in undergraduate students by Schouwenburg and Groenewoud (2001). They took measures of self-reported motivation to study and resistance to temptation associated with five common study distractions (e.g. an unexpected invitation to go out with friends in the evening). They also monitored the hours the students spent studying over a 12-week (84 days) build up to a course examination. Sure enough, motivation to study, resistance to distractors and studying hours all increased with proximity to the exam. Here's the more alarming thing: they didn't increase steeply until the last 14 days of a study period of 84 days. Furthermore, the steepest rises in motivation, resistance to distraction and hours of study occurred just a few days before the exam. "A-ha", I hear the astute and awake among you cry. "This is self-report data. Does actual studying behaviour also follow these trends?" Yes, it certainly appears to! Howell, Watson, Powell and Buro (2006) asked undergraduate students to provide measures of self-reported procrastination, perceived academic control, implementation intention and say-do correspondence. They compared these measures with the timing of the coursework submissions from the students. As expected, the number of submissions increased (at an increasing rate) as the deadline drew closer. This was particularly pronounced for students who identified themselves as procrastinators. That's an unfortunate thing about procrastination: simply being aware of it isn't a defence against it.

Thus far we've identified four things that make it more likely that you'll reach for the TV remote control rather than your lecture notes. These are: perceived efficacy; person-task characteristics; sensitivity to delay; and timing of rewards and punishments. However, the challenge for understanding procrastination has not been identifying individual explanations for its occurrence. I doubt any of the outcomes of the research previously touched on came as a surprise to you. In fact, at several points, you may have even thought: "Well, duh! I could have told you that without the research." However, it may have also occurred to you that you rarely perceive yourself as unlikely to be able to do a task, yet still put it off. Maybe you don't think of yourself as a particularly impulsive person generally, yet still procrastinate terribly when studying? Does this mean that there is a problem with any of the explanations given thus far? No, it just means that there is no single determinant of procrastination across all individuals and in all situations. It's more likely that these explanations interact with each other in determining an individual's odds of procrastinating in a given situation. Think of the explanations provided thus far as individual pieces of a puzzle. The big challenge for procrastination research has been figuring out how to put those pieces together into a complete picture. This picture would account for procrastination across different people and in different situations. If we can broadly explain procrastination, our chances of predicting and preventing it are that much greater. Assuming, that is, we've not already drifted off into watching the latest box-set of *Game of Thrones*.

The theory of everything (about doing nothing constructive)

Key advice: procrastination works like an equation; you can get a very different result by fiddling with one of its values

The strongest candidates for providing a general explanation of procrastination come from research on motivation. A key question for this line of research is: on what basis do people make decisions? Procrastination is, after all, a decision to leave until tomorrow that which can be done today. Of the array of available motivation theories, temporal motivation theory (TMT) (Steel and König, 2006) seems to provide the most complete explanation of procrastination to date. It's too bad that the authors were only one letter away from a way cooler acronym and being able to say that they had an explosive theory. I digress. TMT brings together the findings related to procrastination that we've just reviewed. It argues that a person will base a decision on whether to do something subject to the benefits of doing so (hang on, there's more). Judgements about benefits are derived from an assessment of four values. First, the expectation (E) of achieving the desired outcome, you'll recognise this as self-efficacy. Second, the value (V) attached to that outcome, this corresponds to the person-task characteristics. Third, the delay (D) in the timing of the outcome. This relates to the timing of the rewards/punishments associated with a task. Finally, a person's impulsiveness (I) or, to put it in familiar terms, their sensitivity to delay. I know, this is starting to sound like procrastination is being reduced to an equation. Well, that's because it is! In fact, it looks like this.

$$\text{Motivation (Utility)} = \frac{E \times V}{I \times D}$$

And you thought your issues with mathematics ended with long division! I know what you're thinking: "Is that it? Given the misery procrastination has caused me, I was hoping for something a little bigger and more impressive looking!" At this point I would remind you that Einstein's famous equation for special relativity is shorter. I also feel compelled to admit that this is about all I know of special relativity. Look, I was going to get around to reading Stephen Hawking's *A brief history of time*, but *sighs* you know how it goes. So, now you have the equation. Does this mean you can simply dust off the calculator to work out the odds that you'll get around to mowing your lawn before the council declare your garden a wildlife sanctuary? Maybe, but you don't need to. The purpose of showing you the equation was to illustrate how the explanations of procrastination we've previously covered interact with each other. I can't believe I just said that mathematical notation might have uses in print. Urgh, let's get this over with.

Look at the numerator of the equation (top row). It captures the degree to which we expect success (E) and the value associated with the task (V). Ideally, we'd like to do things that we are confident we can achieve and that are high in value (e.g. are enjoyable). Think of it using the cream cake conundrum. A cream cake is hard to resist, isn't it? You're sure you'll be able to cram it into your cake-hole, aren't you? Thus, your expectation of success is high. Sure, there is a slight risk of respiratory obstruction if you don't chew. However, it'd be worth the trip to casualty because you're sure that the cream cake will be delicious. In other words, eating that cream cake has a high value attached to it. Even if things go *really* pear-shaped, just think of your death certificate. Cause of death being attributed to "shoved an oversized cream cake into their gob" sounds way cooler than "died peacefully in sleep, without cream cake". If you can get that image out of your head, now look at the denominator in the equation (bottom row). This captures the sensitivity to delay of the individual concerned i.e. how impulsive they are (I) and the delay between the task and its associated rewards/consequences (D). Ideally, we would have a scenario where there is little to compete for our attention on the task at hand and where the rewards for that task come sooner rather than later. As we all know, NOTHING competes for your attention when a delicious cream cake is present. The reward from eating the cream cake (i.e. enjoyment) is immediate. Conversely, the punishment associated with eating that cake (i.e. the extra heft around the waistline) is distant and the problem of some future version of you. Sucks to be them! Now we have all the parts of the equation in place we can demonstrate how it accounts for procrastination.

A high motivation (utility) score for a task is generated when the numerator of the equation has high numbers (representing high expectancy and high value) and the denominator contains low numbers (representing low impulsivity and delay between task and associated rewards). Fiddling with any one of these numbers can have a significant effect on the motivation score for the task at hand. This is why the inclination to revise tends to spike the closer you get to the exam. The equation changes such that the figure corresponding to the delay between the revision and its consequences (D) decreases. This change to the equation raises the motivation score that it produces.

Hopefully, this simple example has achieved three things. First, it demonstrates how the components of the equation neatly account for individual differences in procrastination. This is important, as we all bring different things to any given scenario. For example, some people like revising. I know, weirdos! Equally, some people dislike revising, but can say no to that night at the pub. Second, it also shows you how the likelihood of procrastination can vary within an individual for a specific task over time, as exemplified in the revision scenario. Third, and most importantly, it demonstrates that you don't have to address all the factors implicated in procrastination to affect the likelihood of it occurring. As with all equations, fiddling with even one value can have a big effect on the outcome! Now we understand the workings of the procrastination equation, let's consider how we can fiddle the numbers in our favour.

A procrastinator's guide to fiddling the numbers

It's not that we don't appreciate Shia LaBeouf's enthusiasm in his infamous YouTube motivational video. It's just that we suspect that overcoming procrastination is going to take a little more than paying an actor to shout "JUST DO IT" at us. Be that as it may, you might be surprised to learn that reviews of the effectiveness of interventions for procrastination are quite scarce (Rozental & Carlbring, 2014). To make matters worse, I have a few constraints on what solutions I can advocate to you, dear reader. Some of the researched interventions involve proprietary programmes or therapy! Having paid for this book, you might feel a little short-changed if the advice given in this chapter amounted to "pay for therapy". Happily, that won't be necessary. We've established that the likelihood that we'll procrastinate is the result of an interplay between several factors, namely our: perceived efficacy; the value of the task and outcome; our sensitivity to delay; and the delay between the action and its associated rewards or punishments. Let's examine what we can do in respect of each of these factors to defeat the urge to slack off!

Key advice: use implementation intention to increase your effectiveness at self-regulation

Let's consider how you might address the issue of perceived self-efficacy first. You might assume that the best advice in this respect would be to improve your skill at the thing you're avoiding doing. For example, if you procrastinate when writing essays then you could resolve this by improving your knowledge of essay composition. Fast-forward to Chapter V of this book and send the author a generous gift in the post. Unfortunately, it's not quite that simple. Don't let that discourage you from sending the generous gift though! Whilst improving your perceived efficacy at the task of essay writing would be helpful, you'll find it hard to work on this if the thing that causes you to procrastinate most readily is, well, essay writing! There is a bigger issue that you need to address here: your perceived self-efficacy at self-regulation.

Self-regulation refers to your ability to initiate, execute, monitor and, if necessary, modify your learning endeavours. Its importance was demonstrated in a study by Klassen, Krawchuk and Rajani (2008). They recorded the academic performance of a sample of undergraduates in addition to administering a series of questionnaires that examined the following things. First, academic self-efficacy. This was ascertained by the level of agreement with statements such as: "I am confident I can understand the most difficult material presented in the reading for my classes." Second, academic self-regulation. This was determined by the level of agreement with statements such as: "If course materials are difficult, I change the way I read the materials." Third, perceived self-efficacy for self-regulation. This was assessed via the response to questions such as: "How well can you finish assignments by deadlines?" Finally, a measure of procrastination behaviour was given. Surprisingly, the results of the study indicated that perceived academic efficacy did not strongly predict procrastination, nor did the objective measures of the academic performance of the students involved in the study. In contrast, perceived self-efficacy for self-regulation strongly predicted procrastination. Students who were more confident in their ability to self-regulate their studying reported less procrastination behaviour. As Klassen et al. argued, knowing what you're doing, or believing that you know what you're doing, doesn't always reduce the odds of you procrastinating when doing it! That's most inconvenient! We'd better look at ways of improving our perceived self-efficacy at self-regulation, I guess.

A study by Owens, Bowman and Dill (2008) illustrates a principle you can use to improve your ability to self-regulate. They invited students into a study ostensibly involving the administration of a questionnaire examining the tendency to procrastinate. However, there was more to the study than this. Just as the students were about to leave the laboratory they were informed that they could earn extra course credit by participating in a second study. Willing students were then randomly assigned to one of two groups. One group were given a sign-up sheet containing ten timeslots for the second study. They were simply asked to identify one convenient timeslot for their participation in the following study by specifying it on the sheet. In the other group, the participants were given the same sign-up sheet, but with the following opening written instructions:

> You are more likely to keep your appointment if you commit yourself to arriving to the assigned room at one of the times listed above. Select now the time at which you plan to come for the second experiment, write at the bottom of the second page, and return that page to your instructor.

The researchers then compared how many students from each group turned up for the second study. Do you think the two groups differed in the number of returning students? Remember, the task for the participants was the same in both groups. Only the presence of the above passage of text on the sign-up form distinguished the second group from the first group. Effectively, the same instructions were being issued, i.e. sign up for a timeslot. Only 18% of the participants from the first group turned up for the second study. The life of a research assistant is not always a happy one! So, a similar proportion of participants from the second group turned up, right? Wrong! Of the second group, 61% of the participants turned up for the second study. That's eight times more students than the first group. What made the second group of students so much more likely to show up than the first group? Gollwitzer, Gawrilow and Oettingen (2008) argued it's because the participants in the second group had been experimentally induced into making what's referred to as an 'implementation intention'. An implementation intention differs from a goal-based intention in that it explicitly states how the actions that contribute to the goal intention will be achieved. Think of an implementation intention as having two crucial components: an 'if' and a 'then'. The identification of a future goal relevant situational cue is represented by the 'if' component. The response to that cue is represented by the 'then' component. The participants in the second group of the Owens et al. study were given the following implementation intention: IF I commit to the second experiment by signing up THEN I will turn up at this location at 'x' time and 'y' date.

At this point you're probably feeling a bit incredulous that something as simple as generating an implementation intention could possibly improve your self-regulatory skills; I know I was! However, the situation gets even more curious. The 'if' and 'then' format of an implementation intention is particularly important to its effectiveness. Oettingen, Hönig and Gollwitzer (2000) conducted a study in which participants were asked to undertake tedious math homework at a specific time every week. They manipulated the way in which participants were instructed to articulate their intention to complete the homework. One group of participants were told to use the 'if/then' implementation intentions: "If it is Wednesday at 8:30, then I will perform as many arithmetic tasks as possible." The other group articulated the intention by specifying the date, time and objective, but did not use the 'if/then' format. Their stated intention read: "I will perform as many arithmetic tasks as possible each Wednesday at 8:30." The experimenters were interested in the extent to which students in each group would procrastinate in starting their homework each week. This was measured as the deviation between the intended and actual commencement of the homework by the participants in each group. On average, the participants in the 'if/then' implementation condition deviated from the intended start time by 1.5 hours. In contrast, those who didn't articulate their intentions using the 'if/then' format deviated from the intended start time by an average of eight hours!

Why should the 'if/then' format of implementation intentions be important for their success? A brief explanation will have to suffice here. You can look at Gollwitzer, Gawrilow and Oettingen (2008) for further elaboration. The if/then implementation intention format seems to work in several ways. First, it appears to cue people to attend more closely to the critical situation (the if part of the format) should they encounter it. Second, it seems to make for stronger associations between situations and responses. This removes some of the deliberation that can occur when an individual encounters an obstacle to a goal. Third, it seems to help negate some of the issues associated with self-regulation that are detrimental to goal achievement. You can find a fuller account of such issues in Wieber and Gollwitzer (2010). For now it suffices to point out that research suggests you're more likely to initiate an action towards a goal if you are specific about when, where and how you will get started. You're also more likely to continue to execute an action if you've thought about how you will deal with distractions. There is a greater likelihood you will successfully monitor the effectiveness of your actions if you've thought about how you will seek and respond to feedback. Finally, you're less likely to deplete your capacity to self-regulate if you're working towards achieving your goals in a more systematic and organised fashion. I know it seems too good to be true, but the research is very consistent in its support for the use of implementation intentions. A meta-analysis of 94 studies on their use indicates they are effective in bridging the gap between intention and action (Gollwitzer & Sheeran, 2006).

So, it would seem that a good first start in defeating procrastination is just being a bit more explicit in how you set up your goals, specifically using the 'if/then' format to specify where, when and how you will go about achieving a goal. I'd suggest a bit of practice might be in order here. Repeat after me: "If I set a goal, then I will start by specifying when, where and how I will enact the behaviour required to complete the goal." Give implementation intentions a go. It's not like they require any real effort on your behalf and you might get a shock at how well they work for you.

8

Key advice: reward yourself frequently for progress

Let's turn to interventions concerning the value of the task/outcome now. We've covered the intuitively appealing notion that people tend to procrastinate more on tasks they deem boring, resent doing or find frustrating. I could, of course, advocate that you simply avoid these tasks. That's all well and good unless studying, or some part of it, is what produces boredom, resentment or frustration within you. It's not like you can just avoid reading, taking notes, writing or revising. Well, not if you want a degree! Of course, doing these tasks more effectively will make them much less likely to engender boredom, resentment and frustration. However, instruction on things like effective reading and note-taking etc. is the remit of subsequent chapters in this book. For now, let's examine how you can reduce the odds of procrastinating on tasks that seem about as appealing as a pub that exclusively serves pints of cod liver oil. That way, you can still fend off procrastination for tasks that remain unappealing even when you become more proficient at them. To achieve this, we're going to turn to one of the pillars of psychology: behaviourism.

If the mention of B. F. Skinner doesn't ring any bells, it's safe to say that you're new to psychology. Now is not the time for a history lesson, but you should know that Skinner was one of the chief proponents of behaviourism. This approach argues that psychology is a science and, as such, must only be concerned with things that can be objectively observed and measured. Therefore, behaviourism focuses on the interaction between the environment (stimulus) and behaviour (response). It argues that all behaviour, no matter how complex, can be broken down into stimulus, response associations. These associations are governed by reinforcement (positive and negative) and punishment. Behaviour that is reinforced tends to be repeated. Behaviour that is punished is less likely to re-occur. Let's have a look at how this works in the case of procrastination. Say you have some revision to do, but you've found revision boring previously. The revision is associated with punishment (boredom). Simultaneously, the big reward for revising (i.e. good grades) is in the dim and distant future. At least, you hope it is! In contrast, that episode of *24* is looking much more tempting. You've enjoyed watching previous episodes, so that behaviour has been positively reinforced via the reward of enjoyment. The reward you get from watching *24* is also immediate. It's looking pretty obvious which of the two behaviours is more likely to re-occur, isn't it? But wait, there's more! By taking the watch-episode-of-*24* option you are also avoiding the boredom associated with revision. Thus, your behaviour is also being negatively reinforced. It's a double whammy! Each time you procrastinate, you're increasing the likelihood of future procrastination because you're inadvertently strengthening that behaviour via positive and negative reinforcement. Beautifully simple explanation of why procrastination is so hard to shake off, isn't it?

The good news is that once you're aware of the mechanisms of reinforcement and punishment, you can start to use them in your favour. The first and most important thing to point out is that you can self-reinforce your behaviour. Reinforcement isn't just something that happens to you, you can also dictate when, where and how you reward or punish yourself. Indeed, over 20 years ago, Ferrari and Emmons (1995) conducted research indicating that individuals who reported more frequent self-reinforcement also tended to report less frequent procrastination. What was the nature of the self-reinforcement measured in this research, you ask? A weekend away? Dinner at a Michelin star restaurant? Nothing remotely as extravagant! The measure of reinforcement was how likely an individual was to enjoy a self-administered pat on the back! I know, that's rather disappointing given the surname of the first author of that research! The point is that if you can reward yourself with something this basic, think about what you might be able to do with something a little more enticing. That's a tea break for me, then! In specifying your own reward, just remember one of the lessons from temporal motivation theory: you'll prefer a reward that is small but immediate over one that is bigger but more distant. If you reward yourself for progress on a task rather than just when you've completed it, you are shrinking the delay between the task and its payoff. This is a good way to combat procrastination for academic tasks, where there tends to be a long gap between effort and reward!

Rewards can come in unlikely packages. Believe it or not, the self-testing I advocated in Chapter I can be a source of reinforcement. You'd be forgiven for thinking that a test, no matter how informal, is a terrible reward. However, consider the times you have spent hours with your nose in textbooks wondering if your efforts are paying off? Not a particularly pleasant feeling, is it? Disconcerting at best, downright demotivating at worst. Consequently, your study practices are, effectively, being punished by their association with this doubt and negative rumination. Now, consider what might happen if you sought evidence of your knowledge by testing yourself? Maybe you wouldn't do so great at first, but you'd probably get some answers right. The association of even a modicum of achievement with your studying would positively reinforce it, making further studying more likely. Now your subsequent reading also has a specific goal: addressing the things you didn't recall correctly. As we'll see in Chapter III, this is a much better approach than just reading aimlessly hoping something will sink in. Following more reading, you take the test again and likely get even more answers right. Now we're cooking with gas. You've positively reinforced your studying with the satisfaction (and relief) one gets from having evidence of improvement. Perhaps you might reward yourself with some more reading? "Back.The.Truck.Up." I hear you cry. "It was all going well until that point, but how could more reading possibly be a reward? A cream cake, that's a reward. A nap, that's a reward. More reading? That sounds like a punishment." Well, if you associate reading with no progress then, yes, it would be. However, now you're starting to associate reading with the satisfaction that comes with evidence of the fruits of your labour. Because your reading has been positively reinforced, cracking on with that next chapter no longer seems quite so aversive. Perrin, Miller, Haberlin, Ivy, Meindi and Neef (2011) conducted an interesting little study looking at the effect of the availability of study materials (in the form of practice tests) on student procrastination in a seven-day period prior to an examination. They assigned students to one of two conditions. In one condition, new practice tests for the exam were available daily at 6:30 am. In the other condition, following the release of the first practice test, subsequent practice tests were released daily at 6:30 am, but only for the students who had completed the previous day's practice test. The results indicated that the students in the condition that had unrestricted access to the practice tests tended to leave completing them to the 11th hour before the final exam. Students who had to earn the release of the additional practice tests distributed their studying more evenly in the run up to the final exam. When asked about their experience of taking the practice tests, 80% of the students said that they felt more prepared for the final examination having engaged with them. Unfortunately, when asked to express a preference between free access or having to earn the right to complete subsequent tests by completing previous tests, 90% of the students opted for free access! Who was it that said that we are all conspirators in our own undoing?

Another approach to harnessing the principles of reinforcement to make tasks you've historically found aversive more palatable is using piggybacking (Ainslie, 1992). This means incorporating something you enjoy into the more aversive task so that it becomes associated with a reward, rather than a punishment. For example, if you often find socialising an all too tempting alternative to reading, you might try and create a study group. The aversive activity of reading then becomes associated with the more enjoyable activity of getting out of the house and interacting with others. I'd suggest you choose your venue carefully. If you insist on meeting at a pub, might I suggest a quiet one and that you refrain from hitting the shots until after the study session has concluded. You can then use the drinks as a reward for completing the session. Somehow, I'm not sure that my colleagues in the field of health psychology are going to thank me for suggesting this reward. Those of you who are into technology and apps can find a way to use them to positively reinforce your studying. Such technology can even be used to negatively reinforce studying by making it a means of escaping something aversive. This possibility was investigated by Davis and Abbitt (2013) who used a custom SMS text service to send students reminders to complete a course quiz. Here's the twist, the reminders got more frequent the closer to the deadline for the quiz completion got. On the day of the deadline the students got 13 reminders! They could stop these reminders at any time by simply completing the quiz. In other words, completing the quiz was being negatively reinforced by the removal of the annoying SMS messages. Using spam to get people to stop procrastinating is an innovative idea. However, you should know that humans are cunning creatures when it comes to avoiding punishment and negating negative reinforcement. Having read the above study, it probably occurred to you that the participants could have easily blocked the number that was sending the texts. Assuming, that is, they wanted to be particularly bloody minded! On a similar note, the participants in the above study may have procrastinated less in doing the quiz, but that's not the same as benefiting from it. You might think that a great way of beating study related procrastination is to pitch studying against something more aversive (e.g. the hoovering). However, just because you're hitting the books doesn't mean you're doing anything useful with them. In the above instance, your motivation for studying was not to make progress with your learning, but rather to avoid making progress with the hoovering! Positively reinforcing progress in studying is a much better bet than negatively reinforcing the act of sitting down to study.

9

Key advice: remove the sources of distraction from your study environment

We now move on to the thorny subject of addressing the sensitivity to delay aspect of procrastination. I fear you're not going to like the advice in this section much. I'll try and convince you that what I'm going to advocate is a necessary evil by describing a scenario that illustrates the big problem at play. You've finally sat down with your laptop and you *are* going to write that paper! *Ding!* There goes your work e-mail alert. Better look at that. It might be something other than one of your colleagues calling the boss a pain in the a** for the third time this week. Mental note: send them a memo about the freedom of information act, not as a friendly service, just to see the look on their face. Where were you? Oh yes. *Ding!* Oh, that's a notification of a new post by one of your 100+ Facebook friends. OK, well you can just like it and that will be that. *Ding!* Apparently, someone else has just liked that same post. Did you really need to know that? Hang on, it was your ex. Business just picked up! You should check out their profile to see how they are getting on, purely out of humanitarian concern of course! They're looking quite a bit older since you split up and their recent pictures are neck up only photos. This can mean only one thing: they have put on weight. Excellent! *Ding!* Speaking of photos, there's the alert indicating you've just been tagged in one. Better check it out. Eurgh, it's *really* unflattering. Poetic justice, I guess. *Ding!* Instagram notification. OK, you're not interested, but that reminds you that you still haven't posted those holiday pictures. Well, you have, but they could really use the application of a filter or two. *Ding!* That's your Google mail notification. Please god, not another online bill or more e-mails from the African Army General. You know, the one who wants your bank details to transfer half the proceeds of the will of someone with the same surname as you. Remember? The one who recently died in a tragic mining accident! Yep, it's the African Army General again. This time it's to share the proceeds of a rich industrialist who died in a tragic skiing accident. Hmmm. *Ding!* Text message this time, apparently the local pizza outlet misses your custom. You're not sure this reflects well on your lifestyle choices! *Ring, Ring!* Wow, how quaint: a phone call! Turns out it was a PPI salesman. Maybe you should give them the African General's number? *Ding Dong!* The doorbell, it's the thing you ordered from Amazon when you should have been writing yesterday. OK, now you can make a start. Your fingers hover over the keyboard, the cursor winks at you on the still blank page. You type the title of your assignment, resisting the temptation to mess around with font types. A new paragraph is about to be born. *Ding!* It's WhatsApp, your best mate is asking why you're ten minutes late for the rendezvous at the pub. Blimey, is that the time? Go get that beverage, tiger. You've earned it!

I'll concede that I'm using a bit of artistic licence in the above example. The point is that we've all invited an array of things into our lives that intrusively compete for our attention. Unfortunately, we often don't deal with interruptions to demanding activities (like studying) that well. Interruptions increase the time taken to do the original task, make continuing with that task more difficult than it would have otherwise been and make errors more likely in both the original and interrupting tasks. The most disruptive kinds of interruption are those that you didn't instigate and that compel you to respond to them before you return to the original task. So, that's pretty much every alert you get from any social media or communication app/device. Whoops! Sorry folks, but the jury isn't out on this one: multitasking between studying and multimedia is not helpful. The interested reader is referred to May and Elder (2018) for a good review. Such reviews indicate that when it comes to technological interruptions, we are our own worst enemy. Students often recognise the likelihood that media multitasking will have a detrimental effect on their ability to study. However, they typically underestimate the magnitude of this effect and carry on regardless! What's to be done in the face of all these competing demands for our attention?

It probably won't surprise you to learn that distractions are harder to resist if they are closer to hand. This is an issue for the kind of temptations that are present when you're studying. The very PC you're using to study is also a portal to a world of friends, shopping and cat videos! Willpower is a finite resource. If you expend a lot of self-regulatory effort in avoiding one temptation, when another one comes along shortly after, your self-regulatory reserves are diminished. This was very neatly demonstrated by Vohs and Heatherton (2000). In their study, participants were chronic dieters (who should have been avoiding treats) who were assigned to one of several different temptation conditions. They were first asked to watch a wildlife video in a room where a bowl of sweets was either placed within their arm's reach (high temptation condition) or about ten feet away across the room (low temptation condition). The participants were then either told they could "help themselves" to the sweets or "not to touch" them. In the help-yourself condition, it was up to the participants to self-regulate their behaviour. In the do-not-touch condition the regulation of their behaviour had been imposed on them. After watching the video, the participants were taken to another room and told that for the next ten minutes their task was to taste and rate the flavour of a series of large tubs of ice cream. Oh, and they could have as much as they wanted because there was tons of the stuff out the back. Also, the experimenter would leave the room, so no judgement. If you're thinking this experiment was a bit sadistic, you may have a point! Anyway, after ten minutes elapsed, the experimenters returned and measured how much ice cream the participants had eaten (hopefully not in front of them!). Comparing the high versus low temptation conditions for the dieters who were told they could help themselves to the sweets revealed a striking finding. Participants who previously had the sweets placed within their reach subsequently ate about 60% more ice cream than those who had the sweets placed across the room. Having initially had the sweets so close to hand meant the participants in the high temptation condition had exhausted their self-regulatory reserves. When they were subsequently presented with the opportunity to tuck into the ice cream, they simply caved in. The problem with having so many tempting distractions to hand when you're studying is that it's not a matter of if you yield to one of them and procrastinate, it's when! If you've ever been studying and managed to ignore a few e-mail alerts, but then immediately pounced on a text message that arrived shortly afterwards, you'll relate to this.

Running low on your self-regulatory reserves affects more than just how prone you are to temptation. Your capacity to persist when faced with challenging tasks is also reduced. In the second part of their experiment, Vohs and Heatherton substituted the ice cream tasting task for a puzzle that, unbeknownst to the participants, was unsolvable. They were interested in the effect that prior exposure to the high or low temptation condition would have on the willingness of the participants to persist in their efforts to complete the puzzle. The dieters who had previously had the snacks placed within their reach and told they could help themselves persisted at the puzzle for around 20% less time than those who had the sweets placed across the room. In this instance, the effort the participants in the high temptation condition had put into resisting the sweets meant that when they needed to call upon their self-regulatory reserves to persist with a difficult task, the tank was empty! The problem with having lots of tempting distractions close to hand when you're studying is that the effort it will take you to 'just say no' will likely mean that the moment you encounter a rough patch in your learning, you'll call it quits for the day.

Unfortunately, it's not just resisting temptation that depletes your self-regulatory reserves. If it requires self-regulatory effort, it's draining your supplies. Part three of Vohs and Heatherton's experiment demonstrated this. On this occasion they replaced the bowl of sweets portion of the experiment with an alternative form of sadism. Now, participants were asked to watch a moving scene from a film and either supress the expression of their feelings (i.e. expend effort in self-regulating their emotional reaction) or let it all hang out. They then conducted the ice cream tasting part of the experiment. Guess which group contained the participants who scoffed about 36% more ice cream after watching the sad movie scene? Yes, it was the group who were asked to supress their feelings. It looks like just trying to pretend that you're not tempted to check your Amazon account for the latest unmissable deals isn't going to help you avoid procrastinating. Trying to supress the despair of missing out on all those bargains is taking its toll on your self-regulatory reserves, even if your bank manager greatly appreciates your efforts.

The message from research such as that described above is clear: you should lighten the burden on your self-regulatory reserves. The most obvious way of doing this is to jettison whatever distractions you can from wherever you're studying. Unfortunately, as previously noted, this won't always be possible for every potential source of procrastination, or maybe even the biggest culprits. It's unlikely you'll fancy reverting to the stone age to do your research, take notes or compose your essays. You could disable notifications, so that at least technological temptations aren't reaching out to you quite as intrusively. However, you know they are still close to hand. Even worse, because you've switched off your notifications, who knows what you might be missing out on? You can take the self-regulation burden off yourself by using technology that prevents you from succumbing to the siren call of those pesky social media sites and applications. There are numerous free applications available from the internet (ironic, I know) that allow you to either block access to the web, specific sites or applications for periods of time that you've put aside for studying. The one that jumped out at me (because I have a big juvenile streak) is called 'Go F***ing Work'. It's an extension for the Chrome browser that will block any sites that are not productive and give you a sarcastic and foul-mouthed reprimand. If that's not your cup of tea, then have a look for a suitable alternative. Just maybe not when you should be working though, eh?

At this point you may be thinking: "If self-regulatory resources are finite, then surely I need to be taking regular breaks to recuperate?" Well, yes and we've alluded to the possibility of using (tea) breaks as a reward previously. Be honest though, how often have you knocked off for that well-earned 15 minutes break for a cuppa only to witness it become a much less-well-earned two-hour break on the couch watching TV with potato chips. Screw it: diet starts tomorrow, right? You've probably now guessed why that happens. It's because breaks place demands on self-regulatory resources too. You must: plan your break schedule; keep an eye on the time; initiate the break; monitor the passing time whilst you're on the break (no small feat if you're doing something engaging) then disengage with the break and re-start work at the scheduled time. Oh, and you need to repeat that process for each break you take. Fortunately, the websites/applications that can block access to distractions also often have features that help you schedule and regulate your breaks. Alternatively, you could go old-school and just use an egg timer! If you can find a way to use one of those to procrastinate, you've earned it!

If you're finding it difficult to distance yourself from sources of distraction, you can try manipulating either the way you view the task that's causing you to procrastinate or the distraction you're using to avoid what you should be doing. If you mentally re-appraise that unappealing task as an opportunity to develop a skill, or the call of that distraction as a test of fortitude, you'll be more likely to stay on task. I know, this sounds like wishful thinking of the highest order, almost akin to believing if you stare at your coursework long enough it will turn into a winning lottery ticket. However, an experiment by Leroy, Grégoire, Magen, Gross and Mikolajczak (2012) suggests otherwise. In their study, participants were invited into the laboratory and given ten minutes to learn key information about 20 different wines. They were then given a questionnaire that assessed their enthusiasm for the task and a memory test to assess what they had just learned. The participants were then allocated to one of two conditions: a control condition or a task reappraisal condition. In the control condition, the instructions for the next part of the experiment were simply: "Please do your best at the next learning task." In the task reappraisal condition the instructions were: "In order to do your best at the next learning task, I suggest that you envisage this task as an opportunity to train and improve your memory, which is an important key to success at university." Participants were then taken to a different room in the laboratory and asked to learn about 20 different wines. This room had distracting stimuli either in the form of pictures on the wall, or a TV playing funny adverts. After ten minutes had passed, participants were, once again, given a questionnaire that assessed their enthusiasm for the task and a memory test to assess what they had just learned. Additionally, they were also given a test of their recall of the pictures (or TV adverts) present in the laboratory to assess their engagement with these distracting stimuli. General visual memory was also tested for all the participants. This was done to rule out differences between the control and re-appraisal groups being due to ability to recall visual information per se. The results indicated that the participants who re-appraised the learning task maintained more enthusiasm for it, attended less to the distractor stimuli and exhibited superior memory for what they had studied. Leroy et al. also conducted a version of the above experiment where the distraction, as opposed to the task, became the focus of the participants' re-appraisal efforts. They did this by advising participants that to maximise their performance on the task, they should view distractions as a test of their willpower.

The same pattern of results was observed. Those who re-appraised the distractions attended to them less, exhibited more enthusiasm for the learning task and demonstrated superior memory for what they had studied. So, if it's not possible for you to strip the biggest sources of distraction from your study environment, try re-appraising them. It's not like the process exemplified in the above study is complicated!

10

Key advice: break complex tasks down into their component parts

Congratulations! You've reached the part of the chapter addressing what you can do to fiddle the final part of the procrastination equation in your favour. I'm referring to the delay between the task and outcome. Here's the thing about most academic tasks: they usually have a long delay between the effort you have to put into them and their ultimate payoff. This makes them so much less gratifying than activities with more immediate rewards. Consequently, we procrastinate until the delay between getting things done and receiving our just deserts shrinks to the point we can put things off no longer. You may recall this process being referred to as hyperbolic discounting. Would you believe that hyperbolic discounting has a partner in crime? An enabler, if you will, that supports its endeavours to get you to leave things until the 11th hour. This accomplice is known as the planning fallacy (Kahneman & Tversky, 1977) and it refers to our tendency to significantly underestimate the time required to complete a task. I'm going to zero in on the planning fallacy in this section because the solution to it also serves as an effective intervention for hyperbolic discounting.

If you want to see some spectacular instances of the planning fallacy in action, construction projects are a good place to start. The most commonly cited example is the Sydney Opera House. In 1957, it had a projected cost of seven million dollars and an anticipated completion date of 1963. The eventual cost would be 15 times higher than the original estimate and construction would take a decade longer than planned. Oh, and even then, the finished building was less ambitious than originally planned. To paraphrase the old (and somewhat politically incorrect) adage about the opera: "It ain't over until the fat lady is bankrupt!" I'll admit that I'm being slightly disingenuous in giving you this grand example of the planning fallacy. The Sydney Opera House was not designed and built by one person, despite what the hideous over-run might suggest. There were, no doubt, other factors also at play. However, I was hoping this example might put the issues with the construction of your patio into perspective.

The planning fallacy is a very relevant consideration in addressing procrastination when studying. If you underestimate the time required to complete a task, there is much less impetus not to leave it until the last minute, hence its partnership with hyperbolic discounting! A comprehensive demonstration of the planning fallacy in action with undergraduates was provided by Buehler, Griffin and Ross (1994). They asked final year students to predict, as best they could, when they would submit their thesis. They were then also asked for two further estimates. One of these estimates was based on everything going as well as it possibly could. The remaining estimate was to account for the possibility that whatever could go wrong, would go wrong. The experimenters then simply recorded when the students submitted their work. The average best guess (not best-case scenario) students gave for how long it would take them to complete their thesis was 33 days. The average time taken for students to write their thesis was 55 days (i.e. 40% longer). More worrying was the fact that even the average estimates given by participants for the worst-case scenario was six days lower than the average time taken!

Buehler et al. included several other experiments to try and tease out the cause of the planning fallacy. For example, in a variation of the original experiment, they asked participants to estimate when they would submit a piece of work and verbalise whatever thoughts occurred to them in the process of doing so. They were then asked to recall a past occasion when they had failed to complete a project by the anticipated deadline and explain why their estimate was inaccurate. The results indicated that participants were able to recall previous instances where their estimates had been inaccurate. However, these recollections did not inform their subsequent estimates. Effectively, they weren't learning from their mistakes. If we fail to consider prior inaccuracies in our predictions when making subsequent estimates, then a timely reminder of these previous errors should take care of the planning fallacy, right? Unfortunately, no. Buehler et al. did exactly that and the participants persisted in underestimating the time required to complete the task in question. That's a remarkable, and slightly depressing, finding. Even when we have our noses rubbed in evidence that should make us more conservative with our estimates of task completion, we persist in being hopelessly optimistic. What's going on here?

When Kahneman and Tversky first identified the planning fallacy, they suggested that it was likely to reflect a fault in perspective taking. When making estimates about how long it will take to complete a task, we tend to adopt an internal perspective where we concentrate on generating a narrative of how we will complete that task. This sounds perfectly reasonable. However, we do this at the expense of taking an external perspective where we compare the task at hand to previous tasks and look to such comparisons to inform our current estimates. This sounds less reasonable! As Buehler et al. pointed out, taking an internal perspective is associated with three things that impede our ability to learn from experience in giving estimates of task completion time. First, by its very nature, a request for an estimate of how long something will take tends to get us to focus on the future. This makes it that bit harder for us to dredge up memories that would inform our narrative about how the task at hand will go. Second, even if we do have access to memories of underestimating task completion time, as Buehler and his colleagues demonstrated, we're not very good at taking them into account. When making judgements, we tend to ignore background generic data in favour of case-specific data. This is known as the base rate fallacy. Consider the following (totally made up and very simplistic) example:

> One hundred percent of people that have failed a degree level assessment through procrastination own an iPad. One percent of the people that own an iPad have failed a degree level assessment through procrastination. Billy is an undergraduate student and owns an iPad.

If you give someone this scenario and ask them whether, based on the above information, it is likely that Billy has failed a degree level assessment through procrastination, one of two things will likely happen. First, they might punch you right on the nose for being a smart arse and trying to catch them out. Second (and preferably) they will answer: "Yes, it is likely that Billy has failed an assessment." This is because they'd likely have fixated on the "100% of people who have failed a degree level assessment own an iPad" element of the scenario. This is the case specific to the failure outcome statistic. In focusing on this, they would likely fail to consider the base rate of iPad owner statistic in their judgement. This would make them overlook the greater likelihood that Billy is part of the 99% of people who own an iPad, but have never failed a degree assessment via procrastination. I do hope I've explained that well enough, because there is no way I'm going to be able to afford the lawsuit from Apple for lost revenue if I haven't! Last, but not least, we turn to the third obstacle to experience informing estimates of task completion time: attribution error. As part of their research, Buehler et al. asked participants to explain previous inaccurate estimates they had given. In doing this, they attributed the cause of their erroneous estimates to unpredictable, irregular events outside of their control, e.g. an unplanned visit from a relative. In contrast, when the participants were asked to account for previous inaccurate estimates given by a friend, they attributed the cause to predictable events, within their control and which they'd brought on themselves. How convenient, not to mention unwise! If you believe your previous estimation errors are attributable to unpredictable things that you didn't bring on yourself, then you are likely to disregard them in your future estimates as being unrepresentative of the normal state of play. However, if you attribute your prior estimation errors to predictable things that you brought on yourself, then you're more likely to take them into account in giving future estimates because they can't be dismissed as "one-offs". Apparently, when it comes to estimating the time it will take us to get a job done, learning from our mistakes is not something we're that keen on doing. This is yet another reason why procrastination can be so hard to kick.

Having established that you will struggle to learn from experience in accurately estimating how long a task will take to complete, the obvious question is: how do you fix this? The solution lies in highlighting the connection between your previous and current task performance. In a further study, Buehler et al. replicated the scenario where participants were asked to give an estimate on how long a task would take to complete before performing that task. However, this time they split the participants into two groups. One group were just asked to recall past instances of engagement with similar tasks in giving their estimates. The other group had to explicitly use their recall of previous engagement with similar tasks to generate a narrative about how they would complete the current task in giving their estimates. As expected, the group that simply recalled past instances of engagement with similar tasks exhibited the planning fallacy. They substantially underestimated how long the task at hand would take to complete. However, the group that generated the narrative about completing the task by explicitly referencing past engagement with similar tasks did not display the planning fallacy. Their estimates were much more in keeping with the time they subsequently took to complete the task. Making the connection between past and current tasks explicit appears to be key in generating more realistic estimates of task completion. This is useful to know, because underestimating the amount of time it will take to get a task done is conducive with procrastinating until the 11th hour. The clear lesson from Buehler et al.'s work is that you should ensure any estimates you make concerning the time required to complete a task explicitly call upon evidence from previous engagement with similar tasks.

Ensuring that your estimates of task completion time are evidence-based is a good way of reducing the risk of being way too optimistic in your projections. However, its effectiveness depends on the quality of your reflection on what a task involved. Think of the last time that you looked back on a completed task in trying to estimate how long it would take you to complete a similar task in the here and now. Did you think of the task as a single entity, or did you break it down into its constituent sub-tasks? Let's consider this with respect to the task of writing an essay. If you just think of the essay as a single entity, then your essay to-do list looks like this.

1. Write essay.

End of list. This is not a good basis for reflecting on your experience of writing past essays in arriving at an estimate of how long a future essay will take you to complete. Ostensibly, this to-do list makes the process of writing an essay look very straightforward, doesn't it? You could totally understand why someone might look at this and think it's possible to write an essay at the 11th hour. You can also understand how having a to-do list like this plays right into the hands of hyperbolic discounting. There is only one reward on offer in the above breakdown of the task, and it's at the point of completion. Where's the fun in that? However, if you break down essay composition into its constituent sub-tasks, the to-do list looks very different.

1. Familiarise yourself with the essay title and retrieve relevant lecture materials and course notes.
2. Conduct a literature search.
3. Collate and print out/retrieve the most useful sources based on your literature search.
4. Read the sources in detail, retain those that are still helpful, discard those that are not helpful.
5. Produce an essay plan that establishes an academic discourse around the essay title.
6. Compose the first draft.
7. Review the first draft and make necessary amendments. This step might require several iterations.
8. Proofread the final draft (at least a few days before the deadline).
9. Check the in-text citations and the references section.
10. Complete a final proofread.

Suddenly, the task of composing an essay looks like a *lot* more work, doesn't it? This is a much better basis upon which to arrive at an estimate of how long the essay is likely to take you. When you break it down like this, leaving an essay until the 11th hour is up there with punching a grizzly bear on the nose in the grand scheme of bad ideas. It's clear that you can't do all the above at the last minute. Not properly, at least! On the plus side, breaking down the task in the above way presents a great opportunity to intersperse the task with opportunities for more frequent rewards. This could go a long way to counter hyperbolic discounting. Two for the price of one! So, is there any evidence for this divide-and-conquer approach to defeating procrastination?

Kruger and Evans (2004) argued that the planning fallacy could be thought of as a *really* myopic internal perspective resulting in the size and complexity of a task being substantially under-represented. This is exemplified in the first of our essay to-do lists. Kruger and Evans reasoned that if they could induce people to unpack tasks into their constituent parts, as we did with our second essay to-do list, then they might be able to reduce the planning fallacy. To investigate this possibility, they conducted an experiment involving the manipulation of an unformatted Word document to make it correspond with the formatting on a paper-based version of the same piece of text. This formatting task was extensive and involved several sub-tasks, e.g. changing margins, indenting paragraphs, highlighting text and attending to missed capitalisation. All pretty standard, but monotonous, tasks. Before they were set to work, the participants were asked to estimate how long the task would take them. This is where the experimental manipulation came in. Half of the participants were instructed to unpack the task by listing all the changes required to the Word document before giving their estimates. The other half of the participants were asked to unpack the task after giving their estimates. If Kruger and Evans were correct in their hunch, then the planning fallacy should be diminished for the participants who unpacked the task before making their estimates. The results indicated that all the participants underestimated the time that the formatting task would take. However, unpacking the task before giving an estimate reduced the size of the planning fallacy by more than half.

If unpacking works by revealing the constituent parts of a multifaceted task (thus making it seem bigger) then the more multifaceted the task, the bigger it will seem when unpacked. This should mean that the benefits of unpacking for the accuracy of estimates of task completion time increase with the complexity of the task, i.e. the number of parts that it can be broken down into. Kruger and Evans tested this by replicating the Word document formatting experiment, but this time they manipulated how complex the formatting task was by changing the number of sub-tasks it entailed. Participants assigned to the simple formatting task had 56 changes to make, split over two formatting sub-tasks. Participants assigned to the complex formatting task had to make 244 changes split over four formatting sub-tasks. The effects of unpacking on the planning fallacy were modest for the simple formatting task. However, for the complicated formatting task, the discrepancy between the predicted and actual times was three times smaller for the unpacked task. Kruger and Evans were right, the benefits of unpacking increase with the complexity of the task. Rhetorical question: how many components did we say essay writing entailed? Get unpacking! Unless you want to be a victim of the planning fallacy, that is!

Summary

Putting an end to procrastination

We've covered quite a lot of ground in this chapter. So, let's distil its contents into a concise summary of anti-procrastination advice relating to the themes of self-efficacy, value, sensitivity to delay and delay that we've previously explored.

Increasing your self-efficacy

Often, it's our perceived inefficacy to self-regulate that makes us procrastinate. Address this by doing the following:

- Use implementation intentions to be explicit in how you set up your goals. Specifically, use the 'if/then' format to specify where, when and how you will go about achieving a goal. For example: "If I turn on my PC then I will do 30 minutes of work on my essay before anything else."

Increasing the value of a task

We procrastinate at tasks we find boring, frustrating or resent undertaking. Address this by doing the following:

- Use rewards to positively reinforce your efforts at a task. Small, frequent rewards are preferable to larger, less proximal ones.

- Remember that rewards can be academic in nature. Use self-testing to evaluate your learning and then reward your progress with actions that enable further attainment, e.g. access to more reading.
- Use piggybacking to incorporate something you enjoy into tasks you find more aversive, so the aversive task starts to become associated with a reward, not just a punishment.

Reducing sensitivity to delay

Our self-regulatory reserves are finite. When these are depleted, procrastination beckons! Address this by doing the following:

- Remove as many sources of procrastination from your study environment as possible. Use technology (such as website blockers) to help you manage sources of procrastination that are otherwise difficult to mitigate without compromising the things you use to study (e.g. the internet).
- Re-appraise the task at hand to increase its appeal and/or re-appraise sources of distraction to reduce their appeal. For example, examine the short-term benefits of completing a task rather than focusing solely on its role in the bigger picture.

Reducing delay

Academic tasks are often characterised by a long delay between the work that goes into a task and the rewards associated with that task. This increases the chances of procrastination until the 11th hour and is compounded by our tendency to underestimate how long complex tasks will take. Address both issues by doing the following:

- Ensure that your estimates of task completion times and narratives about how you will go about a task are explicitly linked to, and informed by, previous experience of undertaking similar tasks.
- Unpack complex tasks into their constituent sub-tasks when reflecting on your prior performance. Similarly, break down the task at hand into its component sub-tasks, this will greatly increase the accuracy of your estimate of the overall task completion time. It also gives you the opportunity to intersperse the task with rewards, rather than waiting until the task is completed to receive any payoff.

There you go. Simple, eh? When I consider how much of an issue procrastination has been for me, I almost want the solutions to be more elaborate! I'm reminded of something a counselling psychology lecturer once told my class about clients sometimes objecting to the suggestion of shorter programmes of therapy. The clients argued that it had taken them decades worth of work to get as screwed up as they were, so the idea of it all being sorted out in a few weeks was a bit threatening! Maybe my reaction was borne of the same thinking and I was secretly hoping for a luxury procrastination rehabilitation retreat in a hot, far-away land! If you feel like some of the advice on negating procrastination is too simple to be true (even after having had some exposition of the research) then I would remind you of the hindsight bias that we discussed in Chapter I! I'd also invite you to honestly reflect on how many of the tips just proposed you've previously rigorously implemented? I'll bet very few, if any! I know I certainly hadn't made use of them. Sure, I'd figured that breaking down big tasks into smaller components was probably wise, but did any of my planning reflect that? Err, no. I knew that it was wise to take breaks during studying, so I did. Every five minutes! Also, each break unintentionally ended up being about 30 minutes. On reflection, I think I got that one the wrong way around! In this chapter, we've seen that procrastination is a pervasive, pernicious and multifaceted problem, but that its workings are not exactly rocket science. Therefore, it shouldn't be surprising that the solutions to it are correspondingly simple. If you put some concerted effort into implementing the simple tips I've provided, I'd wager you will be surprised at their impact on how productively you use your time.

References

Ainslie, G. (1992). *Picoeconomics: The strategic interaction of successive motivational states within the person*. Cambridge University Press.

Blunt, A. K. & Pychyl, T. A. (2000). Task aversiveness and procrastination: A multi-dimensional approach to task aversiveness across stages of personal projects. *Personality and Individual Differences, 28*(1), 153–167.

Buehler, R., Griffin, D. & Ross, M. (1994). Exploring the "planning fallacy": Why people underestimate their task completion times. *Journal of Personality and Social Psychology, 67*(3), 366.

Davis, D. R. & Abbitt, J. T. (2013). An investigation of the impact of an intervention to reduce academic procrastination using Short Message Service (SMS) technology. *Journal of Interactive Online Learning, 12*(3), 78–102.

Ferrari, J. R. & Emmons, R. A. (1995). Methods of procrastination and their relation to self-control and self-reinforcement: An exploratory study. *Journal of Social Behavior and Personality, 10*(1), 135–142.

Gollwitzer, P. M. & Sheeran, P. (2006). Implementation intentions and goal achievement: A meta-analysis of effects and processes. *Advances in Experimental Social Psychology, 38*, 69–119.

Gollwitzer, P. M., Gawrilow, C. & Oettingen, G. (2008). The power of planning: Effective self-regulation of goal striving. New York University, manuscript.

Howell, A. J., Watson, D. C., Powell, R. A. & Buro, K. (2006). Academic procrastination: The pattern and correlates of behavioural postponement. *Personality and Individual Differences, 40*(8), 1519–1530.

Kahneman, D. & Tversky, A. (1977). *Intuitive prediction: Biases and corrective procedures.* Decisions and Designs Inc.

Kim, K. R. & Seo, E. H. (2015). The relationship between procrastination and academic performance: A meta-analysis. *Personality and Individual Differences, 82*, 26–33.

Klassen, R. M., Krawchuk, L. L. & Rajani, S. (2008). Academic procrastination of undergraduates: Low self-efficacy to self-regulate predicts higher levels of procrastination. *Contemporary Educational Psychology, 33*(4), 915–931.

Krause, K. & Freund, A. M. (2014). Delay or procrastination: A comparison of self-report and behavioral measures of procrastination and their impact on affective well-being. *Personality and Individual Differences, 63*, 75–80.

Kruger, J. & Evans, M. (2004). If you don't want to be late, enumerate: Unpacking reduces the planning fallacy. *Journal of Experimental Social Psychology, 40*, 586–598.

Lay, C. H. (1992). Trait procrastination and the perception of person task characteristics. *Journal of Social Behavior and Personality, 7*(3), 483–494.

Leroy, V., Grégoire, J., Magen, E., Gross, J. J. & Mikolajczak, M. (2012). Resisting the sirens of temptation while studying: Using reappraisal to increase focus, enthusiasm, and performance. *Learning and Individual Differences, 22*(2), 263–268.

May, K. E. & Elder, A. D. (2018). Efficient, helpful, or distracting? A literature review of media multitasking in relation to academic performance. *International Journal of Educational Technology in Higher Education, 15*(1), 13.

Oettingen, G., Hönig, G. & Gollwitzer, P. M. (2000). Effective self-regulation of goal attainment. *International Journal of Educational Research, 33*(7–8), 705–732.

Owens, S. G., Bowman, C. G. & Dill, C. A. (2008). Overcoming procrastination: The effect of implementation intentions. *Journal of Applied Social Psychology, 38*(2), 366–384.

Perrin, C. J., Miller, N., Haberlin, A. T., Ivy, J. W., Meindl, J. N. & Neef, N. A. (2011). Measuring and reducing college students' procrastination. *Journal of Applied Behavior Analysis, 44*(3), 463–474.

Pychyl, T. A. (2013). *Solving the procrastination puzzle: A concise guide to strategies for change*. TarcherPerigee.

Rozental, A. & Carlbring, P. (2014). Understanding and treating procrastination: A review of a common self-regulatory failure. *Psychology, 5*(13), 1488–1502.

Schouwenburg, H. C. & Groenewoud, J. (2001). Study motivation under social temptation: Effects of trait procrastination. *Personality and Individual Differences, 30*(2), 229–240.

Steel, P. (2007). The nature of procrastination: A meta-analytic and theoretical review of quintessential self-regulatory failure. *Psychological Bulletin, 133*(1), 65–94.

Steel, P. & König, C. J. (2006). Integrating theories of motivation. *Academy of Management Review, 31*(4), 889–913.

Van Eerde, W. (2003). A meta-analytically derived nomological network of procrastination. *Personality and Individual Differences, 35*(6), 1401–1418.

Vohs, K. D. & Heatherton, T. F. (2000). Self-regulatory failure: A resource-depletion approach. *Psychological Science, 11*(3), 249–254.

Wieber, F. & Gollwitzer, P. (2010). Overcoming procrastination through planning. In C. Andreou & M. D. White (Eds.), *The thief of time: Philosophical essays on procrastination* (pp. 185–205). Oxford University Press.

Academic reading and note-taking

What we can all learn from *50 Shades of Grey*

An error does not become truth by reason of multiplied propagation,
nor does the truth become error because nobody will see it.
Mahatma Gandhi

You've probably heard the adage that you read for a degree. This is unquestionably true. Sorry! However, you may have inferred from this that a degree is a thinly veiled reading contest and the more reading you do, the better mark you'll get. This is not true and can be refuted by reference to a scenario that any lecturer will recognise.

> STUDENT: Hey Professor x, I read that whole chapter on long-term memory that you set us at the end of your lecture.
> PROFESSOR X: Excellent, what did you learn from your reading?
> STUDENT: ......

The disconcerting thing about the above scenario is the look of surprise and disappointment on the student's face when the lecturer doesn't just congratulate them on reading the chapter. It's almost as if the reading itself was perceived to be the objective of learning rather than the means to the objective.

Undeterred, the lecturer will probably ask how the student took notes on the chapter. At this point one of two things will happen, the first of which involves the lecturer being met with a blank (and slightly apologetic) face. Alternatively, the student will proudly throw a rainforest worth of notes at the lecturer. A quick examination of the remnants of the rainforest usually reveals lots of extensively highlighted photocopies and/or text that is a verbatim reiteration of the author's words. Neither scenario has helped the student recall any of what they have read. The latter scenario reflects a 'never mind the quality, feel the width' approach to studying.

Before I start looking like a condescending old git, I should concede that I was as guilty of ineffectual reading and note-taking practices as anyone before I took my degree in psychology. I mean, I was taught to read at school, I'd passed exams and got into university. Surely, that was evidence that my academic reading and note-taking were up to scratch? They weren't! Being skilled in reading and writing is one thing, understanding how to use those skills optimally to learn is quite another. Achieving this requires some understanding about the nature of memory. When it comes to both memory and your degree level studies, it's not a question of how much you've read, it's how much you've understood that matters.

What you need to know about memory: it doesn't work like a camera, so you might want to stop studying as if it did

1

Key advice: you don't reproduce information with your memory, you reconstruct it

I'm going to start this chapter with a demonstration. This will require a bit of effort on your part because I'm going to ask you to read the short story below and then try and recall it. Your efforts will be rewarded with a demonstration of one of the fundamental characteristics of human memory. If not, then you will have the dubious honour of being the person who successfully undermined the findings of one of the seminal experiments in cognitive psychology. The following Canadian Indian piece of folklore is called War of the Ghosts and was used in research by Bartlett (1932).

> One night two young men from Egulac went down to the river to hunt seals and while they were there it became foggy and calm. Then they heard war-cries, and they thought: "Maybe this is a war-party". They escaped to the shore, and hid behind a log. Now canoes came up, and they heard the noise of paddles, and saw one canoe coming up to them. There were five men in the canoe, and they said:
>
> "What do you think? We wish to take you along. We are going up the river to make war on the people."
>
> One of the young men said, "I have no arrows."
>
> "Arrows are in the canoe," they said.
>
> "I will not go along. I might be killed. My relatives do not know where I have gone. But you," he said, turning to the other, "may go with them."
>
> So one of the young men went, but the other returned home.
>
> And the warriors went on up the river to a town on the other side of Kalama. The people came down to the water and they began to fight, and many were killed. But presently the young man heard one of the warriors say, "Quick, let us go home: that Indian has been hit." Now he thought: "Oh, they are ghosts." He did not feel sick, but they said he had been shot.

> So the canoes went back to Egulac and the young man went ashore to his house and made a fire. And he told everybody and said: "Behold I accompanied the ghosts, and we went to fight. Many of our fellows were killed, and many of those who attacked us were killed. They said I was hit, and I did not feel sick."
>
> He told it all, and then he became quiet. When the sun rose he fell down. Something black came out of his mouth. His face became contorted. The people jumped up and cried.
>
> He was dead.

I know what you're thinking: "Well, that made more sense than most episodes of *Twin Peaks*!" If you want to have a go at Bartlett's experiment, make yourself scarce for 15 minutes. In your absence, grab a pen and paper or just something that you can record your voice with if you're feeling averse to writing. After the 15 minutes have passed, either write down or dictate your recollection of the story. You're on your honour not to peek at the story as you're trying to recall it! Then, compare your version to the original.

My instructions to you broadly correspond to what the participants in Bartlett's study were asked to do. Upon examining their recollections of the War of the Ghosts story, Bartlett made several important observations. First, the recalled stories tended to be shorter than the original. Second, although the gist of the original story had been retained, the participants' recall of its contents was distorted. These distortions weren't random; they were purposeful. The participants had changed certain elements of the story so that it made more sense to them with respect to their knowledge, experience and cultural expectations. For example, the participants tended to omit details that did not seem meaningful or significant. In your recollection of the story, did you remember that the two men hid behind a log, or that they heard paddles? Participants also tended to expand upon details to enhance meaning. For example, did you recall the story in its original highly fractured and disjointed way, or did you embellish it to make it a more conventional narrative? Participants rationalised ambiguous or esoteric material into a form that could be more easily understood given their own experience and expectations. Did you accurately recall the more supernatural parts of the story, e.g. the bit where: "something black came out of his mouth"? Perhaps you translated this into something like: "vomit came out of his mouth"? Whatever the specific details of your recollection of the story, comparing it with the original version should yield one clear conclusion: your memory did not passively reproduce the story verbatim. It did not function like a camera and faithfully reproduce the scene through its view-finder. Instead, it actively reconstructed the story in accordance with your own personal experience and expectations. Sticking with the photography analogy, the crux of Bartlett's contribution to the study of memory was that memory is not about generating megapixels, but rather about generating meaning. I've started this chapter with Bartlett's research because its chief implication underpins everything that follows: your memory doesn't function like a camera, so stop studying as if it did. If the function of memory is to construct meaning, then approaches to reading and note-taking need to be orientated accordingly. With that in mind, let's look at some issues with academic reading and note-taking practices and see what can be done to remedy them. We'll start off by focusing on some errors associated with reading practices.

Maximum effort, minimal gains: why the most popular method of studying is not what it's cracked up to be

2

Key advice: repetition is not the most effective means of committing information to memory

It's 9 pm and you've just finished the fourth read-through of the paper your tutor has asked you to be familiar with for tomorrow's seminar. You don't feel any more clued up about its contents than when you finished the first read-through. It just won't sink in! Still, fifth time's a charm. If you repeat something often enough, eventually osmosis will kick in, right? Well, if you believe that repetition is your best friend when it comes to committing something to memory, then you're in good company. Karpicke, Butler and Roediger III (2009) found that 83% of the undergraduates in their study reported using re-reading when studying and 54% of the sample identified it as their number one study method. Here's the problem: it doesn't seem to work that well compared to other methods of studying. At this point, you might be reeling at the suggestion that repetition is not all it's cracked up to be. However, this is old news within psychology. Craik and Watkins (1973) wanted to establish whether the length of exposure to a stimulus, or the amount of repetitions it received during that period, affected an individual's ability to recall it. They devised a very elegant experiment in which participants were verbally given word lists to commit to memory and asked to be vigilant for a target letter. Upon hearing a word containing this target letter, they were asked to rehearse that word out loud (at a set tempo) until they heard the next word in the list containing the target letter. This approach allowed the experimenters to manipulate the length of exposure to the target words and the number of repetitions they received. Following a one-minute distractor task and a ten-minute break, participants were asked to recall as many of the words they had heard as possible. The test results indicated that neither the duration of exposure nor the number of repetitions associated with a target word predicted the likelihood of it being recalled. Craik and Watkins went on to make the distinction between maintenance and elaborative rehearsal. They argued that increasing length of exposure and number of repetitions is effective for the maintenance of material in short-term memory. An example of such a scenario would be when you are trying to remember a phone number whilst you find a pen and paper to scribble it down on. However, exposure and repetition, in and of themselves, are ineffective for retaining information in the longer term. In this scenario, what you do with the information you're exposed to becomes much more important than how long you spend with it, or how many times you rehearse it.

3

Key advice: thinking is the key to memory

Having learned of the Craik and Watkins study, you might wonder if the reason repetition did not improve recall performance was that the target words were not particularly memorable. For example, maybe they happened to be more esoteric or difficult. That would be a good suggestion, but experiments involving word lists as tests of memory do control for factors such as familiarity and difficulty. However, in contemplating what words were used in this study, you're engaging in a potent catalyst for memory: thinking. Craik and Tulving (1975) argued for the levels of processing framework of memory (Craik & Lockhart, 1972). This proposed that it was the depth of an individual's engagement with a stimulus that best determined whether it would be recalled in the long term. Shallow engagement with a stimulus that was achieved by, for example, examining its appearance is not conducive to being able to remember it in the longer term. In contrast, deep engagement with a stimulus, achieved by interrogating its meaning, would produce a much more durable memory. Craik and Tulving tested the levels of processing theory with a simple experiment. Once again, participants would be presented with word lists, with each word appearing sequentially. The presentation of each word was preceded with one of three types of question that induced a certain type of processing for that word. The first type of question required the participants to focus on the structural aspects of the word. For example: "Does the word appear in capital letters?" or "Is the word in italics?" The second type of question required the participants to focus on the phonetic quality of the word. For example: "Does the word rhyme with train?" The third type of question required the participants to focus on the semantics (meaning) of the word. This was achieved in one of two ways. One way involved asking the participant about the word's category membership, for example: "Is the word an animal?" The other way required the participant to put it in a sentence, for example: "Would the word fit in the following sentence? The girl put the ______ on the table." When the presentation of the words concluded, the participants were given a short break. Following this, they received a sheet of paper containing all 40 words they had just been presented with mixed up with 40 novel words. Their task was to identify as many of the words they had originally been presented with as possible. Participants were most successful at recognising words that had previously been presented with a question that required them to be processed semantically, i.e. by their meaning. In fact, words from the list that had been processed semantically were as much as five times as likely to be recognised as words that were processed structurally. The take-home message of this classic piece of psychological research is that engagement with the meaning of what you read (i.e. deeper processing) is optimal if you want to remember that information.

Never mind the width, feel the quality: elucidating meaning from your reading

4

Key advice: if you want to remember something, work on explaining it

At this point you might be wondering how you can translate research on memory for obscure folklore or word lists into more effective reading practice. Well, if we're arguing that thinking about content facilitates our ability to remember it, the question is: "What is the best catalyst for promoting thinking when we're reading?" Pressley, McDaniel, Turnure, Wood and Ahmad (1987) were among the first to demonstrate a technique to encourage readers to engage more deeply with text, called elaborative interrogation. This technique simply requires the reader to generate an explanation in response to specified facts within a text. In their experiment, Pressley et al. asked undergraduate students to read 24 sentences. They split the participants into three groups. One group read base sentences where the relationship between the subject and the action was seemingly arbitrary, e.g. "The fat man read the sign". Another group read versions of those sentences embellished with a precise elaboration, identifying the significance of the relationship between the subject and action. For example: "The fat man read the sign warning about thin ice." The final group were asked to read the sentences and then answer a question accompanying them. For the base sentences like "The fat man read the sign", the question would be: "why would the man do that?" This type of question prompted the participants to reply with an imprecise elaboration, e.g. "Because he was heavy". For the sentences featuring precise elaborations like: "The fat man read the sign warning about thin ice", the question would be: "How did the last part of that sentence make clear why that particular man did that?" This type of question prompted the participants to reply with a precise elaboration of their own, e.g. "The thin ice sign explains why the fat man looked at it. He wanted to avoid inadvertently stepping on ice that might not be able to support his weight". The participants' memory was tested by factual questions about each of the 24 sentences presented. The question for the base and precise elaboration example sentences given above was "Who read the sign?". The correct answer was: "The fat man." The results of the experiment indicated that the participants who were given the precise elaboration version of the sentences achieved higher scores on the memory test than those who were given the base sentences. However, the improvement was only moderate and limited to when the participants weren't told that they were going to be tested. In contrast, participants who generated their own elaborations in response to the questions about the sentences displayed substantially better performance on the memory test. The best performance was achieved by participants who had to give precise elaborations in response to questions. The effect of the participants providing their own elaboration on the text occurred irrespective of whether they knew they were going to be tested.

Pressley et al.'s findings make perfect sense when you consider them in relation to the proposition that deep processing of information is superior to shallow processing. The participants who had a precise elaboration provided for them had the requisite information to see the meaning in the text. Therefore, they were at an advantage over those who only had the base sentences available. However, the meaning of the text was given to them; they didn't construct that meaning for themselves. Consequently, they were still processing the information in a shallow way because they weren't active in thinking about the material. Rather, they were the passive recipients of meaning. This was reflected in modest gains in their memory performance. In contrast, the participants who were generating their own precise elaborations were active in producing meaning for themselves. They were processing the material deeply, which generated bigger gains in memory performance. The participants who answered questions based on precise elaboration were at an additional advantage because they were being induced to think about the mechanism of the relationship between the subject and action explicitly. This prompted the deepest level of thinking about the material and, thus, the best memory performance.

A reservation sometimes raised about elaborative interrogation is the possibility that it might only benefit students who are highly motivated by their interest in a topic, or those who already have a good working knowledge of it. However, a study by Ozgungor and Guthrie (2004) suggests this is not the case. They gave undergraduates questionnaires to assess their prior knowledge of (and interest in) the subject of phantom limb pain. Before being given a 1,500-word passage to read on this subject, the participants were assigned to one of two reading groups. The experimental group were given a version of the text where each of the paragraphs was interspersed with questions about preceding information. An example of such a question would be: "How does the evidence support this assertion?" This manipulation required the students to use elaborative interrogation in reading the text. The control group were just given the standard passage of text with no prompts to elicit elaborative interrogation. Instead, they were told to read the passage twice at a rate that would best enable them to understand its contents. After reading the text, both groups were given tests of their recall, ability to form inferences based on the information presented and ability to generate coherence (links) between the concepts covered. The students who used elaborative interrogation when reading the text outperformed those who just re-read the material in all three of these tests. Most importantly, the use of elaborative interrogation remained a significant predictor of memory performance even when prior knowledge and interest in the topic were controlled for. The lesson from the research on elaborative interrogation is simple: questioning serves as an effective catalyst for engaging with material more deeply. Simply reading your course materials will provide you with another author's understanding of a topic, but that's not optimal in fostering your own understanding. Elaborative interrogation is a good way to get you processing what you read at a deeper level and, in doing so, extract the meaning from your source materials for yourself. However, it's worth remembering that it doesn't occur automatically. In research, the use of elaborative interrogation is imposed by an experimenter. You won't have one of those standing over you when you study. If you do, I'd suggest that the first elaborative question you ask is: "How did you get into my house?" or: "Are you familiar with the laws relating to stalking?" We'll return to the topic of how to use questions to invigorate your studying a bit further on in the chapter. First, let's address some things that don't work as well as you might think when note-taking.

Take note: your note-taking might not be working for you as well as you think

5

Key advice: taking notes from a source verbatim is no more effective than just reading it, but a lot more effort!

We've established that simply reading (and re-reading) course materials superficially, without actively extracting meaning from them, is not a good idea. This approach constitutes shallow processing, which is not conducive to memory. However, there is an approach to note-taking that promotes similarly shallow processing that I need to try and dissuade you from using. I'm referring to the practice of note-taking that is based on verbatim (word-for-word copying) of content. If you subscribe to the 'never mind the quality, feel the width' approach to studying, then verbatim note-taking makes a perverse kind of sense. Even a 15-minute lecture would translate to pages of notes if transcribed verbatim. I can well imagine that looking at such a wedge of paperwork feels like hard-won progress. But wait just a minute! Producing notes only represents progress if you've gotten something out of the process, other than repetitive strain injury and/or insomnia! Real progress equates to improvements in your knowledge and understanding of the topic at hand. So, does the research indicate that people are any the wiser having used verbatim note-taking? Also, how does it compare to other methods of note-taking?

Research into the effectiveness of note-taking is certainly not a recent development. An influential early study by Bretzing and Kulhavy (1979) provided some illuminating insight. They asked students to read a 2,000-word text about a fictitious tribe in a period of 30 minutes. They assigned their participants to one of five note-taking groups. A summarisation group were asked to write three lines of text that best captured the main points of the piece immediately after reading each page. A note-taking group were given the same instructions, with the exception that they could summarise during (not just after) reading each page of text. A verbatim-copying group were asked to copy (word for word) the three most important lines of text from each page. A letter search group copied up to three lines worth of all the words featuring capital letters within the piece. Finally, a control group were just told to read the paper with no additional instructions. The students were tested either immediately following the study period or one week later via 25 questions that probed their recall of the contents of the text. The results indicated that the recall scores for students in the verbatim note-taking condition were no better than those of participants in the reading only condition. That finding is even more damning than it sounds, as this experiment utilised a generous definition of verbatim copying. The students in the verbatim copying condition had discretion about what they copied. Therefore, they were at least thinking about what material might have been most important to copy word for word, as opposed to just taking down everything. As you might have guessed, the students who exhibited the best recall scores in this experiment were those in the note-taking and summarisation conditions. These conditions were differentiated from the verbatim condition by the participants writing their notes in their own words. So, is this a ringing endorsement of any form of note-taking where you use your own words to summarise the important points of course materials? Nope, not exactly. It's better to view the above study as a good demonstration of what not to do when taking notes than being instructive on what to do.

It might surprise you to learn that research on summarisation over the last 40 years has been rather inconsistent in supporting its use as an effective method of studying. As part of an excellent literature review of commonly used study strategies, Dunlosky, Rawson, Marsh, Nathan and Willingham (2013) surveyed the evidence concerning the implementation and efficacy of summarisation. They concluded that it was a method of study with low utility. At this point you're probably wondering why summarisation hasn't been unequivocally supported by the research. After all, I have emphasised the reconstructive nature of memory, and indicated that effective study practices need to take account of this. Isn't summarisation doing exactly that? Don't worry, there is a very simple explanation and it can be easily illustrated if you've either: (a) ever worked in computer programming, or (b) asked someone else to describe the plot of a film they've seen recently.

6

Key advice: the effectiveness of summarisation is contingent on the summaries being good!

Consider, if you will, the film *Batman, the Dark Knight*. Ask me to summarise that film and I might tell you the following. It's about the superhero Batman, the alter ego of one of the financial pillars of Gotham City, and his nemesis the Joker who is a maniacal anarchist who terrorises the citizens of Gotham. However, the subtext of the film is much deeper and darker. It alludes to the symbiosis of good and evil and the inevitable escalation when either side arises. It's also about the capacity of injustice and despair to corrupt a noble man. This is exemplified in the transition of Harvey Dent from the District Attorney of Gotham into the supervillain Two Face. Contrast this summary with the synopsis of the film given by the website postmodernbarney.com: "Wealthy man assaults the mentally ill." His version is much funnier, I'll give you that. However, were this summary to be the basis of notes for learning about the plot of the film, I think it would prove a little less useful than mine. This example illustrates the main reason for the variable success of summarisation as a strategy. The effectiveness of summarisation is fundamentally tied to how well it is done, and individuals can vary considerably in terms of the quality of the summaries they produce. This was illustrated quite nicely in a study by Bednall and Kehoe (2011). In this study, an entire cohort of undergraduate students were given a web module on logical fallacies to complete as homework. A logical fallacy is a common flaw in the process of reasoning. For example, believing that if an outcome (like feeling better following a bout of flu) follows an action (like taking a remedy) then the action must have caused the outcome. Of course, we don't know this unless we do a well-designed experiment that rules out the recovery being due to other things, like time! This is called a post-hoc fallacy. The web module given to the students contained six different logical fallacies, each fallacy was accompanied by a workbook. Each of these workbooks contained descriptions of a fallacy, examples and explanations along with advice on negating it. In taking this module, students were assigned to one of four study conditions. In an explanation condition, participants were asked to provide a written account of the reasoning error present in each example of the fallacy and then compare their explanations to the ones provided in the workbook. They were then invited to review all their explanations again. In the summarisation condition, participants were asked to compose a written summary of the fallacy upon concluding its workbook. This summary was available to them each time they returned to that page of the workbook. In the explanation and summarisation condition, the participants both explained and summarised each fallacy in their workbooks. Finally, participants in the control condition were left to study their workbooks without any intervention. Upon completion of the module, participants were given a series of three tests of their knowledge of the fallacies and their ability to spot them in both the scenarios already covered in their workbooks and in novel contexts. Participants were also given measures of their enjoyment of, and interest in, the topic. Additionally, the experimenters also took a measure of how easy the students perceived studying the material to be. The headline finding of the study was that, unlike explanation, summarisation did not significantly improve test performance. Also, ratings of ease of learning were significantly lower for the summarisation group than the explanation group, even though their interest and enjoyment ratings were the same. When the experimenters examined the content of the summaries, they found substantial variation in their quality. For example, they noted that only 64% of the summaries provided a correct definition of the fallacies. Only 58% had provided supplementary information such as examples of each fallacy. As you would expect, the accuracy and amount of supplementary information within the summaries was correlated with performance at testing. Students who had more accurate definitions and provided more in the way of supplementary information tended to do better when assessed. Summarisation only being as good as the person who uses it doesn't rule it out as a candidate for an effective study strategy. However, it does serve as a caution and impetus to ask what you can do to improve your ability to summarise. Well, let's start by looking at something that students often use to facilitate the generation of summaries (and note-taking generally). I refer to highlighter pens. Spoiler alert: the news is not great!

Marker pens aren't magic

7

Key advice: be sceptical about the effectiveness of highlighting. Less is more

At one point, most of us have reached for a highlighter pen in researching a topic. Hartwig and Dunlosky (2012) found that 72% of the undergraduates surveyed identified regularly using highlighting or underlining in their studying repertoire. It does seem like an intuitively good idea. Unless you don't own the book you're colouring in, that is! Retailers have a no-refunds policy on academic texts that have been turned into a work of modern art. In principle, highlighting is a good idea. It's neither necessary, desirable or even possible to remember everything that you read. What matters more is whether the important points have been understood accurately. Therefore, identifying and highlighting the most important points of a text should facilitate the note-taking process. However, like summarisation, the research on the effectiveness of highlighting has been anything but unequivocally supportive.

An influential early study on the effects of highlighting on memory for academic text was reported by Fowler and Barker (1974). They asked undergraduates to read published journal articles about city life and boredom within an hour. The participants were randomly assigned to one of three conditions. In an active highlighting condition, they were free to highlight as much of the text as they wished with the instruction that they should highlight particularly important material. In a passive highlighting condition, participants were yoked to another participant in the active highlighting condition. This meant that they read the text that had already been highlighted by the other participant; they did not do any highlighting of their own. Finally, in a control condition, participants simply read the text with no highlighting permitted. After a period of one week, participants returned and were allowed ten minutes to review the text (complete with the annotation in the highlighted conditions) before taking a multiple-choice question (MCQ) test. Overall, participants in the highlighting conditions did not perform any better than those in the control condition. Where relevant information was highlighted, participants in the active group performed better than those in the yoked group for the applicable questions. This is not surprising, given that participants in the active condition were having to think about the importance of the material they read in deciding what to highlight. In contrast, participants in the yoked group had no discretion about what they highlighted. As with summarisation, it seems that the effectiveness of highlighting is very much tied to how well someone can identify the important information.

When it comes to highlighting, research indicates that less is more. Excessive highlighting can be indicative of issues with other aspects of studying, e.g. poor reading practices. As with taking verbatim notes, poor use of highlighting creates an illusory impression of how much effort you've invested in studying. Brandishing pages of highlighted text makes it look like you've really got stuck into the material, but doesn't necessarily mean that you've done anything more than colouring stuff in! Bell and Limber (2009) studied undergraduate student propensity to use highlighting, in addition to how well they used it. They found that students with poorer reading skills reported more reliance on highlighting. They used highlighting more extensively than their more skilled peers and were deemed less capable of identifying important information by course tutors. Even studies that have found a positive effect of highlighting have supported the less is more philosophy. Yue, Storm, Kornell and Bjork (2015) asked undergraduates to read a passage from the US geological survey website under one of two conditions. In a highlighting condition, participants were told to highlight text in a manner consistent with their usual practice when studying material for a class. In a control condition, they simply read the text with no highlighting permitted. The students then had the opportunity to read the text again, before being given a questionnaire to assess their use of highlighting in their studying repertoire. One week later, the participants were given a test that contained phrases from the text they had previously read, but which featured missing keywords. Their task was to recall the missing words. When the experimenters analysed the results, they made three interesting discoveries. First, the students who used highlighting heavily did not perform as well on the test as those who used highlighting lightly. An examination of the annotation from the heavy highlighters indicated that they were less efficient than light highlighters at identifying keywords. Second, participants who reported using highlighting as a study strategy most frequently highlighted more words than those who reported using it less frequently. Third, the performance of the students who were most positive about highlighting did not differ significantly between the highlighting and control conditions. In other words, a student's tendency to use highlighting did not translate to improved skill in implementing it, or improved performance when using it to study. In fact, only those who were unsure about the benefits of highlighting significantly profited from its use. Taken together, these results indicate that it's not the act of highlighting per se that seems to confer any benefits. Those who just confidently turn their reading material into a work of modern art by merrily highlighting anything that seems vaguely relevant do not benefit from the process. Those who are less sure about the benefits of highlighting and who invest more effort into thinking about what to highlight, and why, benefit more. There's that 'thinking' word again! Are you seeing a pattern developing here?

Treat yourself, test yourself

8

Key advice: self-testing should be an integral part of your reading and note-taking

At this point in the chapter, you'd be forgiven for getting the impression that the news is bleak when it comes to advice on reading and note-taking. I've spent most of this chapter telling you that the most common reading and note-taking strategies aren't optimal and that your trusty highlighter pen won't invariably transform your note-taking for the better. That's all well and good to know, but explaining what doesn't work well is only half the battle. Let's turn to what does work and how you can use it! To do this, we need to re-visit something we first touched on at the end of Chapter l. I'm referring to the testing effect. You might remember this as the finding that repeated testing (i.e. retrieval practice) of material produces superior recall to an equivalent period re-studying that material. A recurrent theme in this chapter has been that the amount of effort you put into thinking about material is critical to the likelihood you'll remember it. We've also identified that the findings on elaborative interrogation indicate that asking questions is a potent catalyst for thinking. So, it's not hard to see the rationale for making use of the testing effect in the context of reading and note-taking. There is an extensive body of research attesting to the effectiveness of retrieval practice in the retention of academic material. An overview of the literature is well beyond the scope of this chapter (the interested reader is referred to Karpicke, 2017). However, it's worth looking at an example of the research demonstrating the effectiveness of retrieval practice before considering how to incorporate it into your reading and note-taking.

Butler (2010) conducted a series of experiments examining the efficacy of retrieval practice in the retention of facts and concepts. The basic experimental set up involved asking students to read a series of six passages of information. Each of these passages addressed a different topic. The experimenters extracted two different categories of questions from each of the passages of text. First, factual questions, e.g. "Approximately how many bat species are there in the world?" (p. 1121). Second, conceptual questions, e.g. "Some bats use echo-location to navigate the environment and locate prey. How does echolocation help a bat to determine the distance and size of objects?" (p. 1121). Each student studied all six passages of text. Two of the passages were repeatedly studied (re-read), two were repeatedly tested with the same questions (same test) and two were repeatedly tested with differently worded questions requiring the same answers (different test). In the re-testing conditions, the participants were given feedback on each of their attempts at the tests. One week later, they took a final test to assess their learning. In Butler's first experiment, passages studied by retrieval practice yielded significantly better performance on the final test, for both factual and conceptual questions, than passages repeatedly studied. This applied irrespective of whether the retrieval practice tests used were consistently worded between each attempt. The final test featured the addition of a third inferential category of question. Inferential questions involve the application of learning within the same knowledge domain. So, for the passage of text that explained the process of echo location, an inferential question was: "An insect is moving towards a bat. Using the process of echolocation, how does the bat determine that the insect is moving towards it?" (p. 1121). Performance on these inferential questions was also superior for passages that had been studied by retrieval practice than for those simply re-read.

In the second experiment, Butler wanted to rule out the possibility that the superiority of retrieval practice might be due to the amount of time students spent studying relevant information. This was necessary because when participants were learning via retrieval practice, the questions directly specified the information relevant to addressing them. In contrast, when students were learning by re-studying passages, they had to find the relevant information within the passage. Butler levelled the playing field by adding a further learning condition where students only re-studied the isolated facts that the questions were based on. Once again, performance on both factual and conceptual information was significantly better for the passages that were repeatedly tested than those that were repeatedly studied. The performance of participants who repeatedly studied isolated facts was no better than those who repeatedly studied the entire passage containing those facts.

In the third and final experiment, Butler wanted to ascertain whether what had been learned via retrieval practice could be transferred to a new, but related, subject domain. This was investigated by adding transfer questions to the final test. For example, one of the passages would provide exposition about the merits and drawbacks of the wing structures of bats and birds. A transfer question would ask the students to identify how the wing structures of bats and birds might inform the design of wings for fighter jets. The students obtained the highest scores for the passages of text that were studied via repeated testing for these transfer questions. I think you'll agree that Butler provided a comprehensive demonstration of the power of repeated testing as a method of studying. His work illustrates a very important point about retrieval practice. It is not simply a cynical exercise in learning to the test that is limited to scenarios where you know what questions will be featured in a subsequent exam. In Butler's study, using different questions between iterations of retrieval practice did not negate the testing effect, neither did the use of unfamiliar questions in the final test. The effectiveness of retrieval practice was not simply limited to facts, it also extended to concepts. Finally, retrieval practice was more conducive to the transfer of knowledge to a new domain. So, how does it work?

One of the principle reasons for the effectiveness of retrieval practice is its impact on that all-important concept of metacognition, referred to in Chapter I. Effective learning is contingent on having an accurate idea of what you know and what you don't know. This is a bit more involved than it sounds, because our judgements of our knowledge aren't always black and white. Rather, they are based on subjective levels of confidence. Let's illustrate this point with an example. You emerge from a multiple-choice exam and immediately do the one thing that all academics tell you not to do: compare answers with your peers. A classmate asks you what you put for the final question and you remember that, initially, you had a feeling that the answer was 'b'. However, option 'd' ended up resonating with you a bit more. You were a bit more confident that it was the correct answer, so chose it instead. Your classmate immediately looks smug and tells you they know for a fact that you should have gone with your gut, as 'b' was definitely the right response! Appropriately enough, the correct response to this realisation also starts with a 'b'! The point is that it's possible to be right and not be sure of it. Uncertainty can lead to avoidable errors. Testing can be just as helpful in addressing these instances as it is in addressing those occasions when you're wrong but are confident you are right.

Butler, Karpicke and Roediger III (2008) demonstrated the capacity of retrieval practice to correct metacognitive judgements of knowledge in a couple of neat experiments. In experiment one, a group of students were given an initial MCQ test on general knowledge involving the provision of feedback on half of the questions, but not the other half. Another group of students were assigned to a no-test control group. For the participants who received the initial test, specifying a response to each question was mandatory (even if it was a guess). They were also asked to numerically rate their confidence in each of their answers. For questions featuring feedback, the participants would be shown the correct answer before moving on to the following question. For questions featuring no feedback, the next question would be displayed in a time-frame equal to questions where feedback was provided. Following the completion of the practice test and a five-minute delay, participants were then given a final test, which consisted of the 40 items in the MCQ practice test and 20 previously untested items. Not surprisingly, the greatest proportion of correct responses in the final test was achieved by the students in the initial testing condition for the questions where feedback was given. Also, as one would hope, initially incorrect responses benefited from feedback, being corrected for the final test. As importantly, initially correct responses were maintained for the final test. When the experimenters examined how feedback and confidence interacted, they made an important discovery. Feedback doubled the likelihood that an initially correct response with little confidence attached to it would be retained in the final test, relative to when no feedback was provided. Butler et al. extended their findings by replicating their experiment. This time they also asked participants to rate their confidence in the answers they gave in the final test, as well as the initial test. In addition to this, they extended the period between the initial and final test from five minutes to two days. The results were consistent with the first experiment. However, they also demonstrated that feedback served to enhance the accuracy of the participants' confidence in their responses. So, where a participant had initially given a correct response but not been confident in their answer, feedback increased their confidence in responding to the corresponding question in the final test. Retrieval practice with feedback allows you to more accurately judge what you do know from what you don't know, i.e. it improves your metacognitive awareness.

Unfortunately, the capacity of retrieval practice to improve metacognitive awareness is not reflected in its uptake as a preferred study strategy. You might recall that the research referred to in Chapter I highlighted the relatively ineffectual method of re-reading as being the preferred method of study. In contrast, students were much less inclined to administer a spot of self-testing. This means that, for many students, their principle source of metacognitive information is the result they get on the formal test that they'd been studying for. Too little, too late! It's no wonder students often view the idea of testing as about as appealing as dental surgery. The trick is to stop viewing tests as something that are formally done to you to assess how much you've learned. Rather, view them as something you do informally to yourself as an integral part of the process of learning. Let's have a look at a method of reading and note-taking that will help you achieve this that also calls upon the methods of elaborative interrogation and summarisation that we've previously covered.

The read, recite, review method of studying

Once you start to view testing as less of a foe and more of an ally, you can take ownership of it and incorporate it into your studying. With that in mind, let's examine a method you can use to unobtrusively incorporate retrieval practice into your reading and note-taking: the Read, Recite, Review (3R) method (McDaniel, Howard & Einstein, 2009). The beauty of this method is its simplicity; the steps are all covered in its name! McDaniel et al. conducted two experiments to evaluate the effectiveness of this technique. In the first experiment, students were asked to learn a series of educational texts. They were allocated to one of three studying conditions. In a re-reading condition, they were instructed to read each passage twice. In a note-taking condition, the students were asked to read each passage twice and take notes on it, using a separate piece of paper, whilst they were reading. In the 3R condition, they were told to read each passage once, recite as much as they could remember from it into a tape recorder, and then read the passage again. After a period of three minutes spent performing a series of distractor tasks (e.g. mental arithmetic) they were given a test of their ability to recall the material, immediately and then one week later. Participants in the 3R condition exhibited superior recall of the passages compared to their counterparts in the re-reading and note-taking conditions. This finding was replicated in a second experiment involving test materials that went beyond simple factual information and included passages of text and engineering diagrams. Participants were tested on both their recall of information and response to inference questions requiring they apply what they had learned to solve problems. Once again, the performance of the participants using the 3R method proved superior to the note-taking and re-reading groups. Of particular note was the observation that the 3R method was less time-consuming than the note-taking approach. I'm going to advocate you use a slight variation of the 3R method to that outlined in the previous experiment. It involves the same three basic steps, with a few small refinements that I will explain as we encounter them.

Step 1: Read, but decide what you want to get out of the material first!
First, decide what you want to get out of the material you're about to read. For example, maybe you want to learn about a particular theory. This gives your reading a purpose. I know, this sounds like a blindingly obvious piece of advice. However, be honest, how many times have you dived into a source recommended by a tutor with nothing other than the general aim of learning something and just read it from start to finish? Why? If you haven't thought of any questions then the material in the text, by definition, can't provide you with any answers. You're reading aimlessly! It's generally not a good idea to read academic material the same way as fictional material, unless that fictional material happens to be something like *50 Shades of Grey*. Err, I should probably explain! What was the first thing you did when you picked up *50 Shades of Grey*, or a similar title? You skimmed over the contents looking for the good bits, didn't you? It's OK. So did I, before I got politely asked to leave the bookshop. The point is that you were reading it with the intention of locating the material that was salient to the goal at hand (no pun intended). In this case, that goal was titillation. Why not take the same approach when reading an academic text? No, I don't mean look for racy content! I mean think of what you specifically want to get out of the source so that you can audit what you read for its fitness of purpose and focus in on the most salient bits. Having decided what you would like to get out of the material you're reading, you then read it (bet you didn't see that bit coming!)

Step 2: Recite, but do it in writing!
Following reading the source material, you should place it somewhere out of sight. Then, try and recite its contents. By doing this you organically incorporate self-testing into your studying. It encourages you to try and commit more manageable chunks of reading to memory, rather than biting off way more than you can chew. Only a card-carrying masochist would try and recite an entire book chapter. There are several good reasons I'm advocating that you recite the material by writing down what you can remember rather than just verbally reciting your recollection. First, as we've seen from the literature reviewed, note-taking can be effective if it's done well. Integrating self-testing into the note-taking process naturally exploits the principles of interrogative elaboration and summarisation referred to earlier. Second, having the process of self-testing documented also facilitates its metacognitive benefits. It's much easier to compare a written (as opposed to verbal) response to source materials in the review phase of 3R when trying to establish what you do and don't know. You can then use this

information to re-focus your reading and refine your notes. Finally, by basing your notes on your written recall of information, you automatically avoid the ineffectual practice of verbatim note-taking from the source. Moreover, translating ideas into your own words forces you to think about the material (engage with it more deeply) so that you can articulate it.

Step 3: Review and then act on the information!

In the review stage, you compare your notes to the source material and consider whether you have answered the questions you set out to address originally. If so, are your answers accurate? You might find that your first attempt at recitation is pretty hopeless. If so, give yourself a pat on the back! I'm serious! The point is that your perception of your state of learning (i.e. your metacognitive awareness) is now based on evidence rather than guesswork! When you have a better idea of what you know and what you don't know, you can orientate your subsequent efforts to read the material and refine your notes accordingly. You do this by repeating the 3R process iteratively until your notes answer the questions you had at the outset of your reading and faithfully reflect the facts (not the wording) of the source material. As we've seen from the study by Butler, Karpicke and Roediger III (2008), memory performance benefits from feedback. Making the testing process iterative is a good way of achieving this. It also lets you refine your notes to a point that you can rely on them in consolidating what you have learned rather than the source material.

I know this approach to the 3R method sounds like a lot more work than good old re-reading. However, this is not necessarily the case. Dickinson and O'Connell (1990) surveyed the total time spent studying between a group of high- and low-attaining students. They found that the differences in the time the two groups devoted to studying amounted to only one hour per week. Both groups invested a similar amount of time reading and reviewing. Where they differed, however, was in the amount of their study time they spent engaged with articulating sources in their own words, creating their own connections between concepts and furnishing their thinking with examples. It's not that the high-attaining students were spending a lot more time studying per se. Rather, they were just spending a greater proportion of that time actively and deeply engaging with the material rather than passively and superficially reviewing it.

Summary

Never mind the breadth, check out the depth

Early on in this chapter, I made the assertion that your memory doesn't work like a camera, so you might want to stop studying as if it did. I argued that memory was reconstructive, not reproductive, so to get the most out of it you need to be an active participant in the process of studying. Let's review some of the do's and don'ts in this respect.

- Don't just re-read information. The important word in this piece of advice is 'just'. The problem isn't so much with re-reading per se, as much as an over-reliance on it as the primary, or even sole, method of studying. When it comes to trying to commit academic information to memory, simple repetition doesn't cut it.
- Use elaborative interrogation. Asking your own questions of material is a potent catalyst for thinking about what you are reading. Try and focus on questions that require you to provide explanations, and endeavour to show how the explanation has been derived from the source material.
- Don't copy your notes verbatim from existing text. The value of note-taking is derived from the meaning you extract from the source text. Reiterating existing content passively is no better than just re-reading it, not to mention a lot more work!
- Summarise information, but do not assume that your summaries are accurate or comprehensive until you have verified them against the source text. With summaries, less is not always more. Their usefulness is invariably tied to whether they capture the key information and their accuracy.
- Highlighting information alone won't help you remember it. The less discriminating you are about what you highlight, the more ineffective the process becomes. What limited value highlighting has is derived from the discretion exercised in its use, i.e. thinking about why you've highlighted something.
- Make extensive use of retrieval practice (self-testing) as part of your approach to studying. Testing isn't just something you do to assess learning; it's what you do to promote and guide your learning. If you don't have the metacognitive awareness that comes

from retrieval practice, you can't orientate your subsequent reading and note-taking effectively.

- Use a method such as 3R to organically integrate elaborative interrogation, summarisation and self-testing into your reading and note-taking: read with a purpose, write down what you can recall, compare your notes to the source and then use this comparison to guide the next iteration of this process. Repeat until your recall and your notes capture your understanding of the source material.

Perhaps some of the above advice has come as a bit of a shock to you? Maybe up until now you'd have considered yourself a firm advocate of re-reading and highlighting? You'd certainly be in good company; previous research has indicated that students can show a reliance on ineffective practices, such as re-reading (e.g. Gurung, 2005). I'm aware that extolling the virtues of incorporating systematic self-testing into your studies is probably not the advice you were hoping to hear. However, as a means of encouraging you to give this advice a try, I'm going to conclude this chapter by referring to a study by Einstein, Mullet and Harrison (2012). They conducted a retrieval practice study with a bit of a twist. They gave a group of undergraduate students a series of passages to read. Some of them were simply re-studied and others were studied using retrieval practice. They also asked the students to rate how well they thought they'd learned the material. All pretty standard so far. Einstein et al. then gave them surprise quizzes about the contents of the passages. As usual, memory performance was better for the passages that had been studied using retrieval practice. However, the results also indicated that the students believed they had performed equally well, irrespective of whether they had simply re-read the passages or used retrieval practice. Here's where the twist comes in. The experimenters then got their participants to analyse the data from the experiment as the basis for one of their lab classes, so they could see the evidence for retrieval practice themselves. At the conclusion of the academic semester, they asked the students to report how often they had used self-testing as part of their studying repertoire compared to the start of the semester. Eighty-two per cent of the students reported that they had used self-testing more often in their studying since having seen the testing effect in action. As for the other 18%. Well, they were probably still mad at the experimenters for getting them to do their statistical analysis!

References

Bartlett, F. C. (1932). *Remembering: An experimental and social study*. Cambridge University Press.
Bednall, T. C. & Kehoe, E. J. (2011). Effects of self-regulatory instructional aids on self-directed study. *Instructional Science, 39*(2), 205–226.
Bell, K. E. & Limber, J. E. (2009). Reading skill, textbook marking, and course performance. *Literacy Research and Instruction, 49*(1), 56–67.
Bretzing, B. H. & Kulhavy, R. W. (1979). Notetaking and depth of processing. *Contemporary Educational Psychology, 4*(2), 145–153.
Butler, A. C. (2010). Repeated testing produces superior transfer of learning relative to repeated studying. *Journal of Experimental Psychology: Learning, Memory, and Cognition, 36*(5), 1118–1133.
Butler, A. C., Karpicke, J. D. & Roediger III, H. L. (2008). Correcting a metacognitive error: Feedback increases retention of low-confidence correct responses. *Journal of Experimental Psychology: Learning, Memory, and Cognition, 34*(4), 918–928.
Craik, F. I. & Lockhart, R. S. (1972). Levels of processing: A framework for memory research. *Journal of Verbal Learning and Verbal Behavior, 11*(6), 671–684.
Craik, F. I. & Tulving, E. (1975). Depth of processing and the retention of words in episodic memory. *Journal of Experimental Psychology: General, 104*(3), 268–294.
Craik, F. I. & Watkins, M. J. (1973). The role of rehearsal in short-term memory. *Journal of Verbal Learning and Verbal Behavior, 12*(6), 599–607.
Dickinson, D. J. & O'Connell, D. Q. (1990). Effect of quality and quantity of study on student grades. *The Journal of Educational Research, 83*(4), 227–231.
Dunlosky, J., Rawson, K. A., Marsh, E. J., Nathan, M. J. & Willingham, D. T. (2013). What works, what doesn't. *Scientific American Mind, 24*(4), 46–53.
Einstein, G. O., Mullet, H. G. & Harrison, T. L. (2012). The testing effect: Illustrating a fundamental concept and changing study strategies. *Teaching of Psychology, 39*(3), 190–193.
Fowler, R. L. & Barker, A. S. (1974). Effectiveness of highlighting for retention of text material. *Journal of Applied Psychology, 59*(3), 358–364.
Gurung, R. A. (2005). How do students really study (and does it matter)? *Education, 39*, 323–340.
Hartwig, M. K. & Dunlosky, J. (2012). Study strategies of college students: Are self-testing and scheduling related to achievement? *Psychonomic Bulletin & Review, 19*(1), 126–134.

Karpicke, J. D. (2017). Retrieval-based learning: A decade of progress. In J. T. Wixted (Ed.), *Cognitive psychology of memory, Vol. 2 of Learning and memory: A comprehensive reference* (J. H. Byrne, Series Ed.) (pp. 487–514). Academic Press.

Karpicke, J. D., Butler, A. C. & Roediger III, H. L. (2009). Metacognitive strategies in student learning: Do students practise retrieval when they study on their own? *Memory*, *17*(4), 471–479.

McDaniel, M. A., Howard, D. C. & Einstein, G. O. (2009). The read-recite-review study strategy: Effective and portable. *Psychological Science*, *20*(4), 516–522.

Ozgungor, S. & Guthrie, J. T. (2004). Interactions among elaborative interrogation, knowledge, and interest in the process of constructing knowledge from text. *Journal of Educational Psychology*, *96*(3), 437–443.

Pressley, M., McDaniel, M. A., Turnure, J. E., Wood, E. & Ahmad, M. (1987). Generation and precision of elaboration: Effects on intentional and incidental learning. *Journal of Experimental Psychology: Learning, Memory, and Cognition*, *13*(2), 291–300.

Yue, C. L., Storm, B. C., Kornell, N. & Bjork, E. L. (2015). Highlighting and its relation to distributed study and students' metacognitive beliefs. *Educational Psychology Review*, *27*(1), 69–78.

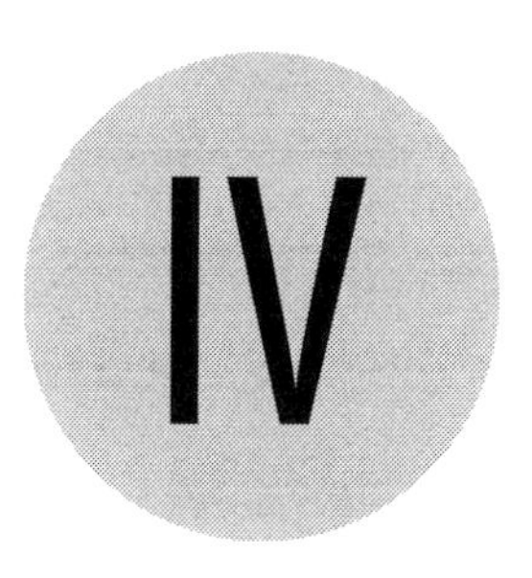

Academic integrity, citation, quotation and referencing

Credit where credit is due

If you have integrity, nothing else matters.
If you don't have integrity, nothing else matters.
Alan Simpson

1

Key advice: make learning about academic integrity a priority. It is fundamental to your success and to the success of academia generally

Let's start this chapter off with a bit of trivia. Who invented the telephone? No, put that smart phone down! If you said Alexander Graham Bell, prepare for a surprise; that's not the correct answer. Well, not exactly. Alexander Graham Bell does have the patent for the telephone, that much is true. However, in 2002 the US Congress passed a resolution to acknowledge Antonio Meucci's role in the invention of the telephone in 1871. This was some five years before the patent from Alexander Graham Bell was filed. It transpired that, being a poor man, Antonio was unable to afford the cost of a full patent application at the time. Therefore, he had to submit what was effectively a notice of intention to file a patent (a caveat) that had to be renewed to remain valid. Unfortunately, life was not kind to poor Antonio. In 1874, having sunk most of his life's savings into developing the telephone and being responsible for the care of his wife who was stricken with severe arthritis, he was no longer able to afford to renew the caveat. To make matters worse, Antonio had stored his working models at the Western Union Affiliate laboratories and when he asked for their return, he was told they had been lost. In 1876, Alexander Graham Bell, who had also been conducting research at the Western Union labs, was granted the patent for the telephone. In 1887, a move to annul the patent was remanded for trial by the Supreme Court. Regrettably, Antonio died in 1889 and the trial was subsequently declared moot, which meant that Alexander Graham Bell retained the patent for the telephone. The issue of whether Antonio's design for the telephone was stolen by either Alexander, or someone acting on his behalf, is unresolved and remains controversial to this day. However, the US Congress made it clear in its resolution that had Antonio been able to afford the fee to renew his caveat in 1874, Alexander Graham Bell would not have been awarded the patent. If only *Dragon's Den* had existed in the Victorian era, eh? The patent for the telephone is still widely regarded as the most lucrative patent issued to date, so next time you indulge in a beverage of your choice raise a glass to Antonio Meucci. As the congressional resolution noted: "the great Italian inventor who had a career that was both extraordinary and tragic" (H.Res. 269, 2002, p. 1). If my choice of opening quote for this chapter seemed strange, re-visit it now and prepare for a hit right in the feels.

The point of the above example was to illustrate just how unfair it can be when an individual does not receive due credit for their work. Universities need to make money to remain financially solvent, of course, but the real currency of academia is words and ideas. As Park (2004) points out, academic integrity is part of the foundation of the reputation of a university. Consequently, it is intrinsic to the value of the degrees a university awards. Accordingly, you should take the attribution of credit for words and ideas (i.e. academic integrity) very seriously. Your university certainly will! Therefore, making you aware of expectations with regards to academic integrity is an important first step before we move on to consider topics like academic writing and presentations. The purpose of this chapter is to elucidate the meaning of academic integrity and introduce the tools of citation, quotation and referencing. I'll explain the principles underpinning the use of these tools and provide some advice on adopting study habits that are most conducive to good practice in respect of academic integrity. This chapter will not contain a detailed guide on each of the different styles of referencing (e.g. Harvard, Oxford, Chicago) simply because the style you will be asked to use in your studies depends on your degree subject. Providing a guide to each of them would make this book circa 1,000 pages long and about as interesting to read as a shipping forecast. It would also be unnecessary, as the purpose of this chapter is to impart fundamental advice about academic integrity and referencing that is applicable across all the referencing styles. For purely selfish reasons, the style I have used in the book thus far and will continue to use in this chapter is the American Psychological Association (APA) format.

Because words and ideas serve as intellectual currency within academia, there is the expectation that academics don't steal this intellectual currency from each other. Intellectual theft is called plagiarism. Plagiarism occurs whenever an individual engages in any form of writing practice that fails to appropriately acknowledge the words or ideas of one or more other authors. Park (2003) identified four principal methods of plagiarism:

1. When someone takes material obtained from another source and presents it as if it were their own work.
2. When someone takes material obtained from another author/s (with their knowledge) and presents it as if it were their own work.
3. When someone copies material from a source and includes the appropriate reference, but does not use quotation, thus giving the erroneous impression that they have paraphrased

the original author when, actually, they have used their words verbatim.

4. When someone paraphrases material from one or more sources, but does not give the original author/s credit for their ideas

2

Key advice: academic integrity transgressions are often the product of ignorance, but ignorance isn't a defence

The first of the above four scenarios can be distinguished from the other three in terms of premeditation. It would be very difficult for you to argue that you intended no impropriety if you purchased or stole an essay from another person. However, you could fall foul of the other three scenarios simply because of ignorance of the appropriate citation and referencing conventions, without the intent to do anything improper. Let's illustrate this point with a little test based on some research by Murray, Henslee and Ludlow (2015). I'm going to give you a piece of source text from yours truly, then three hypothetical scenarios based on that text. Your job is simply to state whether you think each scenario is legitimate academic practice or plagiarism. If you don't know, then just note that you couldn't decide.

Source text

Alexander Graham Bell does have the patent for the telephone, that much is true. However, in 2002 the US Congress passed a resolution to acknowledge Antonio Meucci's role in the invention of the telephone in 1871. This was some five years before the patent from Alexander Graham Bell was filed. It transpired that, being a poor man, Antonio was unable to afford to submit a full patent application at the time. Therefore, he had to submit what was effectively a notice of intention to file a patent (a caveat) that had to be renewed to remain valid.

Scenario (1): if the following extract were to appear in an essay, would it constitute plagiarism?

As noted by Penn (2018), Alexander Graham Bell does have the patent for the telephone, that much is true. However, in 2002 the US Congress passed a resolution to acknowledge Antonio Meucci's role in the invention of the telephone in 1871. This was some five years before the patent from Alexander Graham Bell was filed (p. 113).

a. This is acceptable practice (providing there is a corresponding entrance in the reference section) because the original author's work has been cited and the page reference for the quotation given.
b. This constitutes plagiarism, as quotation marks have not been used to denote the author's original words.
c. I'm not sure.

Scenario (2): if the following extract were to appear in an essay, would it constitute plagiarism?

Alexander Graham Bell does possess the patent for the telephone, that much is affirmed. It turned out that Antonio, being an impoverished man, was unable to afford to submit a full patent application at the time, so had to submit what was, in essence, a notice of intention to file a patent (a caveat) that had to be renewed to continue to be valid.

a. This is acceptable practice. The original text has been paraphrased so the author does not need to use quotation marks.
b. This constitutes plagiarism, as only a few words have been changed from the original source.
c. I'm not sure.

Scenario (3): if the following were to appear in an essay, would it constitute plagiarism?

As noted by Penn (2018) "Alexander Graham Bell does have the patent for the telephone, that much is true. However, in 2002 the US Congress passed a resolution to acknowledge Antonio Meucci's role in the invention of the telephone in 1871. This was some five years before the patent from Alexander Graham Bell was filed" (p. 113).

a. This is acceptable practice as the words of the original source have been delineated via quotation marks, the original source has been cited and a page reference given for the quotation.
b. This constitutes plagiarism. It's not permissible for the author to use the wording of the original text, even if the use of quotation marks and citation is technically correct.
c. I'm not sure.

How do you think you did in that little quiz? In their experiment, Murray et al. asked first-year undergraduate students to rate themselves on their ethical behaviour and record whether they had experienced previous training or education about cheating, plagiarism or student misconduct. They then gave them the same scenarios that I've just given you (albeit with different subject matter) and asked the students to comment on their legitimacy. Students predominantly identified themselves as being ethical, with only 5% giving themselves a rating below the mid-point on the ethical scale used. Furthermore, 93% of them reported having previous training or educational experience in academic integrity. However, 40% of the students failed to identify the first scenario as plagiarism, 62% of them failed to identify the second scenario as plagiarism and 13% of them failed to identify the third scenario as legitimate conduct. Similarly, Newton (2016) found a discrepancy between undergraduate student confidence in their knowledge of plagiarism and their performance on quite rudimentary tests of referencing. The implications of the above research are clear. Your knowledge of academic integrity may be deficient, even if you identify yourself as a highly ethical person and have had previous educational exposition on the subject. Such deficiencies can lead to transgressions in academic integrity born of ignorance rather than deliberate dishonesty. Unfortunately, just because you didn't intend any wrongdoing doesn't mean that you won't be held accountable for it. It's these kinds of transgressions that this chapter will equip you to avoid. Let's start off by introducing the fundamental tools of academic integrity: citation; quotation; and referencing.

The fundamentals of citation, quotation and referencing

Realising the importance of ensuring authors get credit for their work is half the battle, but you also need to know how to achieve this appropriately. Claiming that you heard about this theory from this bloke in a journal with a blue cover is clearly not going to help anyone else find that source! To prevent such ambiguity, several styles of citation, quotation and referencing exist (e.g. Harvard, Oxford, APA). These styles differ in the details, but the principles are always the same. Despite what you may have heard, these principles are all very simple. Let's look at citation first. Again, please remember that the specific examples I will be giving are in APA style.

Citation

A citation is simply an explicit pointer to another author's work. It means that you are referring to the work of someone else, but are describing that work in your own words. For example:

> Penn (2018) proposed a theory about how to optimise undergraduate ability to cite and reference appropriately. According to this theory, for a student to be receptive to learning about academic integrity, one must first address....

From reading this excerpt, we immediately know that the theory being referred to was proposed by Penn (2018) because of the citation. In addition to this, we also know that Penn's theory is being described in the words of the author of this excerpt. This is because none of the text is encased in quotation marks and there is no page reference present.

Quotation

In contrast to a citation, a quotation is an explicit pointer to the presence of the words of another author. It uses a citation, but supplements it with quotation marks and a page reference. For example:

> Penn (2018) argued that: "Sound metacognition is the foundation for the development of academic integrity. As with any other topic, students will be disinclined to spend time studying how to cite and reference appropriately if they perceive themselves as already being competent" (p. 103).

From this extract, we immediately know that, once again, the author of the excerpt is referring to the work of another author. Wouldn't you know, it's that very handsome and charming Penn character again! However, note the use of quotation marks. The author of this excerpt is using these to indicate that they are presenting an argument from Penn (2018) and that the wording of this argument has been taken directly from that source. The use of quotation marks might seem like a small detail, but they are essential. This is because quotation marks are used to clearly distinguish between the words of the author responsible for the source text and the words of the author writing about that text. You'll note that the quotation also features a page number. When you're using someone else's words directly, you need to make it easy for the reader to locate the origin of that quotation. They can then check its accuracy and examine its context.

Referencing

Only having citations to use in locating source material would not be especially helpful. You need more specific details about where you can obtain a copy of that material. This is where references come in. References give the reader the details of every piece of source material cited in a manuscript so that they can easily locate those sources for themselves. The details provided by a reference depend on the type of publication in question. Some details are common to all sources, for example: the date of publication and the names of the authors. Other details are specific to particular sources, for example: the volume and part number for a journal article. Here's an example of a reference for a journal article.

> Glenberg, A. M., Wilkinson, A. C. & Epstein, W. (1982). The illusion of knowing: Failure in the self-assessment of comprehension. *Memory & Cognition*, *10*(6), 597–602.

Of course, there is no way you'd want to include this level of detail in the body of your work, unless the objective was to get your efforts thrown out of the nearest window! Therefore, references are presented separately from the text of your composition. Depending on the style of referencing used, they might be included in footnotes or, as with APA style, have their own dedicated section at the end of a piece of work. Whatever style you use, anything you have cited in your work needs to have a corresponding reference entry.

Citing and referencing secondary sources

Thus far, we've considered how you give credit for work in scenarios where you have read the original source material as composed by the author you are citing and referencing. This is known as a primary source. Basically, as the adage goes, you've got the information from the horse's mouth. However, you'll also often encounter work composed by a third party about a primary source. This is known as a secondary source. For example, when you read about someone's work via an introductory course text written by a different individual, you're using a secondary source. The use of a secondary source has implications for the way that you cite and reference that material. The differences between citing and references for primary and secondary sources exist for good reasons. If you were to just cite and reference a secondary source, the credit for the original work would be wrongly attributed to the secondary source author. Conversely, if you only credited the author of the primary source for the work, then you would create the misleading impression that you had read the original author's work. This would also mean you would not be acknowledging the work of the author of the secondary source. The distinction between primary and secondary sources is usually dealt with very parsimoniously by referencing styles. Let's work through a fictitious example. Say you had read about an experiment by Smith (2001) from an introductory course text by Jones (2007). Here's how you would deal with this scenario using the APA format. For the citation, you would need to acknowledge both the primary and secondary authors, thus:

> In Smith's 2001 study (as cited in Jones, 2007).

For the reference section, you would simply reference what you had read, i.e. the Jones (2007) source, thus:

> Jones, A. A. (2007). *An introduction to psychology*. London: Routledge.

Wherever possible, it's always best to go to the primary source if you can. You'll get a more comprehensive overview of the original author's work this way. This approach also removes the chances of you inadvertently perpetuating any mistakes or oversights in the secondary author's account of the primary source. As with regular conversations, the more individuals that academic information passes through, the more distorted that information can get.

So, that's the basic principles of citation, quotation and referencing in a nutshell. However, to develop your knowledge of these principles further, you need to examine their implementation. This means that we need to look at paraphrasing, because using citation, quotation and referencing appropriately depends on knowing what constitutes acceptable paraphrasing practice when writing about the work of other authors.

Citation, quotation and referencing in practice: the thorny issue of paraphrasing

3

Key advice: recognising and developing sound paraphrasing practice is a critical part of academic integrity and developing your voice as an author

As Park (2003) noted, issues with plagiarism tend to come less from students being uncertain about the definition of plagiarism, as from ambiguity about its application in academic contexts. A principle source of such ambiguity concerns distinguishing between paraphrasing and plagiarism. Roig (1997) conducted some seminal research in this regard. In his study, students were given an original piece of text followed by a series of ten re-written versions. Eight of these re-written pieces contained some form of plagiarism, ranging from the blatant (e.g. verbatim copying with no quotation) to the subtle (e.g. the text was inadequately paraphrased). The remaining two compositions were adequately paraphrased and featured the correct citations. The participants were set the task of reading the pieces of text and correctly classifying each one as either plagiarised or appropriately paraphrased. The results indicated that some of the examples were misclassified as appropriately paraphrased by as many as half of the students. They tended to believe that reproducing original text without quotation marks and/or making minor alterations to it was acceptable if there was a citation present.

In Roig's study, examples of acceptable and unacceptable paraphrasing practice were useful in diagnosing issues in the ability of students to distinguish between paraphrasing and plagiarism. Subsequent research has also reported success in using such examples as part of an intervention to educate students on what constitutes appropriate paraphrasing practice (e.g. Moniz, Fine & Bliss, 2008; Landau, Druen & Arcuri, 2002). In keeping with this approach, I'm going to give you an original passage of writing composed by yours truly. Then, I'm going to present several versions of that text that you should treat as having been composed by other authors who read my original composition. Your task is to specify whether each version is acceptable or unacceptable paraphrasing practice.

Original version

Individuals differ in the degree to which they expect reciprocity in a relationship. The moderating effect of exchange orientation (Murstein, Cerreto & Mac Donald, 1977) is likely to be important in an equity-based model of love. Exchange orientated individuals expect immediate and direct reciprocity for any contributions to a relationship. This notion was supported by Buunk and Van Yperen (1991) who found that the perceived equity of a relationship was related to measures of marital satisfaction only for individuals who scored highly in exchange orientation. Put simply, this study demonstrates that the importance of equity in relationships is not uniform across all individuals!

Version one

Authors such as Penn (2018) have pointed to research that contends that people differ in the extent to which they expect mutuality in a

> relationship. The moderating effect of exchange orientation (Murstein, Cerreto & Mac Donald, 1977) is likely to be significant in an equity-based model of love. Exchange orientated people expect immediate and direct pay-back for any contributions to a relationship. This idea was supported by Buunk and Van Yperen (1991) who discovered that the perceived equity of a relationship was related to indicators of marital satisfaction only for individuals who scored highly in exchange orientation. Put another way, this study shows that the importance of equity in relationships is not the same across all individuals!

So, what do you think of version one? Is it an acceptable example of paraphrasing? Well, it starts off well in that it's clear that the author has cited me to acknowledge that they are referring to my composition. However, note the lack of any quotation marks! This means that the author of version one is implicitly claiming the wording of the piece as their own. Is their composition sufficiently different to mine to constitute legitimate paraphrasing? You can certainly see that some words have been changed throughout the piece. However, it's obvious that the author has just rolled out the thesaurus and replaced a selection of words with synonyms. In effect, this version is saying the same thing, in the same order, with very superficial changes to the wording. The changes made are insufficient for this author to claim the text as their own composition. Therefore, they would be vulnerable to an accusation of plagiarism.

Version two

> Authors such as Penn (2018) have identified research from the field of social psychology suggesting that individuals differ in the degree to which they expect reciprocity in a relationship. The moderating effect of exchange orientation (Murstein, Cerreto & Mac Donald, 1977) is likely to be important in an equity-based model of love. This is to say that exchange orientated individuals expect immediate and direct reciprocity for any contributions to a relationship; if they give something to their partner, they expect a commensurate return. This notion was supported by Buunk and Van Yperen (1991) who found that the perceived equity of a relationship was related to measures of marital satisfaction only for individuals who scored highly in exchange orientation. Put simply, this study demonstrates that the importance of equity in relationships is not uniform across all individuals. This also explains why some relationships can be unequitable in one direction, but not dysfunctional.

What do you think of version two? Is it an acceptable example of paraphrasing? Well, there is some content here that is not present in the original piece, no doubt. However, the problem is that the original content is heavily interspersed with material taken directly from the original source without proper acknowledgement. Therefore, although this version is not taken verbatim from the original source, it's still too close to it to be considered legitimate paraphrasing. If you're still a bit fuzzy on distinguishing between acceptable and unacceptable paraphrasing practice, here's a good litmus test. Step one: highlight any overlap between strings of words in your composition and the original source. If you have access to online originality checking software, then this step will be done for you. For the purposes of demonstration, I've duplicated version two below, but this time highlighted the areas of overlap in italicised text.

> Authors such as Penn (2018) have identified research from the field of social psychology suggesting that individuals *differ in the degree to which they expect reciprocity in a relationship. The moderating effect of exchange orientation (Murstein, Cerreto and Mac Donald, 1977) is likely to be important in an equity-based model of love.* This is to say that, *exchange orientated individuals expect immediate and direct reciprocity for any contributions to the relationship*; if they give something to their partner they expect a commensurate return. *This notion was supported by Buunk and Van Yperen (1991) who found that the perceived equity of a relationship was related to measures of marital satisfaction only for individuals who scored highly in exchange orientation. Put simply, this study demonstrates that the importance of equity in relationships is not uniform across all individuals!* This also explains why some relationships can be unequitable in one direction, but not dysfunctional.

Step two: read out loud anything that isn't highlighted, i.e. what's left of the composition after the non-original text has been omitted. It's probably best not to have an audience for this bit, lest they think that all the studying has finally got to you! Step three: ask yourself if what's left still says anything intelligible? Don't get too caught up with citations being highlighted; worry about whether the substance of the text is intact. Do the non-highlighted remnants of version two pass this litmus test? If the answer is no, then the composition does not work in the absence of the original source material. Therefore, it's not been paraphrased well enough and it would likely be considered plagiarised. An important point to make here is that it doesn't matter whether the overlap between your composition is with one or several original sources. If your composition doesn't stand independently of other sources, then you're in the plagiarism danger zone. Great, now I have that tune from *Top Gun* in my head! Let's move on to version three of the original text.

Version three

> An equity-based account of love would postulate reciprocity between romantic partners as a necessary component of a successful relationship. However, this is only true if either partner is predisposed to expect immediate reciprocity for their contributions to the relationship (i.e. is exchange orientated). Indeed, measures of marital satisfaction reflect the perception of equity within the relationship only if the partner being surveyed also scored highly on a measure of exchange orientation. In romantic relationships, not everyone expects to get as much as they give!

What do you think of version three? Is it an acceptable example of paraphrasing? If you apply the litmus test for checking paraphrasing that I've just advocated, I think few would dispute that version three stands independently as a composition. However, there is still an academic integrity problem here. Where have the citations gone? Given that version three is identifying the same lines of evidence and formulating the same argument as me, it would have been good practice to have cited Penn (2018). They most certainly should have cited Murstein, Cerreto and Mac Donald (1977) for the concept of exchange orientation, and Buunk and Van Yperen (1991) for their experiment illustrating its influence on relationships. The underlying lesson here is that even good paraphrasing does not obviate the need to cite people for their work. A simple and safe principle to operate by in your academic career is: if in doubt, cite.

Version four

> At first glance, an equity-based account of love proposes that reciprocity between romantic partners is necessary for a relationship to be successful. However, the concept of exchange orientation (Murstein, Cerreto & Mac Donald, 1977) regulates the importance of equity. An individual who expects immediate reciprocity for a contribution to a relationship will view equity as being more important. This argument has been put forward by authors such as Penn (2018). Evidence for this line of thinking comes from research by Buunk and Van Yperen (1991). This study showed that measures of marital satisfaction only reflect perceived equity within the relationship if the partner being surveyed also scores highly on a measure

of exchange orientation. In romantic relationships, not everyone expects to get as much as they give!

What do you think of version four: is it an acceptable example of paraphrasing? Hopefully, you'll see that this version has cited Penn (2018) for making the argument being put forward previously. It's also credited the other authors with their contributions. Finally, it's been significantly reworded from the original text. This is an example of acceptable paraphrasing practice.

Engineering out study practices conducive to inadvertent plagiarism

Key advice: poor study practices create conditions conducive to inadvertent academic integrity transgressions

Thus far we've looked at two ways that you can inadvertently find yourself in hot water from an academic integrity standpoint. The first way is ignorance of the principles of citation, quotation and referencing. The second way is not understanding what constitutes good practice with respect to paraphrasing. However, there is a third way identified in a study by Breen and Maassen (2005). They conducted interviews with undergraduate students about their views of plagiarism and found that sometimes the way that students approach their studies can significantly affect the likelihood of plagiarism occurring. This section will focus on identifying some of the studying practices that can be more conducive to inadvertent plagiarism and what can be done to rectify them.

I have a confession: my interest in academic integrity stems from sources other than just researching a book on study skills. One of the numerous roles I have taken on during my time as a lecturer was that of Responsible Officer. I was the academic who acted on behalf of my school to oversee first offence cases of plagiarism. Consequently, over a period of about four years, I was involved in hundreds of hearings where students were shown evidence of significant overlap between the contents of their work and that of another author. None of these hearings involved evidence of premeditation, so no assumption of dishonest intent was made. They were conducted as a form of academic intervention where the university's expectations were clearly outlined, and advice was given on the preparation of future work.

The students invited to these meetings were usually shocked and mortified. Many of them were clearly unaware that the standard of academic integrity exhibited in their work was not up to scratch. The one comment I heard most often from students at these meetings was "I did this piece of work in a rush at the last minute", or words to that effect. Indeed, research has indicated that procrastination increases the likelihood of plagiarism occurring. Patrzek, Sattler, van Veen, Grunschel and Fries (2015) conducted a panel study involving many students from different academic disciplines, taken from four German universities. Using a web-based survey and an intermediary (to ensure the anonymity of participants) they asked them to complete a self-report measure of procrastination. Six months later, the same students were asked to report how often they had committed ten different forms of academic misconduct over the preceding six months. The results indicated that procrastination increased the frequency of all types of academic misconduct (including plagiarism). Similarly, in a study by Comas-Forgas and Sureda-Negre (2010) students predominantly identified doing things at the last minute and lack of time as being most relevant in explaining plagiarism. Procrastination and the resultant lack of time exert their effects on the incidence of plagiarism by compromising due diligence in the preparation of work. When you are short on time you are likely to take shortcuts in researching your work. For example, you will be less meticulous in recording the origin of the sources you have found. You will invest less time in the composition of your work, i.e. you will be less diligent in paraphrasing the information you have gleamed from your sources. Finally, you will have less time to check your work thoroughly (if at all) and likely miss any instances of improperly acknowledged material from other authors. Consequently, the first step in being proactive in preserving the academic integrity of your work is to ensure that you minimise procrastination in its preparation. We covered how to do this back in Chapter II. Having just alluded to the research, composition and proofing stages of a piece of work, let's focus on each of these in turn. We can then uncover what practices are more conducive to inadvertent plagiarism. Dodgy research practices are up first.

5

Key advice: avoid relying on online encyclopaedias in researching topics at degree level

Ferro and Martins (2016) note that the first course of action students often take upon being set a piece of work is to hit Google! Now, there is every reason to utilise the power of the internet in the preparation of your work. However, there are some very important caveats you need to be aware of in doing so. Some caveats relate to the quality of the information obtained from different online sources. We'll defer coverage of this matter to the next chapter on the preparation of written assessments. Other caveats are academic integrity related, so we'll deal with those now. As Šprajc, Urh, Jerebic, Trivan and Jereb (2017) point out, an emerging body of literature indicates that digital literacy has developed somewhat independently from the knowledge and skills associated with academic integrity. The multitude of ways that information can now be accessed online complicates the application of citation, quotation and referencing. As we've previously noted, this is something that undergraduate students can already struggle with. The attribution of authorship can be more difficult online than with conventional printed media. I just Googled various terms associated with plagiarism and, then, Scandinavian bridge design. Why on earth that was the first thing that came to mind is something of a mystery! Each time, there was a Wikipedia entry in the first five hits. As an online encyclopaedia, Wikipedia is arguably a tertiary source, i.e. a collection of primary and secondary sources. Well, that's just complicated things a bit; most guides to citation and referencing only cover primary and secondary sources. Wikipedia can be edited by anyone, which means that information can go uncited (or incorrectly cited) for long periods of time. So, we have a bad combination at play here. A very pervasive source of information that is more difficult for students to interrogate from an academic integrity perspective. Research has indicated that the ease of access to materials online creates the erroneous impression that they are public domain and, therefore, exempt from citation and referencing conventions. For example, Baruchson-Arbib and Yaari (2004) conducted a study where a sample of undergraduate and postgraduate students were asked to review a piece of source text followed by several plagiarised versions of the text. These versions were either copied verbatim without quotation marks or paraphrased with no citation given for the ideas contained in the original text. For two of the plagiarised scenarios, the source material was explicitly identified as being from a printed origin. For the other two scenarios, the origin was identified as an online source. The task given to the students was to state whether they felt each example was acceptable, unacceptable or weren't sure. Consistent with earlier research, the ability of students to correctly classify plagiarised work was far from perfect. Moreover, students judged plagiarised material based on print sources as being more unacceptable than plagiarised material based on internet sources. Baruchson-Arbib and Yaari argued that their results were likely due to the ease of internet access, combined with ambiguity about the authorship of online material and the applicable citation and referencing conventions. The implications of the above research for you are twofold. First, you should find primary sources where possible and avoid relying on online encyclopaedias such as Wikipedia. Second, you must remember that there are no exemptions from the need to give people appropriate credit for their ideas and words. If you can't cite and reference, you can't use the source in question.

6

Key advice: never copy and paste material from sources into your notes

It's an understandable scenario: you find a great extract from a piece of digital source material that you'd like to write about in a piece of coursework. So, rather than risk losing track of it, you quickly copy and paste it into your notes. You'll write it up in your own words later. First, you want to conclude collecting the rest of your source material. I mean, it's not like you'll forget that you copied and pasted that information from another source, right? Err, not necessarily! Our recollections about the authorship of a source can be inaccurate. This phenomenon is called Cryptomensia and is nicely demonstrated in a study by Stark and Perfect (2006). Participants were assigned a partner and asked to individually generate four non-conventional uses for a series of four objects (a brick, shoe, paperclip and button). An example of a non-conventional use of one of these objects would be to suggest that a shoe would make a good paperweight. The experimenter chipped in with eight suggestions of their own for each of the objects, requiring that the participants listen to all the ideas to avoid reproducing them. Following generating their suggestions, the participants were given a five-minute distractor task. They were then asked to review the ideas suggested under one of four conditions. In an imagery elaboration condition, participants rated the proposed use for an object on how difficult it was to imagine. In a generative elaboration condition, they were asked to think of three ways to improve a suggested use for an object. In a rich imagery elaboration condition, the participants imagined the improved suggested uses for the objects provided by their partner from the generative elaboration condition. Finally, in the baseline condition, the uses were not presented for review. The participants were then invited back one week later and asked to recall both their originally suggested uses for each object and generate four further uses. You would hope that their recollection of the uses they had originally suggested for the objects (and their newly generated ideas) would not include any of the suggestions originating from the experimenter or their partner. Unfortunately, 75% of the participants appropriated at least one idea that they did not originally generate. Seventy-two per cent of the participants appropriated two or more ideas! Further examination of the results revealed that ideas reviewed via generative elaboration were inadvertently plagiarised significantly more often than other ideas. Apparently, it was the adoption of an idea and thinking about its application that resulted in an increased likelihood of the source of the idea to be misattributed.

The implications of the Stark and Perfect study are rather sinister when applied to the scenario of taking the copy and paste shortcut with your notes. You might think that this is not such a bad thing to do if you at least put your thinking cap on. So, you consider how your ill-gotten notes fit in with what you already know, and how you might articulate the knowledge they contain in your own words when you come to compose your coursework. As we covered in Chapter III, thinking about material is good practice if you want to recall it. Unfortunately, in the absence of an explicit pointer as to the origin of that material, thinking about the application of its contents could mean you mistakenly appropriate it as your own work through Cryptomensia. There are, of course, two simple solutions to this scenario. The first solution is to simply avoid copying and pasting anything into your notes. If verbatim copying isn't an effective means of note-taking, then substituting the process of transcription with a deft press of CTRL+C, followed by CTRL+V is not going to be of any greater benefit to your memory. Moreover, if you don't use the words of others, then the issue of inadvertently appropriating them is precluded! The second solution involves recording the citation and reference for the source you're referring to before you start writing about it in your own words. This prevents you from inadvertently not giving credit for someone else's ideas. To paraphrase Macrae, Bodenhausen and Calvini's (1999) use of the famous Obi Wan Kenobi expression from the movie *Star Wars*: remember, the source should be with you. Always.

It's easy to look at something like Cryptomensia and think that falling foul of it would be much less likely were it not for that dammed copy and paste facility on your PC. Surely, this feature combined with the kind of ambiguities concerning authorship of online material we've alluded to is just setting people up for trouble? Well, Buckley and Cowap (2013) point to a body of literature highlighting that technology and the internet can serve to facilitate plagiarism. However, the operative word here is facilitate. The root cause of these problems is not the technology, but rather poor study practices that the technology has just made easier to implement. The implications of sub-par study practices for academic integrity are often brought into sharp focus at the writing stage of coursework preparation. In a focus group-based piece of research, Breen and Maassen (2005) identified that students often felt frustrated that they were less eloquent than the authors of their sources. They believed that quotation provided a good solution to this issue. However, this is not a wise course of action for you to take. Over-reliance on using the words of other authors (with proper acknowledgement) deprives you of opportunities to practice paraphrasing. This serves to consolidate a dependence on using the words of other authors rather than demonstrating your own ability to articulate information.

There is a reciprocal relationship between study skills and academic integrity; ineffective study practices generally translate to increased risk of issues with plagiarism. For example, verbatim copying when note-taking does not help you remember the material being studied and it also increases the likelihood of plagiarism. Happily, this means that if you adopt effective study practices, you enjoy corresponding benefits in the academic integrity of your work. Let's quickly illustrate this with reference to the example of the 3R method of reading and note-taking covered in the previous chapter. You'll recall that the first thing I advocated was to decide what, specifically, you wanted to get out of your reading. That's your first academic integrity safeguard, as it sets an agenda for interrogating the information, which includes thinking about what kind of information you need and how you might organise the material. Your agenda in, for example, writing an essay on a specific title is likely to be very different to that of the author of the source material. Next, you will recall I encouraged you to put the source material out of sight and try and recall the crux of what you were reading from memory. This prevents you from leaning on the wording of the source, because you can't see it and you won't remember it word for word. Therefore, you'll have to reconstruct it based on your current level of understanding and in your own words. Finally, I said you should review your knowledge acquisition by comparing your recollection to the source material for its factual accuracy only. Focusing solely on whether you've got your facts straight helps prevent you from becoming demoralised if you're not as eloquent as the author of the source material. With 3R, your written recollection forms the basis of your notes. Once you've repeated the read, recite and review process enough times to get your facts straight, you can smooth out any of the rough edges in your composition. Getting started is always the hardest part of writing, refining what you've got in rough form is much easier. A key feature of the 3R approach is that you start with your own words and then refine them. This completely negates any issues with inadequate paraphrasing arising from using the words of another author as a starting point for your composition. There is a big difference between using your own words from the outset and trying to extensively edit the words of another author as the basis of your composition. The latter approach is a fast-track to plagiarism. If you want to develop your own voice as an author, you must practice writing in your own words at every opportunity.

Key advice: embrace originality checking software as a means of developing your own voice as an author

A combination of a working knowledge of citation, quotation and referencing, along with the adoption of good study practices, is usually enough to prevent any form of inadvertent plagiarism. However, slips can still occur. For example, you might forget to clearly delineate a quotation with quotation marks. Therefore, vigilance is necessary when proofreading your work. You'll recall the research cited earlier about handing work in hastily increasing the likelihood of plagiarism. Technology can render some assistance in this respect, for example Badge and Scott (2009) note the pervasiveness of the use of originality checking software in UK education institutions. Students sometimes regard such software as an enforcement tool (i.e. a way to deter deliberate plagiarism). However, it has a more important use as an educational tool (e.g. Graham-Matheson & Starr, 2013). Originality checking software works by cross-referencing the content of a submitted manuscript against its database of previous submissions. It then returns an analysis of how much of the submitted work it has seen before, i.e. what proportion of the current submission is original text. The more work that is submitted to its database, the greater the scope of the cross-referencing it performs becomes. As an author trying to develop their own academic voice, originality checking software can really help you develop your ability to paraphrase. Recall the litmus test for acceptable paraphrasing I provided earlier. I suggested that you read your composition out loud, omitting any content that overlaps with the wording of the original source. Well, originality checking software can make this much easier for you by highlighting the areas of overlap. It is also very useful for identifying quotations, which is your cue to ensure that you have properly acknowledged them in the appropriate referencing style. However, there are limitations associated with originality checking software you need to be aware of, so you do not misinterpret its function or outputs. As useful as this software is, it's not a substitute for the good practice I've advocated thus far, nor is it a panacea for plagiarism.

8

Key advice: originality checking software is not a substitute for academic judgement – don't get caught up with percentages

You may have heard of originality checking software, such as Turnitin, being referred to as plagiarism detection software. This is a misnomer and a very misleading one at that. Software such as Turnitin does not check documents for plagiarism; it checks them for non-original content. That's a vital distinction, because plagiarism and non-originality are not synonymous. Non-original content can be perfectly legitimate. For example, a properly acknowledged quotation is non-original, but is legitimate. A reference in a reference section is highly likely to be unoriginal, but it's also legitimate. In other words, just because something is flagged by originality checking software, does not mean it has been plagiarised. To determine whether plagiarism has occurred, you must examine what has been highlighted and apply your academic judgement.

The application of academic judgement is a particularly important part of using originality checking software, because such software often returns a percentage figure indicating what proportion of the document contains non-original material. It's easy to look at such a figure and be hoodwinked into thinking that there is a threshold number that differentiates legitimate from plagiarised work. However, this is simply not the case. To illustrate why, consider the following example. You review two submissions, both of which have returned a non-originality score of 15%. When you examine submission one, that 15% is entirely accounted for by the reference section of the document. Therefore, this figure represents legitimate non-originality. In submission two, the 15% is accounted for by a paragraph that has been taken verbatim from another author's work without proper acknowledgement. In this instance, the same figure represents plagiarism. You can't base any decisions on the legitimacy of a piece of work solely on the non-originality percentage figure. It's not how much of the work is highlighted that matters per se, but rather what is highlighted. You might be inclined to think that the submission of a piece of work where 15% of its contents has been plagiarised isn't exactly the crime of the century. Maybe so, but smaller amounts of plagiarism, though less flagrant, are still unacceptable. By way of analogy, consider the following scenario. You visit your local electronics store and walk out with a laptop under your arm without paying for it. When confronted by store security you politely explain: "Well, it's not like I'm trying to take one of your 60-inch widescreen TVs, old chap!" Do you think the store would let you off? Neither do I! There is no acceptable percentage of plagiarised content.

A final consideration in using originality checking software is acknowledging that it can only check a piece of work to determine if the wording is original. It has no way of checking the originality of the ideas expressed by the words. If someone were to extensively paraphrase another author's idea, the originality checking software would be none the wiser and likely return a clean bill of health, even though the idea had been plagiarised. Just as highlighted text does not invariably mean plagiarism, non-highlighted text does not always mean an absence of plagiarism. Originality checking software is not a substitute for academic judgement when it comes to being proactive in maintaining your standards of academic integrity.

Summary

Taking responsibility for the academic integrity of your work

Let's summarise the key advice and guidance on academic integrity that you should take from this chapter.

- Read your university's policy on academic integrity as early as possible in your studies. Whilst heeding the advice contained within this chapter will most likely prevent any inadvertent issues with plagiarism, you are bound by the policy of the institution you attend. Therefore, it's important that you become familiar with any rules or guidelines that you are expected to follow.
- Learn the system of referencing used within your degree subject as a priority. You might find that your department/school has its own guides to referencing or identifies a recommended text. If not, there are resources available in print and online, such as *Cite them right* (Pears & Shields, 2016). This book contains guidance on how to use all the major referencing formats.

- When possible, always use primary sources. Avoid relying on online encyclopaedias, such as Wikipedia, because these can present issues with identifying authorship. Remember: just because something appears online does not make it open access. Words and ideas that appear online must also be cited and referenced.
- Never copy and paste material into your notes. Taking information verbatim from a source is a completely ineffective study strategy and significantly increases the risk of plagiarism. As soon as you encounter a useful source, record a citation for it so that you can attribute any ideas to the correct author.
- Write everything in your own words. Don't look at a source as you're writing about it or copy parts of the source and then try to amend them as the basis for your writing. Both these approaches increase the likelihood of you plagiarising content.
- Allow yourself enough time to check your work for any issues with academic integrity. Don't leave things like checking your citations and completing your reference section to the last minute, as this is conducive to issues with academic integrity.
- Avail yourself of any originality checking software your institution has available. This will help you avoid inadvertent lapses in your composition and develop your paraphrasing aptitude. Remember that a non-originality score, useful though it is, is not a substitute for academic judgement in maintaining standards of academic integrity.

So, that's the key aspects of academic integrity and plagiarism covered. I hope that you now understand the importance of giving other authors credit for their words/ideas and the roles of citation, quotation and referencing in achieving this. I think you'll agree that there is nothing particularly onerous or draconian about anything I've advocated in this chapter. Often, effective approaches to studying are also good practice with respect to academic integrity. It's when people take shortcuts that they tend to end up in trouble. If you adopt the advice previously given on reducing procrastination in addition to that on reading and note-taking, you'll already have made significant progress in respect of academic integrity. There are two remaining steps for you to take. First, use this chapter as a catalyst for learning the details of the specific referencing system employed by your degree discipline. Do this as early on in your studies as possible. It might seem like a bit of a chore at first, but with some practice it soon becomes a natural, procedural thing to do. Second, don't beat yourself up if your standard of composition is not as good as the authors of the sources you're using; your tutors don't expect it to be. In fact, they'd probably be out of a job if it was! Cliched as it sounds, the authors whose writing you admire weren't always that eloquent; they developed their prose through years of effort and practice. Above all, they chose to develop their own voice rather than cling on to the compositional coat tails of others. Aim to develop your own voice as an author, the rest will follow! Oh, and there is also some useful advice on academic writing in the next chapter!

References

Badge, J. & Scott, J. (2009). Dealing with plagiarism in the digital age. Retrieved from www.heacademy.ac.uk/system/files/leicester.pdf.

Baruchson-Arbib, S. & Yaari, E. (2004). Printed versus Internet plagiarism: A study of students' perception. *International Journal of Information Ethics*, *1*(6), 29–35.

Breen, L. & Maassen, M. (2005). Reducing the incidence of plagiarism in an undergraduate course: The role of education. *Issues in Educational Research*, *15*(1), 1–16.

Buckley, E. & Cowap, L. (2013). An evaluation of the use of Turnitin for electronic submission and marking and as a formative feedback tool from an educator's perspective. *British Journal of Educational Technology*, *44*(4), 562–570.

Buunk, B. P. & Van Yperen, N. W. (1991). Referential comparisons, relational comparisons, and exchange orientation: Their relation to marital satisfaction. *Personality and Social Psychology Bulletin*, *17*(6), 709–717.

Comas-Forgas, R. & Sureda-Negre, J. (2010). Academic plagiarism: Explanatory factors from students' perspective. *Journal of Academic Ethics*, *8*(3), 217–232.

Ferro, M. J. & Martins, H. F. (2016). Academic plagiarism: Yielding to temptation. *British Journal of Education, Society & Behavioural Science*, *13*(1), 1–11.

Graham-Matheson, L. & Starr, S. (2013). Is it cheating or learning the craft of writing? Using Turnitin to help students avoid plagiarism. *ALT-J: Research in Learning Technology*, *21*(17218), 1–13.

H.Res. 269. 107th Cong. (2002, June 11). Retrieved from www.govinfo.gov/content/pkg/BILLS-107hres269eh/pdf/BILLS-107hres269eh.pdf.

Landau, J. D., Druen, P. B. & Arcuri, J. A. (2002). Methods for helping students avoid plagiarism. *Teaching of Psychology*, *29*(2), 112–115.

Macrae, C. N., Bodenhausen, G. V. & Calvini, G. (1999). Contexts of cryptomnesia: May the source be with you. *Social Cognition*, *17*(3), 273–297.

Moniz, R., Fine, J. & Bliss, L. (2008). The effectiveness of direct-instruction and student-centered teaching methods on students' functional understanding of plagiarism. *College & Undergraduate Libraries, 15*(3), 255–279.

Murray, S. L., Henslee, A. M. & Ludlow, D. K. (2015, June). Engineering students' understanding of plagiarism. Presented at the American society for engineering education annual conference and exposition, Seattle, WA.

Murstein, B. I., Cerreto, M. & Mac Donald, M. G. (1977). A theory and investigation of the effect of exchange-orientation on marriage and friendship. *Journal of Marriage and the Family*, 543–548.

Newton, P. (2016). Academic integrity: A quantitative study of confidence and understanding in students at the start of their higher education. *Assessment & Evaluation in Higher Education, 41*(3), 482–497.

Park, C. (2003). In other (people's) words: Plagiarism by university students–literature and lessons. *Assessment & Evaluation in Higher Education, 28*(5), 471–488.

Park, C. (2004). Rebels without a clause: Towards an institutional framework for dealing with plagiarism by students. *Journal of Further and Higher Education, 28*(3), 291–306.

Patrzek, J., Sattler, S., van Veen, F., Grunschel, C. & Fries, S. (2015). Investigating the effect of academic procrastination on the frequency and variety of academic misconduct: A panel study. *Studies in Higher Education, 40*(6), 1014–1029.

Pears, R. & Shields, G. J. (2016). *Cite them right: The essential referencing guide*. Palgrave Macmillan.

Roig, M. (1997). Can undergraduate students determine whether text has been plagiarized? *The Psychological Record, 47*(1), 113–122.

Šprajc, P., Urh, M., Jerebic, J., Trivan, D. & Jereb, E. (2017). Reasons for plagiarism in higher education. *Organizacija, 50*(1), 33–45.

Stark, L. J. & Perfect, T. J. (2006). Elaboration inflation: How your ideas become mine. *Applied Cognitive Psychology: The Official Journal of the Society for Applied Research in Memory and Cognition, 20*(5), 641–648.

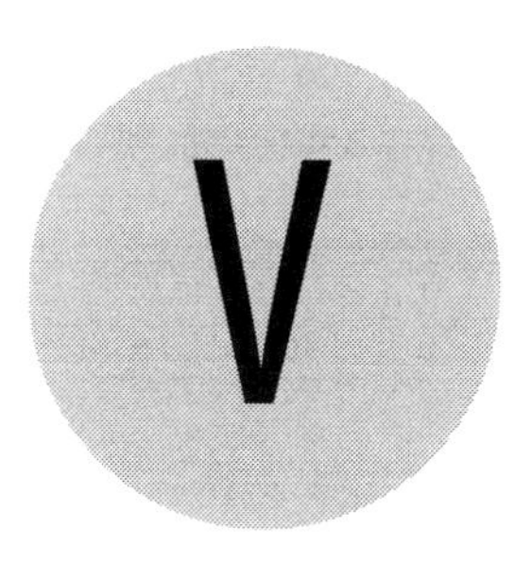

Producing high quality written assessments at degree level

It doesn't have to be rocket science, even if you're studying rocket science

No sympathy for the devil; keep that in mind. Buy the ticket, take the ride ... and if it occasionally gets a little heavier than what you had in mind, well ... maybe chalk it up to forced consciousness expansion: Tune in, freak out, get beaten.

Hunter S. Thompson

I'll freely admit, I did originally wonder if this chapter was feasible. Ostensibly, giving advice on the preparation of written assessments as applicable to students studying history of art as it is to those studying cellular biology, seems a hopelessly ambitious remit. After all, there are numerous different categories of written assessments across degree disciplines. Even when different disciplines use the same types of assessment, their respective expectations in terms of content and style are likely to differ significantly. Then it occurred to me: at a procedural level, you can break down any written assessment into a series of identical sub-tasks. You should: interrogate the relevant assessment documentation; locate suitable sources; plan the contents of your composition; write clearly; proofread your work; and then take account of the feedback you receive. At this procedural level of analysis, it is possible to provide some advice that is useful across the range of degree subjects and written assessment types. So, that's exactly what this chapter is going to do! The literature called upon in the forthcoming sections will go beyond pure (for want of a better term) psychology into allied research within the learning and teaching domain. Full disclosure: much of the research in this area tends to focus on the widely used essay format of assessment. However, the principles and guidelines that I will be taking from the research are applicable to preparing written assessments generally.

This chapter is all about trying to make your life a bit easier by addressing the fundamentals of written assessment production at degree level. At first glance, some of the topics in this chapter might seem almost too basic to merit much attention. Don't be fooled. It's the basics you must get right, as they provide the foundation for the subject-specific material you'll be studying. Think of these fundamentals as being akin to the first few figures in a long equation; if they are wrong, then everything that follows is also wrong. The advice and guidance in this chapter could save your ego (not to mention your grades) from taking a large and avoidable beating. Let's begin by looking at the preparation you should undertake before starting your written assessments.

Know the enemy

Key advice: always locate and examine the marking criteria for an assessment before you do anything else

Back in Chapter I, we explored the concept of metacognition, i.e. one's perception of, and control over, their own state of learning. We also examined the Dunning–Kruger effect, which describes the finding that it's the least competent individuals who usually have the most inflated perception of their competence. You can find a good example of the Dunning–Kruger effect in action when you look at the way that some students treat a critical part of the preparation stage of a written assessment. A quick scenario for you, by way of illustration. You're applying for a job that you would very much like to get. What's the first document you'd look at? Hopefully, it would be the person specification, i.e. the document that contains the criteria against which candidates for the job will be assessed. If you have this information, you can easily anticipate the kinds of questions you might be asked at an interview. This enables you to think about orienting your responses in a way that demonstrates you meet the requirements set out in the person specification. By the same logic, if you have a written assessment that you'd very much like to get a good grade for, then you need to understand the criteria against which your work will be assessed. That way, you can orient your writing to satisfy the requirements of the assessment. That's why the marking criteria is the first thing you reach for when preparing to tackle your written assessments, right? Hello? Is anyone there? If you're currently feeling a bit sheepish, don't worry: you're not alone! The literature indicates that students often lack a sound understanding of assessment expectations (e.g. Rust, Price & O'Donovan, 2003). Unfortunately, it's this understanding of assessment expectations that would encourage students to engage with teaching content on helping them to develop their knowledge of assessment criteria. As it stands, student engagement with such content is, let's be polite and say, non-optimal. Catch-22, Dunning–Kruger style! A grimly amusing example of this was provided by Turner (2018). This article featured a picture of an empty 400-seat lecture theatre, posted online by a lecturer after an entire class bunked off their lecture on demystifying marking and grading criteria. Do you think the confidence exhibited by those students in skipping that session was matched by their objective levels of competence? Neither do I! Unhappily for that class, research has predictably indicated that the greater the discrepancy between tutor and student expectations for an assessment, the worse the mark achieved (e.g. Hounsell, 1997). The lessons for you are twofold. First, upon being set a piece of coursework, you will likely be inclined to dive straight into searching for some good source literature. Instead, do yourself a big favour and start by going hunting for the applicable marking criteria. Second, if your programme offers taught sessions on the marking criteria they use, regard attendance as mandatory. Unless, that is, you have a demonstrable record of high attainment on previous assessments that have used the same marking criteria. Help us to help you. The Dunning–Kruger effect is a cruel mistress! You have been warned!

2

Key advice: practice applying marking criteria to assessment examples and your own work

Obtaining the marking criteria for a written assessment is a critical step in its preparation. However, as Sadler (1989) argued, knowing how your assessment will be marked is one thing, using that information effectively to develop your work is another. Again, think back to Chapter I where we covered the illusion of knowing, which occurs when a person exhibits a discrepancy between their perceived and actual levels of understanding. It's easy for you to fall foul of this when it comes to marking criteria. Let's say you're working on an essay and one of the marking criteria identified in the assessment documentation is 'Relevancy'. The documentation features a marking criteria grid that describes the levels of performance with respect to the relevancy criterion associated with different degree classifications. Of course, you're interested in what constitutes a first-class piece of work. The following description is provided:

> A first-class submission clearly and convincingly responds to the essay title set. The material used in the response is, without exception, relevant to the topic of the essay. The work effectively formulates and presents material in accordance with the instructions of the essay title.

Hopefully, the above seems entirely reasonable and straightforward irrespective of what degree subject you're studying. If you think you understand this marking criteria extract, I have a few questions for you. Do you think you could recognise an essay that met the above criterion, i.e. do you have an idea of what an exemplar of the above looks like? If so, do you think you could use this exemplar to objectively evaluate your own work with respect to the same criterion? If yes, then would you know how to make the appropriate changes to your work to improve it with respect to this criterion? The question of whether you understand the above extract is not quite so straightforward now is it? So, how do you go from just being able to identify the marking criteria for an assessment to being able to use it to accurately evaluate your work? Well, the same way your tutors did: via exposure to examples of assessment, and practice in the application of the associated criteria to such examples. As Sadler (1989) argued, this kind of practice is what helps you develop the explicit and tacit knowledge that you need to accurately evaluate your own work.

A good way of achieving practising the application of marking criteria is to use exemplars of written assessment that tutors often make available for student perusal. Your efforts to do this can serve as a catalyst for a dialogue with a tutor to help you calibrate your application of the marking criteria. Liu and Carless (2006) refer to this process as peer evaluation. It was investigated in a study by Riddell (2015). In this research, participants practised applying marking criteria to essays previously submitted by other students before using the same criteria to mark their own work. The results indicated a reduction in the discrepancies between student and tutor evaluations of work over the course of a semester. If you're really organised with the completion of the draft of an assessment, you can even have a go at applying the marking criteria to it and then using that as a basis for discussion with a tutor. There are three things you should be aware of if you want to take this approach. First, you should make an appointment with the applicable tutor, not just turn up on their doorstep brandishing reams of paper and puppy dog eyes! Second, they won't commit to a grade for your efforts in advance of your work being formally marked (nice try!). However, they will most likely be happy to have a dialogue with you about your use of the marking and grading criteria in evaluating your work. Third, please don't just turn up at your tutor's doorstep at the 11th hour before the work is due to be submitted. Contrary to what you might have been told, tutors aren't big on Martinis infused with the tears of students who have just found out they've made a pig's ear of their essay one hour before it's due in!

Making your (research) connection more reliable

3

Key advice: Google searches should not be your first port of call when doing your research

Having dealt with the need to obtain and familiarise yourself with the marking criteria, you can now move on to locating the required source material for your assessment. In this respect, there is one particularly important issue I would like to draw your attention to: the need to identify and secure high-quality sources for your assessments. To this end, I'm initially going to focus in on using the internet as a research tool because, as we shall see, it presents opportunities and challenges in the identification of high-quality sources for your assessments. However, the advice subsequently given on evaluating the quality of sources applies to online and offline material.

The use of the internet in researching a topic is a no-brainer for undergraduates and rightly so! Gone are the bad old days when research invariably meant trudging to the library and spending long hours sat in front of an antiquated CD-ROM based catalogue. I've repressed the memories of having to retrieve dusty old books and journals from precariously high book shelves via a wobbly ladder. Oh, and then there was the matter of paying exorbitant photocopying fees or taking the material out on loan only to have to return it again a week later. The internet is *so* much more accessible and convenient; everything is just a Google search away. However, let's consider whether convenience is invariably a good thing. The principal issue with the internet, especially for budding academics, is that its accessibility is both its greatest strength and biggest tripping hazard. Anyone with an internet connection can post content that can find its way into Google, without the need to undergo any kind of editorial or review process to ensure the accuracy and academic rigour of that information. Therefore, the quality of the sources available online ranges from rock solid to, well, rock bottom. Research has indicated that, on balance, if it's quality of sources that you're after then just hitting Google is not your best first port of call (e.g. Brophy & Bawden, 2005). Unfortunately, as Perruso (2016) pointed out having reviewed some of the relevant literature, search engines like Google have become the go-to source for undergraduates engaged in academic research. This tendency is by no means restricted to specific disciplines; even the medical students are at it! Judd and Kennedy (2011) found that final year medics were relying on Google and Wikipedia to access biomedical information 41% of the time. It transpired that less than 40% of the sites accessed by students via Google were identified by tutors as being high-quality sources. To be fair, I don't recall the last time I was in the doctor's office and witnessed them hit Wikipedia. If they did, I'd most certainly be getting a second opinion!

Please don't run away with the impression that I'm about to advocate you yank out your fibre wire connections or dispense other advice about as welcome as a baby with an ear infection on a long-haul flight. Nothing could be further from the truth. Studies that have identified the tendency of undergraduates to Google the topics of their assessments do not claim that the use of the internet in academic research is problematical per se. Instead, they highlight issues that make it more likely that students will slip up when looking for sources online. Such issues include: privileging ease of access over quality when searching for information (Connaway, Dickey & Radford, 2011); over-estimating the reliability of information found online (e.g. Colón-Aguirre & Fleming-May, 2012); and using ineffectual criteria to distinguish between reliable and unreliable online information (Currie, Devlin,

Emde & Graves, 2010). In other words, it's not using the internet for research that is the problem. Using sub-optimal methods to retrieve information online and not being discerning enough about the quality of the material you locate is what causes the issues. Let's consider how you might go about more effectively searching for and identifying the good stuff online. Yes, I'm still referring to academic material here!

Research has generated numerous checklists that can be used to evaluate website content, each of which contains measures of quality such as accuracy and completeness. You can see some examples of these checklists in Knight and Burn (2005). However, checklists do run into a few problems, nicely articulated by Meola (2004). For example, some checklist items would be difficult for you to respond to when you are new to a topic and provide little or nothing in the way of guidance when you find yourself in this predicament. If you're not yet familiar with the literature, how are you supposed to make an appraisal of the accuracy or completeness of the information within a website? Some checklist items, such as whether there are contact details for the author of the website, seem sensible but probably won't work in practice. Can you see a teeny methodological issue with contacting an author of the contents of a website and asking them to comment on the accuracy and completeness of the information they've provided? So, what are you to make of the outcome of this checklist item? Sure, you could add more items to the checklist to delve a little deeper into the background of the author, e.g. ascertain their qualifications and professional accreditations. However, that just raises more questions about the legitimacy of what you uncover. Some credentials that sound impressive are, on closer inspection, not worth the paper they are written on. In his excellent book, *Bad science*, Ben Goldacre gives an amusing example of this whereby he obtained a professional membership for an American nutritional society for his dead cat! Quite rightly, he hung it in his toilet! Of course, you could avoid the likelihood of being fooled by such shenanigans by adding yet more items to your checklist to probe the legitimacy of accreditations. However, I would suggest that consulting a 200-item checklist for every website you visit when trawling the internet for information is going to get old, very quickly!

Issues with checklist size notwithstanding, their principal problem is that they're putting more emphasis on capturing superficial indicators of quality from within the website in question. It's more meaningful for you to be equipped with techniques that empower you to evaluate a website from an external perspective. Let's illustrate this with a quick example. Say your extensive enquiries about the author of a website has revealed that their credentials are impeccable. What does this mean? Is it an assurance that everything that author ever composes will be free from error? Does the fact that they are eminently well qualified mean that they are immune to bias, don't make mistakes, or that their interpretation of data is somehow beyond reproach? Of course it doesn't. Meola (2004) argues that to meaningfully evaluate information online, you need to take a context-based approach. This involves the evaluation of a website with reference to information taken from outside of its contents. Giving you a bit of exposition about the techniques that Meola advocates is a better springboard for the development of your website evaluation skills than providing you with a checklist.

4

Key advice: prioritise peer reviewed material in your research

One of the principles of natural justice that provide the basis for the English legal system is that no one can be a judge in their own case. Academia has its own version of this principle: authors do not get to decide whether their work is good enough to merit publication. This stands in contrast to what happens on the public internet, where authors are very often at complete liberty to post their own work without undergoing any kind of editorial process. Therefore, as Meola (2004) argues, the first thing you should be familiar with in learning to evaluate sources is the quality assurance process used in academia: peer review.

As the name implies, peer review involves authors submitting their work to a panel of independent experts in the applicable field to evaluate its quality and suitability for publication within a source. The source in question might be published offline, online or both. The process usually involves the author contacting an editor with their manuscript and requesting peer review with a view to it appearing in their publication. If it falls within the remit of that publication, the editor will invite the submission of the manuscript. When submitting their manuscript, authors are usually required to declare any potential conflicts of interest in the production of the work and identify its source of funding (if it had any). This is a first line of defence against researchers with vested interests getting data that is subject to obvious sources of bias into publication unchecked. For example, if a group of researchers were funded by the manufacturer of a drug to examine its effectiveness, this is an obvious potential conflict of interest that could bias the research findings. Note the use of the word 'potential'. Research conducted under such an arrangement can be perfectly valid and above-board. However, the presence of the risk of bias means that the authors would be expected to be transparent and declare their potential conflict of interest. Being forewarned means you can have a good rummage around the methodology of the study to ensure that it had not been rigged (intentionally or otherwise) to make the drug look good for the sake of not falling out with the people that paid for the research. Upon receiving the manuscript, the editor will remove the author's personal details from the work. This is to ensure that the peer review process is based solely on the merit of the work and not any familiarity (personal or professional) between the authors and reviewers. They will then forward it to several academics within that field who will be asked to rate and comment on the submission with respect to given criteria. Such criteria might include: the appropriateness of the sources used; the methodological rigour of the work; the justification for the conclusions reached; the quality of the writing and so forth. Each reviewer will usually be asked to conclude their comments on the work with an overall decision as to whether the manuscript should be published. Their recommendation options range from outright rejection with no re-submission invited, to immediate acceptance with no revisions required. Once the editor has read the reviewers' comments and recommendations, they have the final say on whether the work gets published and convey this decision in writing to the author. This correspondence includes the comments and ratings given by the peer reviewers. If the decision is that the manuscript should be revised and re-submitted, the author is expected to make the required changes and re-submit their work with a covering letter explaining how they have addressed the reviewers' comments. As you can probably guess, composing such a letter when you might feel a bit aggrieved by some of the reviewer's contributions is an exercise in restraint. Referring to reviewers as pedantic, self-serving, egotistical t***s is generally frowned on by editors.

Sorry for the rather lengthy exposition on the process of peer review, but it's a critical concept to understand because it's considered something of a 'gold standard' in academia. It should certainly be at the forefront of your mind when evaluating online or offline sources. Of course, knowing this is redundant if you don't know how to tell if a source is peer reviewed. Fortunately, this is usually straightforward as peer reviewed publications will almost invariably explicitly refer to the process in their publications. A good shortcut is to look at the guidance notes or instructions to authors, as these will refer to the peer review process (if there is one). If in doubt, simply contact the editor of the publication and ask. You can save yourself a lot of leg-work in this respect by heading straight for your library and finding out what access they have to subscription-based content, which is predominantly peer reviewed. Most universities will use an access management portal to enable their students to obtain journals and other publications that require a subscription. OpenAthens is a good example of such a portal. Your library should be able to give you a login to this kind of service. Once logged in you can search vast online catalogues of peer reviewed content and download full articles from sources that your university has a subscription to. In the event your university doesn't have a subscription to that source, you can still read an abstract/summary of the work and obtain the contact details of the corresponding author of the work.

Becoming familiar with your university's access management portal should be your first step in tracking down peer reviewed content. Most university libraries offer instruction on the use of such services. If yours doesn't, ask a librarian to show you the ropes. You can find additional shortcuts to peer reviewed material by looking at academic social networking sites such as ResearchGate, where authors share digital copies of their work with fellow academics. This can be a useful way of obtaining sources that may have been identified by information access portals, such as Athens, within publications your university does not subscribe to. You can also use this kind of social media software to keep up to date with the outputs from relevant research projects and prominent academics within a field. Of course, there is also a search engine that lets you look for literature on specific subjects too. These sites are free to subscribe to and it's very easy to set up your own profile, which you can tinker with as you progress as an academic. If you must use Google, at least use Google Scholar. As the name implies, this branch of the Google search engine filters search terms for scholarly content, i.e. journals, books and conference proceedings that are likely to have undergone peer review.

5

Key advice: peer review is not foolproof; you must still evaluate sources for yourself

Looking for peer reviewed material is a great first step in developing your information literacy, but it is just that: a first step. Just because a source is peer reviewed does not mean you can assume all is well with it and simply switch off your critical faculty. Peer review, like any process, is only as good as the way it's implemented and the people doing the implementation. An array of things can undermine the reliability of the peer review process, too numerous to cover exhaustively here. To give you an example, manuscripts sometimes get sent out to reviewers who are not suitably qualified to pass judgement on the quality of the work, but who carry on with the process regardless. Conversely, suitably qualified reviewers can sometimes fail to give a piece of work enough attention in the reviewing process, perhaps due to competing professional demands or just having an off day. The peer review process is far from perfect and its effectiveness as a quality assurance mechanism is arguably under-researched. The interested reader is referred to Smith (2006) for an accessible critique of peer review. I think one of my colleagues has the best teaching example of how even papers with glaringly obvious issues can get past peer review. Fair warning: if you object to a spot of toilet humour, you might want to skip the remainder of this paragraph. Still here? Thought so! He refers to a paper that purported to document geographical variations in penis size. Admittedly, it's difficult to get past the question about what purpose such research might serve, other than bragging rights. However, continuing to read the paper generates another question, i.e. what is the meaning of the little asterisk that appears next to selected entries in the league table of willies? Also, why does it frequently accompany the larger figures in the table? Have you guessed the answer yet? Yes, that's right, an asterisk denoted that the adjacent figure was obtained from self-report data! If you're concerned about the implications of self-report methodology for the control over the ambient temperature at the time of measurement, I'd respectfully suggest you're missing a much bigger (no pun intended) issue! Sieber (2006) likened peer review to democracy, i.e. a flawed system, but the best one possible. I wholeheartedly agree with this analogy, but would take it a little further. Like democracy, you should engage with the peer review process enthusiastically whilst always being mindful of its limitations. You should prioritise peer reviewed material in your search for sources, but not view peer review as a cast iron guarantee that the source in question is sound. The onus is always on you to evaluate the quality of your source material. The next section will give you two simple techniques to help you do this.

6

Key advice: corroborate and compare sources when doing your research to develop your critical faculties

Providing advice on critical evaluation equally applicable to students studying different degrees is difficult, as concepts important to the process of evaluation differ between disciplines. For example, knowledge of concepts such as control groups is critical in evaluating the quality of sources for those whose degree calls upon scientific literature. It's less useful for interrogating literature from the humanities. Of course, I can't provide you with pointers on what to look out for in the literature for specific degree disciplines, but I can give you some simple guidance on how to discover such pointers for yourself. Recall that when we discussed the issues with website checklists, one of the problems identified was that they would be difficult for a novice to a topic to use. This is because evaluative judgements are relative: if you ask someone how good something is, they'll usually ask you to specify what the judgement is being made in relation to. The problem is that novices to a topic lack the appropriate reference points required to arrive at a meaningful judgement. Meola (2004) identified two very simple techniques you can use to generate the reference points you need to evaluate sources of information: corroboration and comparison. Let's look at how you can use these to assess a source with respect to the accuracy and completeness criteria identified a little earlier in the chapter.

When we talk about evaluating the accuracy of information, an approach that should come to mind is corroboration, i.e. verifying that information against other sources. An excellent first step is to start by identifying where the information you're using originated from. Recall that in the previous chapter on academic integrity, we made the distinction between primary and secondary sources. Primary sources are first-hand accounts of work, e.g. a journal article containing a write up of an experiment, composed by the researcher (or researchers) responsible for the work. Secondary sources are a second-hand account of a piece of work, composed by another author, e.g. an introductory text book. In obtaining accurate information, wherever possible, it's always wise to locate the primary source. With the best will in the world, authors can inadvertently make factual or interpretive errors when writing about the work of others. In the process of describing the original work in their own words, authors also sometimes fail to convey meaning as faithfully and clearly as they might have done. If you are using a secondary source, you should corroborate the information against the primary source to look for discrepancies. However, a better course of action is to endeavour to use primary sources when you're doing your research. This way, you can eliminate errors associated with secondary sources from the outset.

In corroborating a piece of information, you should attempt to verify it against several different sources. The idea is that the more times independent sources generate the same information, the lower the likelihood is of that information being erroneous. They key phrase here is 'independent sources'. Consistency in the appearance of information between different works from the same author (or research group) does not necessarily mean they got it right the first time. It might just mean they got it wrong initially and were oblivious to this, so simply reproduced the same error in subsequent works. Of course, corroboration is not foolproof. It's entirely possible that several independent sources arrive at the same mistake because no one in the chain of sources did their fact-checking. Consequently, they just re-produced an error made at the start of the chain in good faith. It's even possible, albeit less likely, that several sources could independently arrive at the same error. However, we're playing a game of probabilities here. Independently corroborated information is less likely to be inaccurate than uncorroborated information. Think of corroboration as an integral part of due diligence when doing research for your assessments.

Moving from the question of the accuracy of a source to its completeness, re-visiting the primary versus secondary source distinction is also useful. Rarely will a secondary source contain a comprehensive account of the original material, as to do so would defeat the object of the secondary source existing. For example, the purpose of an introductory text is to highlight and compile information on the fundamental aspects of a topic into a narrative. This gives students new to the subject a broad grounding in that topic and serves as a springboard for them to investigate things in more detail. Within this remit, it's neither possible nor desirable for the author to cover everything they refer to in as much detail as the primary source. Thus, their coverage is necessarily incomplete. You must read the original source and compare it to the applicable secondary source to see what's been omitted in the latter and how that impacts on its completeness. However, it's not just secondary sources that warrant comparisons with their primary counterparts. Primary sources also vary considerably in their completeness. It is, of course, not possible for any one publication to do justice to the entirety of a topic. Some authors are very explicit about this and provide a remit for their coverage at the beginning of their manuscript that makes it more obvious what the limitations of the piece are. This serves as a cue for you to look for complementary work that will fill in the gaps, so to speak. However, even when authors do this, their coverage may still be incomplete in other ways. For example, they may have simply missed relevant source material in doing their own research for their work. Authors might, intentionally or otherwise, favour information from a specific perspective, maybe because it fits in with their own intellectual leanings or happens to fit the narrative of the piece they are writing. The only way you can really identify such coverage limitations is to look at a range of material on the topic. Turns out there is a reason they say you read for a degree.

An effective way of developing your ability to judge the completeness of sources on a topic is to use what's often referred to within academia as the funnel approach. This entails starting with sources that have the explicit purpose of highlighting the breadth of material available on a topic (e.g. an introductory chapter) and then working your way towards material with a narrower focus. Looking at the broader material first will give you a good overview of the different approaches to, and perspectives on, a topic. It's important that you work from broad to specific sources (not the other way around) for two main reasons. First, it will help prevent you get intellectually pigeon-holed into a specific perspective on a topic through lack of awareness of other viewpoints. Second, learning about differing perspectives on a topic is more conducive with the active processing of information we talked about in Chapter III. This is because it invites questions around identifying the differences between alternative approaches and perspectives. As we've previously covered, asking and answering questions about material is an effective memory aid.

I would suggest that you begin implementing the corroboration and comparison techniques by using them with peer reviewed sources. Fishing for sources in these waters is safer in developing an understanding of the conventions and expectations of works within your discipline than hitting the public internet sites from the outset. Once you find your feet using a variety of peer reviewed sources, you will be better equipped to wade into the more treacherous waters of non-peer reviewed material and evaluate their content. It is important to acknowledge that there is a wealth of information online in non-peer reviewed sources that is, nonetheless, still fit for academic purposes. Summarily dismissing such information because it doesn't appear in a peer reviewed publication would mean missing out on potentially useful material. Grounding your corroborative and comparative activities in the peer reviewed literature has another benefit. Looking at examples of work published in reputable sources will illustrate how authors from your degree discipline formulate the literature and their research into scholarly work. This brings us nicely onto the next stage of the process of preparing a written assessment: planning how you're going to use all the sources you've obtained!

Prior planning and preparation prevent pretty poor performance

7

Key advice: planning your writing needs to account for how you are going to use your sources to develop an academic discourse

In some respects, we already touched on planning at the beginning of this chapter with the advice on locating and studying the marking criteria for the assessment in question. However, now we're going to look at planning in the context of the writing process specifically. I'm sure that being advised to plan your written work will come as no great surprise to you. Advice on formally planning what you write is a mainstay of study guides. What might come as more of a shock to you is that the literature on the effectiveness of planning in the writing process is not as large and unequivocal as you might imagine! In one rare example of research on this topic, Torrance, Thomas and Robinson (2000) surveyed students about their strategies in approaching essay writing. They found that students who made detailed plans for their essays received higher grades than those who did not plan their essay in advance, by an entire degree classification. So far, so predictable. However, the average mark for the essays of the students in the detailed planning group was within 1% of the students who simply adopted a think then do strategy. This involved no advance written outline of the essay contents. Well, that's a spanner in the works of conventional wisdom. So, am I about to suggest that you dispense with planning and just spend a bit more time thinking about the topic of your assessment before committing fingers to keyboard? Not exactly. You see, a key feature about the above study is that it only asked students about their planning practices. Torrance et al. didn't examine what the students thought their principal objective was in composing an essay. It transpires that this is rather important.

The way that students often conceptualise academic writing was illustrated in a surprisingly rare piece of work to ascertain which writing practices were predictive of the grades students obtained in their essays. Norton (1990) found that there was a marked discrepancy in what tutors and students identified as the most important criteria in determining the quality of their work. The students were more concerned with the contents of their essays (i.e. the demonstration of knowledge) whereas the tutors were more concerned with the development of an argument (i.e. the use of knowledge). These students were demonstrating deficiencies in their grasp of what Hounsell (1995) referred to as academic discourse. This is characterised by: interpretation of information and development of argument; the use of evidence to substantiate or refute interpretation or arguments; and the use of a coherent and logical structure in the presentation of information. Hounsell's thesis was that before you can plan your work effectively, you must first understand the idea of academic discourse. Moreover, you must think about developing it as the primary goal of your writing. This is because your purpose in writing affects the way you go about planning. Written work that emerges from plans addressing the development of academic discourse gets higher grades than work emerging from plans that only serve as an inventory of contents. Indeed, Campbell, Smith and Brooker (1998) demonstrated this when they interviewed students about their approaches to essay writing and compared their expected and achieved grades. They found that students who composed essays that received higher marks did not view their objective as simply to re-tell knowledge, but rather to reconstruct existing knowledge. At the planning stage, these students thought more about organising their sources into sub-topics or themes. They also used the information they had collated as the basis for building arguments to organise their essays around. Finally, they focused on refining and improving the presentation of these arguments throughout the drafting process. This stood in contrast to the lower attaining students who tended to focus on building information sequentially, according to its location within the sources they used.

So, what are the implications of the research for the way you go about planning your written assessments? Well, I'd argue that the most important lesson that has emerged from the, admittedly limited, literature is that you should think of a plan as a framework for helping you develop your academic discourse around a topic. It's one thing to know that you should be developing an argument or narrative of some kind in planning your composition, but your plan should explicitly identify how you are going to achieve this. By way of example, I'm going to show you my plan for this section of the book.

Objective: to provide fundamentally important advice on planning written compositions for undergraduates.

Narrative and evidence: importance of planning axiomatic in study guides > Research on effectiveness of planning is scarce and not very compelling (Thomas & Robinson, 2000) maybe because students and tutors differ in expectations of written work. Students prioritise contents, lecturers prioritise development of argument (Norton, 1990). > Students often conceptualise purpose of academic writing as knowledge reproduction, rather than academic discourse, i.e. argument (Hounsell, 1995) > Students who conceptualise purpose of writing as regurgitating info go about planning differently, e.g. don't think about developing argument and therefore get poorer marks (Campbell, Smith & Brooker, 1998).

Argument and link to following section: students should view plans less as an inventory of content and more as an academic discourse map. > Give example and explain > Use clarity benefits of planning as a link to writing style section.

Hopefully, in the above example you can see me practising what I'm preaching. Note that the plan for this section is not simply a list of content, but rather a roadmap for the way I use that content to generate an argument. I've achieved this by giving my planning three very simple requirements.

1. State the objective for the section of text in question. Effective writing is much like effective reading in that it tends to happen more readily if you're doing it with a clear objective in mind. My goal was to provide fundamentally important advice on planning written compositions for undergraduates. Note how my objective required that I do something with the information I presented, beyond just presenting it. Just this one-sentence objective gave me a remit for the contents of that part of my work. It set the parameters for what kind of information I would need to review. This enabled me to move onto thinking about the second requirement of the plan.
2. Establish a narrative with supporting evidence. I had to think about how I could tie the information I had found together in a meaningful way. Of course, I could just have described the studies that I found, in the order I found them and have left it at that. However, that would not have achieved the section's objective. Rather, it would have just demonstrated that I'd found relevant material and that I could describe it. Therefore, I had to read the research with a view to presenting a narrative to the reader that enabled them to understand the reasoning behind the advice that was to follow. This enabled me to move onto the third part of the plan.
3. State the argument and link to the following section. Here, I had to use the narrative I had developed to provide an argument in relation to the purpose of the section, i.e. to give you the promised advice on planning your writing.

At this point you might be wondering how to break up your writing into sections, so that you can use the kind of approach I've just advocated to compose an entire document. It's really very simple: you start by identifying the overall purpose of the writing you are doing. Quite often this is stated explicitly in the assessment itself, either in the form of an assessment question, title or brief. This is the bit you absolutely must be clear on. If you set off down the wrong path at this point, every step you take in your writing only serves to transport you further away from the desired destination. If in doubt, seek clarification from a tutor. Once you've identified the overall purpose for your writing, you just think of the contents of your work as a series of sub-sections, each with their own objective, narrative with evidence and argument with link requirements.

Let's take the contents of this chapter as an example of how you might approach planning the contents of a document. I had the overall objective of providing guidance on written assessments at degree level, useful to undergraduates from all disciplines. With that in mind it was immediately obvious that the only realistic way of achieving this was to break the process of academic writing down into its discipline non-specific constituent parts. This suggested several sub-sections for the chapter (e.g. interrogate the assessment documentation, locate quality sources, plan contents, etc.). Each of these sub-sections contributed to the chapter's overall purpose. I tackled the planning for each sub-section in turn, using its objective as an anchor point when reading the literature. This helped me identify the best evidence to use and think about how I could integrate my sources into an argument around the objective and move on to the next sub-section. Repeating this process for each of the planned sub-sections resulted in a game plan for the entire chapter.

Having read about my method of planning the contents of this chapter, you might be thinking that it sounds like a lot of work and will only extend the already substantial amount of time that you need to invest in completing an assessment. In response, I would say that I'm not trying to impose my approach on you. I offer it as an example. I see no reason why you should not experiment with your own methods of planning that might prove more economical. I would, however, issue the following two provisos. First, that you ensure you understand the purpose of the assessment and use this as the basis of your planning. Second, that your plan serves as more than just an inventory of content and addresses how you are going to use your sources to generate an academic discourse around the topic of your assessment. Think of writing plans as being like the academic equivalent of Ordnance Survey maps. Maps do more than just list the names of places you'll go past on your way to your destination. They work because they give you the information you need to generate a route that tells you how to navigate to your destination. By the same token, writing plans need to do more than list the material you'll call upon in your composition. They also need to indicate how you can use the material to generate a narrative that tells you how to navigate an academic argument.

If you still think that planning will only ever extend the time you have to spend on a written assessment, consider the following question. How much longer would car journeys take if you had to figure out new routes as you were driving, rather than have the directions laid out for you by the satellite navigation system? You'll know from bitter experience that being occupied with the act of driving itself compromises your ability to navigate. You are prone to taking wrong turns, getting confused, and having to spend time back-tracking or trying to improvise your way back to the correct route, which involves the risk of going even further out of your way. The result? A longer and more stressful journey. Well, it's the same with writing. Being preoccupied with articulating what you are thinking intelligibly (which is no mean feat) compromises your ability to marshal those thoughts into a coherent narrative. You'll tend to focus on describing the material rather than extracting its meaning, go off on tangents according to what material you find most interesting, back-track and then have to re-write content. The result? The writing process takes longer, not to mention gives you many more grey hairs, than it would have done had you bothered to give yourself some directions. Time spent planning how you are going to use material to create an academic narrative, is usually time saved in the writing process!

Elements of guile

8

Key advice: trying to sound clever is a good way of sounding stupid

I would understand if you were doubtful there was any advice I could dispense on academic writing useful to students across all degree subjects. Certainly, some authors have argued that the development of academic writing is inextricably tied to the discipline being studied. For example, they assert that it's questionable whether lessons on effective communication in scientific subjects are transferable to subjects within the humanities (e.g. North, 2005). I suspect that the more nuanced advice on academic writing is likely to be discipline-specific, or at least would be best illustrated with reference to examples from that discipline. However, there is a piece of advice I can give you that will help you get off to a good start in developing your academic voice, in a manner appropriate for your degree subject. This advice is incredibly simple in principle, but rather harder to implement than you might imagine. Are you ready? When producing written work, aim to be clear above all else!

The necessity of clear writing for success in academia should be self-evident. The primary goal of producing an academic piece of work is to communicate knowledge. If the work is written in an unclear fashion, then it's not effectively achieving this goal. Be that as it may, the clarity of expression in academic writing has been heavily criticised over the last 50 years. This is particularly true of the social sciences, where entire books have been devoted to panning academics for their lack of clarity in published works (e.g. Billig, 2013). Therefore, I'd argue it's important for a book on study skills to do a little something to address this issue with the future generation of academics, i.e. you lot! My contribution to helping you write more clearly involves identifying two of the main culprits for unclear writing within academia. Let's start off with some bullshit! No, really!

I offer you my apologies (but not a refund) for the next passage of writing. It's necessary to demonstrate what I'm trying to discourage. I'll make this brief and promise never to do it again. Well, not deliberately at least.

> In the composition of their manuscripts, students frequently exhibit a proclivity towards circumlocution indicative of a desire to inveigle the favour of their tutors or obfuscate their unsophisticated understanding of the applicable phenomena unaware of the deleterious consequences for the transparency of their composition, or their complicity in perpetuating a problematical orthodoxy that prizes complexity over clarity, conflates impenetrable and verbose prose with profundity and marginalises the reader from engagement with the academic discourse.

Or to put it another way:

> You might be tempted to use unnecessarily wordy composition to impress your tutor or conceal the fact that your understanding of a topic is not as advanced as you'd like. This practice only serves to make your writing unclear. It also suggests you have been lulled into thinking that using a convoluted writing style has inherent academic merit. In fact, it's the clarity of your writing that matters most. Unclear writing makes it more likely that the reader will struggle to understand you, get frustrated and move onto other sources.

Both of the above passages are saying exactly the same thing, but only the first one is what Frankfurt (2009) and I would call bullshit. It's not the message that is at fault; it's the presentation that is the problem. In the first passage I was trying to make something simple sound much more complicated in the way I articulated it: there was deception at play. I relegated the importance of the message to second place behind attempting to manipulate the reader's impression of my intelligence. This practice can be common in students. In a survey of 110 Stanford undergraduates, 86% confessed to having changed the wording of an essay to make it sound more valid or intelligent by using complicated language (Oppenheimer, 2006). This does rather beg the question of why anyone would think that making their writing harder to understand makes them appear more intelligent. One possible reason might be what Sperber (2010) referred to as the guru effect. This effect refers to the tendency to view things that are difficult to understand as being profound, irrespective of whether they make any sense! As I've, hopefully, already demonstrated, obscure writing is a very effective way of making something difficult to understand. Pennycook, Cheyne, Barr, Koehler and Fugelsang (2015) provided an experimental example of the guru effect in action. In this research, the authors asked undergraduates to rate, among other things, nonsense statements randomly generated by a website. An example of such a statement was: "Wholeness quiets infinite phenomena." Over a quarter of the participants identified such nonsense statements as being profound. Before you laugh too hard at the students who were taken in by the bullshit, let me ask you something. Have you ever emerged from the cinema having seen a film that didn't seem to make any sense? Did you attribute this to not being clued up enough on film theory or cinematography to understand the director's vision? If so, did you really have good reason to discount the alternative possibility that what you'd just seen was just, well, bullshit?

At this point, you might be starting to wonder whether making your prose a bit less crystal clear would be such a bad thing. Could you exploit the guru effect with your writing to get extra credit on your assessments? Well, a study by Oppenheimer (2006) suggests that making your language more complicated in the hope you'll appear more intelligent in assessment contexts probably won't work. In this research, the authors took extracts from sample essays composed as part of the admissions requirements for graduate level studies to an English literature course. They then manipulated these extracts to produce two other versions of the text, highly complex and moderately complex in nature. In the highly complex version, a computer programme replaced every noun, verb and adjective with its longest equivalent in Microsoft Word's thesaurus. In the moderately complex version, every third example of each word was replaced.

The only other changes made to the text were to preserve its grammatical structure in view of the replaced words. Participants in the experiment were asked to assume the role of an admissions officer to the English literature course. They were invited to read a text extract, which was presented to them as a sample of a candidate's admission essay for the course. Their task was to decide whether to accept the candidate who composed it based on what they read. They were also asked to rate their confidence in their decision and how difficult they found the passage to read on a scale of 1–7. The results were clear: more complicated essays were judged as being more difficult to read and given lower acceptance ratings (i.e. the authors were judged as being less intelligent) than less complicated extracts. Importantly, this trend was found irrespective of the quality of the essay from which the extracts had been taken. You might assume that only the poorer essays would benefit from being embellished with more complicated language, but this wasn't the case. Using longer words neither redeemed the poor essays, nor further enhanced the good ones. What happened to the guru effect? Well, it's likely that the context of an academic assessment throws a spanner in its workings. As Sperber points out, the guru effect is likely reliant on a reader having reason to believe in the authority of the author who produced the unclear text. Under these circumstances, the reader tends to trust that what the author has said has merit without going to any lengths to evaluate whether this is the case. However, in assessing work, a tutor's role is to evaluate the efforts of a student. The role of a student designates that a person has yet to demonstrate their authority on a subject. Furthermore, the validity of the tutor's evaluation can be examined and questioned by their peers. That's a double whammy for the guru effect: neither the student nor the tutor can conceal shoddy work under the guise of authority. In summary, if you want to sound smart, get your ideas across clearly and achieve better marks, aim to simplify what you write rather than complicate it.

9

Key advice: use readability metrics to help you improve the clarity of your writing

Unclear writing isn't always due to a deliberate intention to deceive readers via unnecessarily complicated language and composition. Often, it just reflects the fact that writing clearly and concisely is blooming hard and very time-consuming. This is especially true when the goal of the writing is to explain something that you know. Do you remember our coverage of the hindsight bias? The tendency to view things that you have previously learned as simple and obvious to others is not helpful when writing an assessment where the purpose is to demonstrate your knowledge and understanding. If you view previously learned material as obvious, your inclination will be to exclude it or cover it very superficially in your work. This is one way you can inadvertently make your writing less clear than it could be and is why it is often unwise to identify a tutor as being the audience for your writing. A tutor will mark your work, that much is true, but if you are writing for an expert on the topic there is a good chance you'll omit exposition of any information that you see as rudimentary. You'd reason that the tutor would already be painfully aware of such information and, therefore, you'd be wasting your word count going over it. However, here's the critical thing: they already have their degree, you don't. They don't have to demonstrate their familiarity with the basics, you probably do. It's usually better to target your composition at an intelligent, but uninformed audience; assume your role is to teach someone else what you now know. This way, you're less likely to omit information that an assessment wants you to demonstrate your understanding of, even if it does seem simple in hindsight.

Seeing the audience for your assessment as an expert can affect the clarity of your writing in more ways than just promoting the omission of material that you should be covering. It's also likely to affect how you articulate your knowledge. If you are writing for an expert on a topic you're likely to be concerned about patronising the reader by using simple and straightforward language. This opens another door to unnecessarily long-winded and complex writing. It explains why even experienced academics from disciplines that you might think would know better are as guilty of unclear prose as anyone! For example, Hartley, Pennebaker and Fox (2003) reviewed 80 *Educational Psychology* journal articles and found that, overall, the papers were classified as being very difficult to read. This type of review does raise the question of how reading ease is measured, and if we can use such a measure as the basis for checking and improving the clarity of our own writing.

Hartley (2008) points to an accessible and popular example of a metric that can help you assess the ease with which your prose can be read: The Flesch Readability Score. If you use Microsoft Word, it's available as part of the spell-checking facility. It works by calculating the length of words and sentences within a piece of text and then uses this information to generate a Reading Ease score between 0 and 100. Ranges of scores (e.g. 90–100) are associated with minimum reading age levels (e.g. 10–11 years old). These ranges are associated with difficulty levels (e.g. very easy) and exemplars of such text (e.g. children's stories). Text achieving a score between 60–69 is classified as being of average difficulty and deemed readable by 14–15-year-olds. A tabloid newspaper would normally fall into this range. A score of between 30–49 would be classified as difficult to read and deemed readable by 18–20-year-olds. An undergraduate essay would fall into this range (Hartley, 2008). Anything that achieves a score of less than 30 is deemed very difficult to read and only suitable for a graduate-level audience. Hartley (2015) went as far as to argue that even specialist academic journals should reject papers that achieve a Flesch score of less than 30 and ask for a re-write. I'm inclined to agree.

I should stress that I'm not pushing the Flesch Readability Score as a panacea for unclear academic writing. Equally, I'm not suggesting that everyone tries to get as close to a score of 100 as possible in all their writing. I'm advocating you use the Flesch score for two purposes. First, as a guide to whether the readability of your work is appropriate for the intended audience. This is a critical point, as the idea of using a metric such as the Flesch Readability Score is not to deter you from using terminology appropriate for your subject. Nor is it to prevent you from producing more nuanced sentences. Academic material is often inherently complex in nature and using subject specific terminology can be appropriate in making your writing clear and concise. Clarity of expression is not the same as dumbing down. It is not about outlawing the use of terminology or complex expression per se; it's about not using it unnecessarily. For example, an undergraduate paper that achieved a Flesch score of 40 is appropriate for its readership. Of course, that's not to say that the paper could not be revised so that it becomes easier to read for its audience. This brings us onto the next purpose of using the Flesch score: it's a convenient yardstick for improving the clarity of a draft of your work. For example, say you're writing an essay and it receives a Flesch Reading Ease score of 30. You know that your work is readable by 18–20-year-olds and is characteristic of an undergraduate paper. However, you also know that the readability score is only one mark outside of putting your paper in the very difficult to read increment. You could be making your work easier to read for your audience. Your initial score gives you a baseline to judge the success of your attempts to improve the readability of your work against. Treat the Flesch score in a similar manner to the spelling or grammar checking facility; as a prompt to have another look at your composition. Use it to identify if there is anything you might have expressed using more common language and in a more straightforward manner.

Having obtained your Flesch score, what can you do to improve it? Well, since the Flesch calculation is based on word and sentence length, you should look at these aspects of your writing first. Are you using complicated phrases or terminology when simpler alternatives would make your writing clearer? If the fancy terminology isn't preventing you from using ten words when one would do, then what purpose is it serving? If the answer to this question is simply "It sounds impressive", then you know what to do. Are you using long sentences, littered with commas? If trying to read your sentences out loud on a single breath leaves you gasping for air, that's a hint! Break your writing down into smaller sentences containing less clauses. Simply doing these two things will significantly improve the readability of your writing. They are considered universally good practice and won't conflict with any subject specific academic writing conventions. You should be aware that some advice on making your writing clearer might conflict with discipline specific academic writing advice. For example, academic writing is often characterised by use of the passive voice and the third-person perspective (e.g. Gillett Hammond & Martala, 2013). However, guides on writing clearly will often advocate you use passive voice as little as possible and address the reader in the first person. I suggest you make your use of terminology and sentence construction priorities in improving the clarity of your writing. You should check any additional writing advice against whatever discipline specific guidance you have been given before you implement it. In addition to using the Flesch score in Word, I found the Hemmingway app (available online) to be a useful tool in examining the clarity of my writing.

Proofreading: measure twice, cut twice, then measure again

10

Key advice: removing your expectations about what should be on the page is the key to effective proofreading

So, after much toil, you have produced a complete first draft of your work. At this point the urge to immediately give it a quick once over and submit it will be strong. Don't do this, under any circumstances. If you want evidence of why this is a bad idea, indulge me and do as follows. Retrieve an example of work that you proofread shortly after completing the first draft and then submitted soon after. The odds are in favour of you being surprised, and a bit dismayed, at the number and magnitude of the mistakes you missed. Chances are we're not talking the odd misused comma here. We're talking about glaring mistakes; the kind of errors that really interfere with the meaning of your writing. How did you miss these errors at the time when they are so obvious now? Are you really that inattentive? Yes, kind of. We all are. This was demonstrated in startling fashion by Simons and Chabris (1999). They conducted an experiment that illustrated just how oblivious we can be to things that are very obviously out of place. They asked participants to watch a video of a group of people throwing a basketball to each other and keep count of the passes that were made. At one point during the video, a confederate of the experimenter walked into the middle of the scene dressed in a gorilla suit. They thumped their chest several times, then walked out of the scene. That's a noteworthy event, I think you'll agree. The participants were asked how many passes they counted and if they had seen anything unusual during the video. You'd think that every single one of them would have replied: "Funny you say that, because I could have sworn I saw some idiot in a cheap gorilla suit." Would you believe that nearly half of the participants reported seeing nothing abnormal? Suddenly, missing that repeated word or dodgy use of the possessive in your work doesn't seem quite so shameful, eh? There is a simple principle at play here. Any visual scene contains way too much information for you to process in its entirety, so you must focus your attention on specific things. What you focus on is up for grabs and can be determined by the salience of the stimuli. For example, a car speeding towards you as you wait to cross the road. However, it can also be determined by your expectations; what you see can be constrained by what you expect to see. In the Simons and Chabris experiment, the focus of the participants' attention was on the individuals playing basketball, due to the request that they count the passes made. When the person in the gorilla suit walked on, many participants were too preoccupied with the thing they were expecting to see to notice something that was neither expected, nor relevant to the task at hand. They missed it because they didn't expect it, so they weren't looking for it and, in any case, it wasn't relevant to the thing they were supposed to be looking for. Psychologists call this inattentional blindness. So, how does this explain why proofreading your own work is so tricky? Well, as with the participants in the gorilla study, it's your expectations that are effectively putting blinkers on you when you're proofreading. When you write something, you know exactly what you are trying to convey and you expect this to be faithfully represented in your writing. Therein lies the problem: you're not really looking at what's on the page, you're looking at what you expected to be there. So, when a gorilla in the form of a missing or repeated word shows up to the party, there's a good chance you'll miss it. The other problem is that inattentional blindness does make it difficult to scan a passage of text for the full range of possible writing errors. In their analysis of the most common composition mistakes, Lunsford and Lunsford (2008) identified 47 types of formal error in a random sample taken from 877 student papers. They then analysed the whole sample to produce a list of 20 of the most common errors. What composition mistake are you looking for when you proofread? All of them? At the same time? Really? Good luck with that!

So, what can you do to overcome inattentional blindness when proofreading? The key to effective proofreading is to take measures that prevent your expectations of your writing from glossing over what's really on the paper. Happily, there are a few very simple ways to do this. First, leave a draft of writing a few days before you attempt to proofread it. The memory of your expectations of what should be on the page will have decayed by then. When your expectations get weaker, they are less able to tell you what should be on the page, leaving you to see what's really there! When you look back upon previous work, this is why you often pick up on errors that went undetected at the time. You've forgotten what you meant to write and are now having to rely on what you actually wrote. It's also why tutors will always tell you not to proofread work at the last minute! They're right. Don't! Another way of undermining your expectations of what should be on the page is to read your draft in reverse. I don't mean read every sentence backwards, I mean read each sentence from beginning to end, but start with the last sentence in a paragraph and work your way back to the first. This forces you to look at the contents of each of the sentences in isolation, as the fact that you're not reading them in the intended order disrupts your expectations of what should be coming next. This helps you to see what's on the page as opposed to what you think should be there.

Allowing time to elapse between drafting and proofreading your work and reading it in such a way that minimises the confounding effect of your expectations are useful practices. However, the issue with these and other proofreading methods (such as using a high contrast background when examining a draft of your work) is that you are still reading the script. Whatever method you use to undermine your expectations of what should be on the page, the chances are that you will remember some of what you were trying to say. These residual expectations can still impair your ability to see what's on the page. Therefore, the best solution is to remove your expectations about what should be on the page from the reading part of the proofreading process. You can do this very easily by using the read aloud function in Microsoft Word to dictate the contents of your work to you. Computers are notoriously fussy things. They have this nasty habit of not being able to read your mind. Instead, they do exactly what you tell them to infuriatingly faithfully! This is rather useful when it comes to proofreading. Crank that volume up and prepare to cringe as Microsoft Word kicks your expectations to the curb and reads out what you've written verbatim. As Marlon Brando said in *Apocalypse Now*: "The horror. Horror." If you don't use Microsoft Word, you can copy sections of text into Google Translate and get it to dictate what you've written. It's equally unforgiving. Still, I guess it does give you the option to hide from your mistakes by asking it to read your work out in a language you don't understand. If you can still tell that what you've written is littered with errors, you should probably have a break from writing! You might be wondering why I'm advocating using a computer over another human. There are three reasons for this. First, even when unfamiliar with what you are trying to convey, people recognise certain phrases and expressions. As soon as this happens, expectations about what should be on the page take the driving seat and momentarily conceal any errors that might exist within the familiar phrase or expression. Second, humans are subject to things like fatigue, lack of motivation, concern for the author's ego, etc. that can impact on their proofreading performance. Computers don't have this problem; if they have power, they are good to go. Finally, delegating the task of spotting your errors takes you out of the proofreading process. Ultimately, the quality control of your work is down to you. You should embrace this and see it as an opportunity to get the most out of your written work. If you pay attention to your proofreading, you can learn a lot about your writing style and the types of errors you are prone to.

In proofreading your work, I would suggest you adhere to the following guidelines.

1. Finish any re-writing of the document before you attempt to proofread it. If you try and rewrite material (as opposed to making corrections) as you are proofreading it, you're likely to create as many new errors as resolve existing ones. You need to get your draft to a point where you are happy with the contents and structure before you can work on spotting errors in the composition.
2. Once you are happy with the contents and structure of your draft, walk away from it for a few days. You want to try and forget as much about what you intended to put on the page as possible; only then can you see what's actually on the page.
3. When you come back to the draft, break your proofreading up into sections, e.g. paragraphs. Don't try and proofread an entire document at once; you'll get fatigued and start to miss errors.

4. Start by looking at the first section of your work for any obvious errors that your word processor has marked up for you, e.g. spelling and grammar errors. Review and, if necessary, correct these now. This will not identify all the errors present, but it should eliminate the most obvious ones and make it easier for you to identify the errors relating to the meaning of your words. Word processors can't reliably detect errors associated with meaning.
5. Next, read the contents of the first section from the last sentence to the first sentence. Correct any errors as you encounter them. If you correct a sentence, re-read the corrected sentence before moving on.
6. After reading the contents of the section backwards, use the read aloud function in Word (or equivalent) to read your composition back to you. Concentrate on the spoken words, not the written text. When you hear an error, pause the playback and address the error in the text immediately. Continue the playback from the sentence before the error you have just identified. This helps to prevent additional errors in composition being caused by corrections.
7. Move on to the next section of your work and repeat steps three to six for each of the remaining sections.

If you think that my approach to proofreading sounds like a lot of work, good: it is! You've likely spent a long time researching and preparing your assessments, don't sabotage your efforts for want of giving the proofreading process the attention it needs. If you don't review your work effectively, you're compromising its clarity, undermining its impact and eroding the good-will of the person marking it. Time invested in effective proofreading always pays dividends in the mark you achieve for your work.

Feedback: live it, especially if you don't love it

Key advice: park your ego when looking at feedback

I'd like to begin the final part of this chapter with an anecdote. In my defence, it contains a lesson that I don't think anyone involved with learning and teaching research would find objectionable. The year was 1995. I was a fresh-faced undergraduate and just about to receive feedback from my tutor on my first essay. I was feeling confident; I had received an A for my A-level psychology course and I had put a lot of effort into the essay in question. I went to the Psychology Helpdesk to collect my feedback sheet, fully anticipating a high grade. Unfortunately, the tutor that marked my work had other ideas! The feedback sheet I was holding featured the mark of a mid-2:2. My essay was average: not good, not bad, average! I won't lie, I was bitterly disappointed. I immediately shoved the feedback sheet in my bag and stormed off. Fortunately, I retained just enough control over my wounded ego to avoid indignantly shouting: "A 2:2? Do they know who I am?" I know, first world problem and all that. On the bus journey home that followed, I was the proverbial teenager that had just failed their driving test and was looking for anyone to blame but themselves. You know, the one that complains that the examiner was "totally biased" even though they had tried to post footage of their emergency stop demonstration to Instagram, whilst performing it! Anyway, I got home and, after a cup of tea, made the first of two decisions that were to be key in my academic career: I looked beyond the mark I had received and directed my attention to the written comments on the feedback. The main point of contention seemed to be that I had not narrowed down the focus of my essay sufficiently and had, therefore, tried to take on too much with my writing. The result? My work was superficial and didn't contain any critical analysis. I wouldn't say knowing this improved my mood much at the time, but it did at least give me hope that I could improve. However, I wasn't sure about the best way to achieve the tutor's suggestion concerning narrowing down the focus of my work. At that point, I made the second key decision of my academic career. I went to see the tutor to ask for advice on how best to implement their feedback. It transpired that there was a very simple solution to my issue: I was to use the introduction of my future essays to specify what aspects of the topic I was going to focus on. This would help me keep the remit of my essay manageable and give me more of the word count to dedicate to critical analysis. To be honest, at the time, this all seemed too simple to be true. Nonetheless, in my next essay I did exactly what the tutor recommended. This time, I received a first-class classification for my efforts.

Key advice: don't think of feedback as a one-way conversation

My feedback anecdote illustrates a potential pitfall when it comes to academic writing and a real area of concern in the teaching and learning literature: student response to feedback. If you're really interested in this topic, Winstone, Nash, Parker and Rowntree (2016) provide a comprehensive overview. For our purposes, I'm just going to point out a consistent theme in the literature, i.e. that students can often lack confidence in how to implement feedback on their work (e.g. Doan, 2013). Knowing that you've done something wrong or sub-optimally is one thing, using that knowledge in a way that pays dividends in future assessments is quite another. Feedback is, after all, only useful if it's used!

I'm going to suggest you do two very simple things to ensure that you benefit from your feedback. The first thing is to avoid viewing your feedback as a one-way conversation. If you don't understand how you might go about addressing an issue that feedback has identified with your work, make an appointment to see a tutor. As obvious as this advice may seem, it's surprising how many students don't take advantage of opportunities to discuss their feedback with tutors, even when explicitly invited to do so. For example, Duncan (2007) found that only 31% of a student cohort engaged with an offer of additional one-to-one based help with their feedback. This occurred even though the authors had promoted the benefits of engagement with feedback, provided ample notice of the assistance and minimised any additional workload for the students. You might think that asking a tutor for a dialogue about your feedback could be seen as confrontational or an imposition, but that's not true. Tutors universally recognise the importance of students acting on feedback and are usually happy to see anyone who needs help in implementing advice on improving their work. You might believe that asking for some help with your feedback will have a negative effect on a tutor's impression of your ability. If anything, seeking help is more likely to have a positive effect because it demonstrates your commitment to learning and improving your performance.

The second thing you can do to help you benefit from your feedback is to be proactive in determining the content of the dialogue between you and the tutor. Just turning up without an agenda might result in a tutor assuming you haven't understood the comments and just reiterating the feedback. Alternatively, they might steer the conversation away from the aspect of feedback that you felt you needed most help with. Therefore, in setting an agenda for a dialogue about feedback, it's helpful to think in terms of the conditions that need to be satisfied for feedback to be useful to you. Sadler (1989) offered some very sage advice in this respect. First, you need to be sure you are clear on what's expected of you. Second, you need to be able to compare your work as it stands to an exemplar of the standard you aspire to. Third, you need to identify what you can do to reduce the discrepancy between your current and desired level of performance. I would suggest you need to achieve these three things for any aspect of your feedback that you're not sure how to implement. Try and remember the mantra: "What's expected? How does this differ from what I've done? What can I do to meet the expectations?" If you can answer these three questions you have the information you need to improve your performance.

Summary

Making the most out of your written work

Let's summarise the key advice and guidance on preparing written assessments at degree level contained within this chapter.

Familiarisation with assessment expectations

- You must always familiarise yourself with the applicable marking criteria for the assessment you're preparing. Practice using it to evaluate exemplars of the assessment and your own work. You can also use the marking criteria as the basis for discussions with tutors about the development of your work.

Obtaining and evaluating sources

- Prioritise peer reviewed material when looking for sources for your written assessments. Use university-based access management portals (such as OpenAthens) to locate peer reviewed material. ResearchGate and Google Scholar can also be useful portals to peer reviewed content. Avoid using Google and encyclopaedias, such as Wikipedia, for academic research.
- Remember that peer review is not an assurance of quality. You must still evaluate these sources. Corroborate and compare the information you obtain from different resources to help you develop your ability to appraise the quality of a source. This will help ensure you don't get complacent around peer reviewed material, or prematurely dismiss non-peer reviewed content.
- When researching a topic, use the funnel approach. Start with broader sources such as literature reviews and introductory chapters. These will help give you an idea of the breadth of work

available and provide context for the material that has a narrower focus. If you begin with the more specific sources, it's easy to lose sight of the wood for the trees and get overwhelmed.

Planning academic composition

- Plan your written work but avoid creating plans that are simply lists of sources or contents. The primary purpose of your plans should be to identify how you are going to use your sources to produce an academic discourse around your assessment title/ question. Writing plans, like maps, only work if they tell you how to get from point 'a' to point 'b'.

Academic writing

- Aim for clarity in your writing first and foremost. Use a readability metric such as the Flesch Reading Ease score to help ensure that you're writing is appropriate for the intended audience. Use shorter sentences and avoid unnecessary jargon to make your writing easier to read.
- Pitch your writing at an intelligent but uninformed person, not an expert on the topic. This will help prevent you from skipping over exposition of material that you should be demonstrating knowledge of. It also reduces the tendency to make your composition more complex for fear of patronising the reader.

Proofreading

- To proofread effectively, you must prevent your expectations of what you intended to write concealing what appears on the page. Do this by: finishing a draft of the work a couple of days before you proofread it; reading each section of your work from the last sentence to the first; and using text to speech functionality to read your work back to you verbatim.

Using feedback

- Implementing feedback is critical for your academic development. If you are not sure how you can use your feedback to improve your work, start a dialogue with an appropriate tutor. Be proactive in setting the agenda for such discussions. For any issues with your work, make sure you understand the expected standard, how your work deviates from it and what you can do in subsequent assessments to address any shortcomings.

I'd like to end this chapter with a bit of tough love. I've tried to provide you with some advice that will give you a solid start in the production of written assessments at degree level. Be that as it may, the process of writing is hard. You will make mistakes and receive criticism (sometimes strong) along with corresponding grades. Mistakes and the associated criticism are an integral (not optional) part of learning. Therefore, they are not something to be ashamed of or unduly upset by. Don't let your ego get in the way of your learning. Embrace criticism with a bit of humility, respond positively to it and you might be surprised at just how quickly it turns into praise.

References

Billig, M. (2013). *Learn to write badly: How to succeed in the social sciences*. Cambridge University Press.

Brophy, J. & Bawden, D. (2005, December). Is Google enough? Comparison of an internet search engine with academic library resources. *Aslib Proceedings*, *57*(6), 498–512.

Campbell, J., Smith, D., & Brooker, R. (1998). From conception to performance: How undergraduate students conceptualise and construct essays. *Higher Education*, *36*(4), 449–469.

Colón-Aguirre, M. & Fleming-May, R. A. (2012). "You just type in what you are looking for": Undergraduates' use of library resources vs. Wikipedia. *The Journal of Academic Librarianship*, *38*(6), 391–399.

Connaway, L. S., Dickey, T. J. & Radford, M. L. (2011). "If it is too inconvenient I'm not going after it": Convenience as a critical factor in information-seeking behaviours. *Library & Information Science Research*, *33*(3), 179–190.

Currie, L., Devlin, F., Emde, J. & Graves, K. (2010). Undergraduate search strategies and evaluation criteria: Searching for credible sources. *New Library World*, *111*(3/4), 113–124.

Doan, L. (2013). Is feedback a waste of time? The students' perspective. *Journal of Perspectives in Applied Academic Practice*, *1*(2), 3–10.

Duncan, N. (2007). "Feed-forward": Improving students' use of tutors' comments. *Assessment & Evaluation in Higher Education*, *32*(3), 271–283.

Frankfurt, H. G. (2009). *On bullshit*. Princeton University Press.

Gillett, A., Hammond, A. & Martala, M. (2013). *Inside track to successful academic writing*. Pearson.

Hartley, J. (2008). *Academic writing and publishing: A practical handbook.* Routledge.

Hartley, J. (2015). Making writing readable. *PSYCHOLOGIST, 28*(4), 254–255.

Hartley, J., Pennebaker, J. W. & Fox, C. (2003). Abstracts, introductions and discussions: How far do they differ in style? *Scientometrics, 57*(3), 389–398.

Hounsell, D. (1995). Marking and commenting on essays. *Tutoring and demonstrating: A handbook.* University of Edinburgh.

Hounsell, D. (1997). Contrasting conceptions of essay-writing. In F. Marton, D. Hounsell and N. Entwistle (Eds.), *The experience of learning*, 2nd rev. edn (pp. 106–125). Scottish Academic Press.

Judd, T. & Kennedy, G. (2011). Expediency-based practice? Medical students' reliance on Google and Wikipedia for biomedical inquiries. *British Journal of Educational Technology, 42*(2), 351–360.

Knight, S. A. & Burn, J. (2005). Developing a framework for assessing information quality on the World Wide Web. *Informing Science, 8*, 159–172.

Liu, N. F. & Carless, D. (2006). Peer feedback: The learning element of peer assessment. *Teaching in Higher Education, 11*(3), 279–290.

Lunsford, A. A. & Lunsford, K. J. (2008). Mistakes are a fact of life: A national comparative study. *CCC, 59*, 781–806.

Meola, M. (2004). Chucking the checklist: A contextual approach to teaching undergraduates Web-site evaluation. *portal: Libraries and the Academy, 4*(3), 331–344.

North, S. (2005). Different values, different skills? A comparison of essay writing by students from arts and science backgrounds. *Studies in Higher Education, 30*(5), 517–533.

Norton, L. S. (1990). Essay-writing: What really counts? *Higher Education, 20*(4), 411–442.

Oppenheimer, D. M. (2006). Consequences of erudite vernacular utilized irrespective of necessity: Problems with using long words needlessly. *Applied Cognitive Psychology: The Official Journal of the Society for Applied Research in Memory and Cognition, 20*(2), 139–156.

Pennycook, G., Cheyne, J. A., Barr, N., Koehler, D. J. & Fugelsang, J. A. (2015). On the reception and detection of pseudo-profound bullshit. *Judgment and Decision Making, 10*(6), 549–563.

Perruso, C. (2016). Undergraduates' use of Google vs. library resources: A four-year cohort study. *College & Research Libraries, 77*(5), 614–630.

Riddell, J. (2015). Performance, feedback, and revision: Metacognitive approaches to undergraduate essay writing. *Collected Essays on Learning and Teaching, 8*, 79–96.

Rust, C., Price, M., & O'Donovan, B. (2003). Improving students' learning by developing their understanding of assessment criteria and processes. *Assessment & Evaluation in Higher Education*, *28*(2), 147–164.

Sadler, D. R. (1989). Formative assessment and the design of instructional systems. *Instructional Science*, *18*(2), 119–141.

Sieber, J. E. (2006). Quality and value: How can we research peer review? *Nature: International Weekly Journal of Science*. Retrieved from www.nature.com/nature/peerreview/debate/nature05032.html.

Simons, D. J. & Chabris, C. F. (1999). Gorillas in our midst: Sustained inattentional blindness for dynamic events. *Perception*, *28*(9), 1059–1074.

Smith, R. (2006). Peer review: A flawed process at the heart of science and journals. *Journal of the Royal Society of Medicine*, *99*(4), 178–182.

Sperber, D. (2010). The guru effect. *Review of Philosophy and Psychology*, *1*(4), 583–592.

Torrance, M., Thomas, G. V. & Robinson, E. J. (2000). Individual differences in undergraduate essay-writing strategies: A longitudinal study. *Higher Education*, *39*(2), 181–200.

Turner, C. (2018, November 12). University lecturer confronted with empty hall after none of her 400 students turns up. *Daily Telegraph*. Retrieved from www.telegraph.co.uk/education/2018/11/12/russel-group-university-lecturer-reveals-none-400-students-turned/.

Winstone, N., Nash, R. A., Parker, M. & Rowntree, J. (2016). Supporting learners' agentic engagement with feedback: A systematic review and taxonomy of recipience processes. *Educational Psychologist*, *52*(1), 17–37.

Working collaboratively

There is no 'I' in team, but there is an 'I' in "I really hate teamwork"

The only consistent feature of all of your dissatisfying relationships is you.

Despair.inc.

Teamwork has, since the mid-1990s, become increasingly prevalent in degree-level studies (Gibbs, 2009). This is due to interest in the role of co-operative learning in student attainment (e.g. Johnson, Johnson & Smith, 2014) and learning communities in the development of generic skills such as communication and critical thinking. It's probably self-evident that the ability to work well in a team is highly prized by graduate employers, without me needing to cite lots of surveys. I have a sneaking suspicion that writing "It's better for everyone concerned if I work alone" in an application will disqualify you from consideration for most jobs. Well, except maybe for the role of a lighthouse keeper! In short, it's almost certain that your undergraduate degree will involve some team-based learning activities and assessments.

Given the importance of effective teamwork, it's disconcerting to find out that the student experience of working collaboratively is far from unanimously positive! Tucker and Abbasi (2016) serves as a good example of the commonly cited problems. They identified issues such as: individuals not doing their fair share; difficulties with collaborative decision making; individual differences in personality; dealing with organisational issues and addressing team conflict. Some studies have indicated that, given the choice, students would prefer to work independently (e.g. Knight, 2004). Other research has even identified a phenomenon called group-hate (Sorensen, 1981) which refers to a sense of deep unease when confronted with the prospect of working in groups (Myers & Goodboy, 2005). There is also evidence that a bad experience of teamwork can result in students holding intransigent negative views about comparable future group-based work (Favor & Harvey, 2016). Are you looking forward to working with your fellow students yet?

Research on student experiences of teamwork seems to contradict old adages such as "many hands make light work" and "a problem shared is a problem halved". Maybe the issue is implicit in such adages: there is an assumption that students are naturally well-disposed towards working in groups and are already adept at doing so. Unfortunately, this assumption isn't supported by much of the research on teamwork, which indicates that undergraduates often feel unprepared by their degrees for working in groups. For example, Wilson, Ho and Brookes (2018) found that less than 60% of the science undergraduates they surveyed felt that their degree was equipping them with teamwork skills. Accordingly, the remit of this chapter is simple. We're going to have a look at some of the psychological research on teamwork with a view to explaining the problems commonly experienced by students and consider what you can do to resolve them. With any luck, we can avoid a situation where your first exposure to working with your fellow students makes you want to quit university and retreat to a life in the wilderness.

Natural born loafers

1

Key advice: individuals are not as well disposed towards teamwork as you might think. Yes, that includes you

A principle issue with teamwork for students (and staff) is when individuals within a team don't do their share of the work. For example, Burdett and Hastie (2009) collected questionnaire and interview data from final year business undergraduates about their experiences of group work and found that the biggest predictor of dissatisfaction was workload related issues. Chief among these issues was people not contributing fairly. To address this complaint, we need to establish if a tendency to slack off when working in groups is something that is documented in the psychological literature. If so, what causes it? A brief foray into some classics in social psychology it is then!

Arguably the first experiments in social psychology were carried out between 1882 and 1887, not by a psychologist, but rather by a French agricultural engineer named Maximilien Ringelmann. To make matters worse, the purpose of his research wasn't to provide any insight into teamwork per se, but rather to look at the relative performance of men, machines and animals in a variety of agricultural tasks. C'est la vie! Incidentally, I'm totally considering changing my first name to Maximilien! Admit it, it's a great name! Anyway, Ringelmann published his work back in 1913, but it wasn't until the last quarter of the twentieth century that Kravitz and Martin (1986) went to the trouble of obtaining the original publication, so that they could translate and describe its contents. Ringelmann was interested in comparing the performance of workers in pushing or pulling a load horizontally. The variable that was of principal interest to him was the method by which this was achieved. However, he also compared individual versus group performance on the tasks in question. He conducted a series of trials in which participants were asked to pull on a five-metre length of rope, attached to a dynamometer, as hard as they could for a period of 4–5 seconds. They performed this task individually, in addition to with 6 and 13 other participants. The method used by Ringelmann to determine if every group member involved in the pulling task was giving it 100% is simple and works for many tasks. First, you establish the maximum level of performance of each individual member of a group for the task in question. Once you have these figures, you measure the combined maximum performance of the group. The combined maximum group performance should be equal to the sum of the maximum performance of each of its members. However, Ringelmann found that his participants were not working to their maximum potential when in a group. Furthermore, the gap between a group's theoretical maximum potential and their actual performance increased as the group got larger! People were slacking off in the presence of others, and they were slacking off even more in larger groups! Ringelmann charitably suggested that the reduction in individual efforts might be due to difficulties in co-ordinating a maximum effort pull with a group of people. In all fairness to his participants, co-ordinating physical effort does become more demanding as group size increases. Ringelmann also speculated that the reduction in effort might be due to motivational reasons. Given a little time, each member of the group might have increasingly trusted their co-workers to complete the task at hand and, therefore, started to go through the motions of doing the task themselves. However, he did not follow up his original study with a further experiment to test these explanations. The Ringelmann effect, as it became known, was not further elucidated by psychologists until the mid-1970s.

Ingham, Levinger, Graves and Peckham (1974) re-visited the Ringelmann effect, replicating his basic experimental set up of participants pulling on a strain gauge, either alone or in different group sizes of up to six members. However, they also modified the experiment to establish whether reductions in individual effort with increasing group size was due to group co-ordination issues. Their modification was simple and elegant: they added an additional pseudo group condition. In this condition, participants undertook the task in groups that, unbeknownst to them, consisted entirely of confederates of the experimenters. These confederates were always located behind the participants and were trained to merely give the impression of pulling on the rope without applying any pulling force. In this scenario, any reductions in participants' pulling efforts as a function of group size could no longer be due to group co-ordination issues, because only the participant was genuinely engaged with the task. The results of Ingham et al.'s study were clear: individual efforts decreased as a function of increasing group size, whether the groups were composed of real or pseudo members. Coordination wasn't to blame; participants just weren't trying as hard when in groups as they were when alone. This phenomenon was subsequently referred to as social loafing (Latané, Williams & Harkins, 1979).

Knowing that people put less effort into a task when in a group is a valuable finding, but knowing why this occurs is necessary if we are to do anything about it. Ingham et al. speculated that the reason their participants loafed was that they may have felt less personally responsible for their performance when in a group. They likely deduced that their individual contributions to the rope pulling task were not identifiable, which gave them the cover they needed to slack off a bit. Perhaps it's a lack of personal accountability that serves as a catalyst for social loafing? Williams, Harkins and Latané (1981) were interested in exactly this question. They opted to use a different task than pulling on a rope to investigate social loafing for several reasons. First, they wanted to determine if social loafing occurred in less esoteric settings. Second, a feature of the rope pulling task was the absence of feedback available to the participants. They weren't overcoming anything, nor were they privy to the readings on the strain gauge. Consequently, their efforts might diminish for motivational reasons. Finally, the readings derived from a rope pull task can be confounded by slight deviations in the technique used. For example, if an individual pulls the rope slightly to the left or right of the centre line, the force reading will decrease even though the effort being applied might remain constant. To overcome these issues, Williams et al. simply asked participants to shout as loud as they could, either alone or in groups consisting of one or five other individuals. They also incorporated pseudo versions of the real groups into their experimental design. In these groups, participants believed that they were being joined by one or five other participants but were shouting at four walls. Yes, the walls were soundproof in case you were wondering what the neighbours must have thought. Each participant in the study wore headsets and blindfolds, so there was no visual or auditory information about their performance or that of the other participants. This served three purposes. First, it enabled the experimenters to generate a fictitious purpose for the experiment, i.e. that they were interested in the effect of sensory feedback on the production of sound in groups. This deception was necessary to prevent the participants from guessing the true purpose of the study and adjusting their behaviour accordingly. Second, it enabled the experimenters to generate the pseudo groups by removing the evidence that participants assigned to those groups were in the lab alone. Finally, presumably it prevented every participant in the study from sinking into a crack in the lab floor from embarrassment! It's a good job that the trusty camera phone hadn't been invented back then! The participants were simply told that the experimenter was interested in how loud they could shout, thus they should do so as loud as they could when alone or with others. They were informed that the sound output would be measured via a single microphone in the room. This is important because it meant that the participants knew that their individual output could only have been monitored when they were on their own. As with the Ringelmann study, participants put less effort into their shouting when they were in a group, irrespective of whether that group was real or imagined (i.e. a pseudo group). For example, in the pseudo group condition, participants shouted only 69% as loud when they believed they were in pairs as they did when they shouted alone. In part two of the experiment, a small but very important change was made. Participants had microphones attached to them individually and were told that even when they were shouting as part of a pair or group of six, it was possible to identify their unique contribution. The instruction remained the same: shout as loud as you can. Have a guess what happened to the social loafing effect. Yep, it disappeared. In a further experiment, Williams et al. replicated the same procedure with the exception that participants were randomly allocated into conditions in which they were told that their contributions were either always identifiable, never identifiable or identifiable only when alone. Sure enough, those in the always identifiable condition tried consistently hard whether alone or in groups. Participants in the never identifiable condition invested consistently lower levels of effort, irrespective of whether they were alone or in groups. Finally, those who were identifiable only when alone put less effort into the task when in groups than when alone. Interestingly, when asked to estimate a percentage value for their efforts throughout the experiment in relation to their absolute maximum shouting capacity, the participants readily gave figures notably less than 100%. However, these figures were consistent across group sizes, suggesting the participants were not aware (or unwilling to admit) that they were putting less effort into the task when in groups and where their efforts were not accountable.

2

Key advice: teams composed of friends don't slack off any less than teams composed of strangers

You might wonder if the social loafing observed in the above studies was due to the participants being strangers. Perhaps loafing is the product of a relative lack of investment in a task resulting from being thrust into a group of unknown quantities? Maybe, if people just work with team-mates of their choosing they will be less likely to loaf, so as not to let their team-mates down? Sorry to break this to you, but the evidence on the antecedents of social loafing would suggest not. Aggarwal and O'Brien (2008) conducted a study involving business school undergraduates who had undertaken a group-work based assessment. They collected data on aspects of the assessment such as: group size; group formation (i.e. whether the groups had been assigned by the tutor or the students); and the use of peer evaluations of each team member's contributions. They also asked the participants to rate the extent to which social loafing took place and their satisfaction with the experience of working in a team overall. The results of the study indicated no differences in the reported incidence of social loafing between assessments where groups were assigned by the tutor and those where they were assigned by the students.

The idea of electing to work with your friends, or at least with people you trust and respect, not being less conducive with social loafing might seem a tad counter-intuitive at first. However, Williams and Karau (1991) conducted a study that probably accounts for why working with known quantities is not an antidote to loafing. They were investigating social loafing in addition to social compensation (the opposite of social loafing) where group members increase their task effort to offset the poorer performance of a co-worker. Their experiment involved a simple idea generation task in which groups of participants had to suggest as many uses for an object nominated by the experimenter as possible. They were told that they should be less concerned about the quality of the uses they generated than the number (the more uses the better). They were also informed that it didn't matter if they inadvertently replicated suggestions from their co-workers. The participants did this task under one of two conditions. In the coactive condition, participants were told that they should write each suggested use for the object on a piece of paper and then place it in their own box adjacent to their seat. The experimenter told them that they would be monitoring how many suggestions each participant generated, i.e. they had individual responsibility for coming up with as many uses as possible. Alternatively, in the collective condition, participants were asked to put each of their suggestions into a team box in the middle of the group's seating arrangement. In this scenario, the responsibility for generating as many suggestions as possible was shared between the group members. Yes, you can probably see where this one is going! In their first experiment involving groups of 4–8 participants, those who worked collectively generated less uses for the objects than those who worked coactively. However, the experimenters also wanted to determine if an individual's expectations of a co-worker would affect the tendency to loaf. They achieved this in a very simple way. The basic experimental set up was modified so that the participants now did the task in pairs. However, unbeknownst to them, the person they were paired with was a confederate of the experimenter. Upon the experimenter leaving the room to retrieve his stopwatch, the confederate would make a statement to the genuine participant to modify their expectations of them. To manipulate a participant's level of trust in them, they would either say that they were going to try really hard at the task or claim that they were not going to put much effort into it. To manipulate a participant's perception of their competence, they would either claim to be very good at the type of task at hand or say that they always struggled with such tasks. The results of the experiment indicated that social loafing decreased in the conditions where participants were paired up with co-workers who they believed were disinclined to put effort into the task or who were less competent at it. This is why working in groups with your friends can backfire. Presumably, you trust most of your established friends to do the right thing by you and you perceive them as generally competent. They probably (or should I say, hopefully?) view you in a similar light. This is all very warm and fuzzy, but it does rather negate any impetus for anyone to counter the tendency to loaf when working collectively!

3

Key advice: use peer evaluation to reduce social loafing when working with others

So, the extent to which a person feels accountable for their contributions to a group is a key factor in the likelihood they will indulge in a spot of social loafing. However, how do you increase accountability in a group without the process degenerating into a witch hunt? Research indicates that using a system of peer evaluation, whereby team members get to rate each other's contributions to a project in relation to specified criteria, can be an effective means of reducing social loafing. For example, in the Aggarwal and O'Brien (2008) study referred to earlier, the authors found that group assessments that featured multiple peer evaluations resulted in reduced levels of social loafing. This replicated the findings of earlier work by Brooks and Ammons (2003). Admittedly, this does rather sound like a recipe for pistols at dawn, but if it's done in the right way it can help ensure that no one ends up feeling hard done by. Research has also found that the use of peer evaluation is predictive of satisfaction with group work (e.g. Pfaff and Huddleston, 2003). To this end, Brooks and Ammons identify three main considerations: the timing of evaluations; their frequency; and the specificity of the criteria being used. Having an evaluation early in the group-work activity is useful as it projects that there will be expected contribution levels and that individuals will be accountable to these from the outset. Having group members rate each other's contribution upon completion of the group task is too little, too late for anyone to act upon. Similarly, as Aggarwal and

O'Brien point out, more than one evaluation is necessary to enable group members to respond to any concerns articulated by their co-workers. If the first evaluation is also the last then, to all intents and purposes, the accountability ends there! Finally, as Gibbs (2009) points out, the criteria against which the contribution of team members are assessed need to be transparent, specific and observable. Brooks and Ammons (2003) provide a good example of an instrument that can be used for peer evaluation. They utilised a survey entailing giving ratings ranging from 1 (meaning never) to 5 (meaning always) in response to statements such as "prompt in attendance for team meetings" and "met deadlines". Note that the statements refer to expected behaviours that can be monitored, so performance can be evidenced. Statements that can be evidenced are conducive with fairer evaluation, especially if they are associated with explicit standards that were negotiated by the group. This prevents individuals from assigning arbitrary or biased ratings. Let's take the example of a statement that refers to group members being prompt in attendance for team meetings. The related expectation might be that group members are expected to attend all meetings. If they can't attend, they should respond to any meeting agenda items within three days of the meeting via e-mail.

Peer evaluation statements and standards are akin to the marking and grading criteria used in your assessments. The marking criteria sets out the dimensions along which your work is assessed, and the grading criteria sets out the standards expected in relation to that criteria. With peer evaluation, it's the students, not the tutors, who are setting the expectations. However, the objective is the same: people need to know what is expected of them and how their current level of performance relates to those expectations (good or otherwise) to improve. Peer evaluation may be a potent way of overcoming public enemy number one when it comes to teamwork, i.e. social loafing, but it certainly doesn't just happen by accident. It requires a clear dialogue between the team, which brings us on nicely to the next common issue with teamwork.

Communication: is this thing on?

Key advice: your contributions to your team are not as conspicuous as you think

Issues with communication can be a major source of student disaffection with teamwork (e.g. Hassanien, 2006). Of course, communication problems come in different varieties. I'm going to pick out a specific issue that is both fundamental and completely within your power to resolve. I refer to the assumption that everything you say within a group is successfully communicated to that group. Unfortunately, people tend to have an inflated view of the conspicuity of their presence within a group and their contributions to that group. This is a big problem when it comes to working effectively within a team. If you mistakenly believe that your team is attending to an important message you're delivering when they're actually twiddling their thumbs, things probably aren't going to turn out well!

Psychologists call the tendency to have an inflated perception of how conspicuous you are the spotlight effect. The seminal study on this effect was conducted by Gilovich, Medvec and Savitsky (2000) who asked groups of 3–7 participants to take part in a group discussion, ostensibly to study group dynamics. They were asked to imagine they were all part of a commission whose remit was to investigate problems associated with inner cities in the United States and then propose some solutions in the form of a policy statement. Participants were assigned 20 minutes for the discussion and ten minutes to create (and all sign) a policy statement. After the completion of the statement, participants were asked to rank each group member (including themselves) according to four criteria. First, the extent to which they advanced the discussion. Second, the number of times they committed speech errors. Third, the number of comments that may have offended another member of the group. Finally, the number of comments that other members might have been critical of. Participants responded to these criteria twice. On one occasion, they were asked to adopt a group perspective by estimating the average rank that would have been assigned by the group for each group member. On another occasion, they were asked to adopt an individual perspective by giving the rank they personally felt was appropriate for each group member. This enabled the experimenters to compare each participant's perception of how they would be ranked by the other group members to how the other group members ranked them. The results clearly indicated that participants ranked their own contributions, both positive and negative, as being higher than the rankings that were awarded by the other members of their group. They believed that their contributions had been more conspicuous to others than, in reality, they had been.

The idea that we are not as conspicuous in the eyes of others as we might think is something of a double-edged sword. It's great in the sense that people might not have noticed our momentary slips and indiscretions. However, equally, people may have also missed out on those times when we were particularly articulate and competent. Either way, where does this assumption of conspicuity come from? Do we all have underlying narcissistic tendencies? If you have at any point taken a selfie of yourself reading this book and posted it on social media then the answer is: "Yes, you are that vain, but many thanks for the free advertising!" However, research on the spotlight effect suggests it has less to do with vanity and more to do with something retailers routinely use to get us to part with cash. Consider this scenario: you're in a shop browsing for a new TV. You spy a particularly good model and immediately check out the price tag. Oh. My. God. The first thing you read on the sticker says that the TV normally costs £1,000, but it's on sale here at £500. You cannot walk away from a bargain this good. I mean, it might be £500, but it's double that outside of the sale! The proprietors of this shop are clearly modern-day saints, more interested in helping you live the life of avarice without the commensurate price tag than in making a profit. Yeah, right! Back in the real world, you're just demonstrating something known as the anchoring effect. This refers to a tendency for an initial piece of information to influence subsequent judgements way too heavily. In the above example, the initial piece of information was the TV's regular price of £1,000. This regular price anchored your subsequent judgement on what the TV was worth. Compared to the regular price, the 50% lower sale price seems amazing. But hold on a minute: what if that regular price was set way above the TV's actual market value by the shopkeeper? In this scenario, what you should have been focusing on was not the difference between the regular price and the sale price, but whether the sale price per se was a good market value for the TV. A TV that should cost £500 being sold for £500 doesn't look like quite such a steal, does it? By the way, retail outlets are unlikely to accept returns on the basis that you now realise that they suckered you in with the anchoring effect. Sorry! Older and wiser, eh?

Gilovich, Medvec and Savitsky (2000) thought that the spotlight effect might be a product of anchoring, so included an experiment to test this theory. Their basic experimental set up was simple and involved participants being recruited as either observers or targets. The observers, directed by a first experimenter, sat in groups at a long table in the centre of a room and were asked to fill out a questionnaire, which was just a distraction task. Meanwhile, the target participant was meeting with a second experimenter in a different part of the lab. They were told that they would be taking part in the experiment in another room but should first don a t-shirt that was then given to them by the experimenter. In the first experiment, this t-shirt featured a large depiction of the singer Barry Manilow. If you don't recognise the name, just know that such a t-shirt would have been regarded as social kryptonite by any self-respecting undergraduate at the time. In the second experiment, the t-shirt featured a face that students would have endorsed as being cool (e.g. Bob Marley). In both experiments, the target participants were then asked to knock on the door of the room containing the observers. They were invited in by the first experimenter, who retrieved a chair for them and placed it opposite the observers. However, before the target participants sat down, the first experimenter claimed that, on reflection, they were joining the experiment a little too late for things to work and that they should wait outside. Upon leaving the room, the participant was re-joined by the second experimenter who told them that the experiment was about incidental memory. They were then asked to state how many of the observers in the room would have been able to name the person on their t-shirt. Meanwhile, back in the room with the observers, the first experimenter was asking each of them individually if they could recall who was on the target participant's t-shirt. Sure enough, the spotlight effect occurred. The target participants over-estimated the number of people who were able to identify the face on their shirt, irrespective of whether that shirt was socially embarrassing or commendable. Gilovich et al. argued that the participants' judgements of their conspicuity was being anchored at a high level by their own immediate and acute positive or negative identification with their t-shirt. Basically, at that moment in time, they felt conspicuous so they assumed that other people would see them as being conspicuous.

If the spotlight effect is due to conspicuity being anchored at high levels, Gilovich et al. argued that allowing participants to habituate to the t-shirt featured in the experiment should reduce their sense of conspicuity and negate the spotlight effect. To test this theory, they ran their experiment again, but with one important change. The target participants were randomly assigned to one of two groups. In an immediate exposure group, they entered the room with the observers right after putting on the t-shirt. In a delayed group, participants waited 15 minutes after donning the t-shirt before entering the room of observers. These individuals spent the 15 minutes in an adjacent lab filling out an unrelated survey. Whilst they were doing this, two experimenters staged a conversation in the corridor outside to create the impression that the lab was a social area. The results of the experiment supported Gilovich et al.'s hunch. When asked to estimate what percentage of the observers noticed their t-shirt, the participants in the delayed condition gave lower estimates than the participants in the immediate condition. The delay had indeed diminished the spotlight effect. The experimenters argued that this was because the participants in the delayed condition had acclimatised to the feelings induced by the t-shirt. Therefore, their anchor point for judging how conspicuous they were was lower than the participants in the immediate condition, who entered the room without the benefit of acclimatisation. The spotlight effect does not mean that we have no awareness that we are probably not as conspicuous as we feel. Ratings of 100% conspicuity are exceptions rather than rules in these kinds of experiments. It just means that our judgement of how conspicuous we are can be anchored at an artificially high level by our subjective perspective. This means that any adjustments we do make to estimates of our conspicuity are often insufficient.

5

Key advice: habituation and external perspective taking help you perceive your conspicuity more accurately

If the spotlight effect is the result of perspective, i.e. people being anchored in their own elevated perception of their conspicuity, can we negate it by getting them to adopt a different perspective? Well, recent research suggests that it may well be as simple as this. In principle, at least! Macrae et al. (2016) conducted a variation of the Gilovich et al. study, with a few twists. In their first experiment, the participants were invited into a laboratory where they were greeted individually by an experimenter who asked them to imagine the following scenario. They were having a conversation near the doorway to a familiar lecture room on campus with a few friends. During this conversation, 40 of their fellow students would walk past them to enter the room. One group of participants were told to imagine that the scenario would be taking place the following day and the other group were told to imagine that it would occur in three years. They were then shown a picture of the t-shirt they were to imagine wearing in the scenario (a white shirt featuring a blue whale). Participants then spent 20 seconds imagining the scenario, after which the experimenter simply asked them to describe the vantage point that they used in imagining it. Of course, the participant could have described it from either a first-person (an actor's) perspective or the third-person (an observer's) perspective. The participants had not been given any prior instructions by the experimenter to this effect. The results indicated that participants who were told that the scenario would occur the following day predominantly adopted a first-person perspective in imagining it. In contrast, those who were told the scenario would occur in three years predominantly adopted a third-person perspective.

In their second experiment, the researchers wanted to find out if they could use the perspective taken by a participant to manipulate how conspicuous they felt. So, they replicated the experiment using the same imagined scenario, but this time gave the participants explicit instructions on what perspective they took (first person or third person). On this occasion, the t-shirt featured a picture of Miley Cyrus on the basis that this would make the garment embarrassing to wear. Sorry, Miley! After participants had imagined the scenario, the researchers asked them what percentage of the 40 undergraduates who walked past them would have noticed their t-shirt. Sure enough, the participants who were asked to adopt a first-person perspective in imagining the scenario gave higher estimates of conspicuity than those who were instructed to use the third-person perspective. The experiment was replicated for a third time with a measure of embarrassment added to the estimate of conspicuity. This confirmed that participants identified feeling more embarrassed when imagining the scenario from a first-person perspective than a third-person perspective.

It's not difficult to imagine how the spotlight effect can occur in a team meeting scenario. A group member makes a point that you want to respond to, but you are doing so off the cuff. You haven't planned what you are going to say, nor have you spent any time mentally rehearsing it. The first time you are trying to articulate your point occurs under the scrutiny of the rest of the team. This is compounded by the fact that you are putting a lot of effort into thinking on your feet to say something vaguely coherent. Consequently, you likely feel rather conspicuous and are, therefore, vulnerable to the spotlight effect. Three solutions are suggested by the research we have reviewed. The first is to spend time rehearsing the point you want to make rather than trying to ad-lib on the spot. If, as will be advocated a bit later in this chapter, an agenda for the meeting is circulated in advance then this is easier from a practical perspective. However, a little mental rehearsal is still possible for unplanned contributions. You can spend time during the meeting mentally rehearsing a point you want to make by letting others contribute first, rather than diving straight in there. Mentally rehearsing your contribution will allow you to acclimatise to it, thus making you feel a little less conspicuous in speaking. In mentally rehearsing what you want to say, you might also like to try and imagine viewing yourself making the point in the third, rather than the first, person perspective. As we've seen, just the act of imagining how you might look from the viewpoint of others tends to make you feel less conspicuous. Another eminently practical way of dealing with the spotlight effect is to incorporate a request for feedback into your contribution. Maybe avoid simply asking whether anyone listened to a blind word of what you just said. That's a tad confrontational! Instead, take the approach adopted by lecturers and ask something that needs the group to consider the implications of what you've just said for the current or planned topic. If everyone suddenly clams up, you know that the spotlight effect has struck. Well, either that or you really should have brought some coffee along to the meeting.

Collaborative decision making: that's another fine (cohesive) mess we've gotten ourselves into

6

Key advice: group cohesion is not always a sign of sound group decision making

Having touched on the importance of being able to decentre from your own perspective as a means of improving the communication of ideas, you might expect that line of thinking to extend through to group decision making processes. Intuitively, it would seem likely that being able to adopt the perspective of other people would facilitate group cohesion and generate harmonious decision making within a group. Indeed, you might assume that the principal determinant of the quality of a group's decision-making process is how much agreement there is between team members, i.e. how cohesive the group seems to be. However, desire for cohesion and agreement between group members above all else can be a recipe for disaster when it comes to sound decision making.

In 1971, Irving Janis investigated a simple question: why do small groups of smart people, who are united in their efforts and goals, sometimes make catastrophic decisions? He considered this question with reference to some of the great (I use the term loosely) military and political fiascos of the twentieth century. For example, Pearl Harbor; the Bay of Pigs Invasion; and the escalation of military action in North Korea and Vietnam. His analysis of the decision making processes involved in these events lead to him identifying something called groupthink. Janis (1982) defined groupthink as: "A mode of thinking that people engage in when they are deeply involved in a cohesive in group, when members' striving for unanimity override their motivation to realistically appraise alternative courses of action" (p. 9). Janis made the broad distinction between the things that were likely to result in groupthink (antecedents) and the signs of the presence of groupthink (observable consequences). In terms of the antecedents, in addition to a desire for the group to be cohesive, Janis identified two further conditions. First, organisational structural faults, such as there being no established procedural norms for collaboration. Second, situational factors, such as working under conditions of stress from external threats. Consider how the antecedent conditions of groupthink relate to an undergraduate student team project scenario. A small team of students take on some assessed project work. They want to get good grades. So, irrespective of whether the members of the group are prior acquaintances, there is a shared interest in not falling out to expedite their chances of success. That's the desire for group cohesiveness antecedent in place. As alluded to previously, undergraduates often lack knowledge about the skills required to work effectively in a team. They aren't familiar with things like how to create agendas and implement peer evaluation. That's a tick in the organisational structure antecedent box. Finally, the students are also working under time pressure and the threat of a poor grade if things don't go well. Bingo, that's the situational antecedents box also checked. So, what do you win? Well, that's where the observable consequences of groupthink come in. Janis differentiated between symptoms of groupthink and associated defects in a group's decision-making process. He postulated eight symptoms of groupthink, which were placed into one of three categories. First, over-estimation of the group, e.g. an impression of its inherent 'rightness'. Second, closed-mindedness, e.g. a collective discrediting of anything contrary to group thinking. Third, pressure towards uniformity, such as self-censorship. Janis identified seven ways in which these symptoms are manifest in defective decision making. These include: failure to adequately assess the objectives of the task; neglecting to work out a contingency plan; and exhibiting bias in dealing with uncovered research. Returning to our student team project example, group members may well have the objective of getting a good grade, but have they properly broken down the task into its subcomponents? They may have thought about the allocation of group members to the task at hand, but have they considered the things that could go wrong with their efforts and generated a plan 'b' for such eventualities? They may have meetings where they discuss their research and progress to date, but are the individuals empowered to take a critical perspective on what is being said? Given the research on student satisfaction with group work, it's clear that the answer to these questions is certainly not a unanimous yes.

The theory of groupthink does have great intuitive appeal and has become very pervasive within psychology, but it's not been without its critics over the preceding decades. A full evaluation of the state of play of groupthink theory is well beyond the scope of this chapter, but if you're interested Rose (2011) provides a good overview. Nonetheless, I present groupthink theory here as the goal of this section is to point out that when it comes to group work, uniformity is not necessarily a sign that all is well. Dissent (or at least the ability to dissent) far from being invariably harmful to a group, can be a characteristic of sound group decision making. This is a notion that even those who have articulated doubts about groupthink should not find objectionable. Also, groupthink theory does generate a series of practical recommendations that can be easily incorporated into the process of teamwork to prevent a group from degenerating into an assembly of 'yes people'.

7

Key advice: when it comes to making good group-based decisions, take a belt and braces approach to promoting polite dissent

The remedies that Janis proposed to minimise the risk of groupthink are, not surprisingly, orientated to negate what he saw as its antecedents, particularly the desire for groups to prioritise being cohesive over constructively critical. Therefore, much of what he suggests are practical ways of creating an environment that requires group members to be proactive in playing devil's advocate. In the interests of transparency, I should say that direct empirical evidence for the effectiveness of these proposals is rather thin on the ground. However, I do think they are useful here for two reasons. First, because of the overlap between groupthink (which is under-developed in the literature) and allied, but more specific, topics such as conformity (which have a highly developed literature). Such literature clearly attests to the risks of individuals modifying or abandoning their judgement to fit in with that of their colleagues. Therefore, anything that explicitly acknowledges this risk and embeds countermeasures against it at the very least has a sound rationale. Second, Janis's recommendations involve making procedural changes to group work that can be easily implemented. This creates a favourable cost/returns ratio! With that caveat out of the way, let's have a look at some of Janis's recommendations.

Janis argued that a group should nominate a leader, but the primary role of this leader should be to foster discussion, i.e. the leader should refrain from stating their own personal preferences and views. Instead, their role is to explicitly create an environment where each member has a responsibility (and is encouraged) to be critical. The appointment of a leader (or chairperson, if you prefer) is necessary to oversee the process of a team meeting. However, the authority implicit in this role can mean that any ideas coming from that person are privileged over the rest of the team. This is an even bigger problem if the member of the team nominated happens to be one of the more outgoing members of the group. Restricting the role of leader to one of ensuring that each group member is encouraged to contribute freely helps avoid a scenario where a group might get freight-trained by an over-zealous member, even if their intentions are good.

Janis also advocates that at least one group member needs to be assigned the role of devil's advocate in each meeting. It is their responsibility to solely generate criticism and ensure that the group considers alternative arguments/perspectives. The problem with just saying that every team member has a role in being critical is that there is a risk of diffusion of responsibility, whereby everyone assumes that someone else will do it. Making playing devil's advocate the sole responsibility of at least one member should help negate this possibility. It also liberates that person from concerns that the group might take a dim view of any dissenting contributions because, well, they've invited them!

Being nominated as devil's advocate might empower team members to be critical without becoming 'that person' in the group. However, their membership of the group can still inhibit them from being effective in this role. Therefore, Janis also suggested that all team members privately discuss important issues arising from meetings with trusted sources who are not part of the group. They should then feedback the results of such discussions to the rest of the group at subsequent meetings. People outside of a group have relatively little, if any, vested interest in endorsing a viewpoint for the sake of maintaining the group's cohesion. Therefore, they can offer a perspective that is uncontaminated by any such concern.

Having people from outside of the group contribute their views is useful in getting a detached perspective. However, a detached perspective is not necessarily an informed one. Therefore, Janis argued that a group should also invite external people with relevant expertise to review and challenge the decisions of the group. Groups are often not composed of experts on matters relevant to those that might emerge in a meeting. Therefore, they can reach ostensibly sensible conclusions that are, nonetheless, unsound. Inviting an expert into a meeting to challenge the group can help avoid a scenario where collective ignorance results in bad decision making. Of course, your tutors can be ideal candidates for this role. Many of them, subject to you making an appointment, would be happy to sit in on a group meeting. If they are critical of the efforts thus far, then that criticism is coming from outside of the group from someone with relevant expertise. This can serve as an excellent wake-up call to the group that might have been difficult for someone inside the group to have delivered.

Interpersonal conflict: there is always one; possibly you

8

Key advice: do not assume that someone's behaviour is a reflection on who they are. Situations often provide much by way of mitigation

Although harmony might not necessarily be a good thing in the group decision making process, it certainly helps if it prevails in the interpersonal relationships between group members. Constructive and respectful differences of opinion are one thing, hostility and interpersonal conflict are quite another and, obviously, not helpful to the team effort. Of course, there are a multitude of possible causes of conflict within a group and trying to address them individually is well beyond the scope of this book. In any case, when it comes to conflict, surely prevention is better than cure? Therefore, I'm going to focus my efforts on letting you in on some classic research in psychology that demonstrates how each of us can be the unknowing agents of conflict. This is due to the way we make inferences about the cause of behaviour we view as problematical or an annoyance. Once you know about this, you are empowered to reduce the chances of any problem with a team member escalating into a full-blown conflict, irrespective of the specifics of the problem.

Consider the following scenario. You are driving home in quite heavy traffic and you approach a two-lane junction controlled by traffic lights. The left lane is for traffic continuing straight ahead and the right lane is for traffic turning right only. You need to go straight on, unfortunately about 15 other cars have the same intention and they are all in front of you. In contrast, the turn right lane is empty. You patiently await your turn and end up at the front of the queue in the left lane awaiting the next green light. Out of the corner of your eye, you notice that a car has pulled alongside you in the right-hand lane, but you just assume they are going to turn right. The lights change from red to amber and the car in the right-hand turn only lane screeches off, cuts across into your lane and continues straight ahead, thus successfully circumventing the queue you've been waiting so patiently in. How would you react to this kind of scenario? What would go through your mind? What would you have attributed the cause of the offending driver's behaviour to? Would you conclude that the driver was just being impatient, selfish and inconsiderate? Would you have used your car's horn in anger and shouted some choice words out of the window? If so, why? Sure, they cut you off at the lights, that much is indisputable. However, why would you automatically attribute this to impatient, selfish and inconsiderate motives? Where is your evidence for this conclusion? How did you know that they hadn't, for example, just had a call from the hospital informing them of a loved one who had been taken ill? If you had a flash of clairvoyance and saw that this was the case, would you have still attributed their behaviour to selfishness and become angry, or would you have viewed their behaviour as being understandable given the situation? Now, substitute the person who cuts you up at the junction with the person who is yet to attend a team meeting, or who maybe hasn't turned up for a meeting properly prepared. The first step in determining whether you respond positively or negatively lies in the inference you make about the reason for that individual's behaviour.

If, in the traffic light scenario, you jumped to the conclusion that the driver's behaviour was a reflection on who they were as a person and neglected to consider a possible situational cause for their behaviour, you're in good company. Back in the late 1970s, Ross, Amabile and Steinmetz (1977) conducted research indicating that we can all be remarkably quick to attribute a person's behaviour to personal (dispositional) characteristics rather than contextual (situational) variables. We do this even in the presence of clear evidence pointing to the greater causal significance of the situation. In Ross et al.'s study, pairs of participants were told that they would be taking part in a quiz show scenario. They were then randomly allocated to the role of either the contestant or questioner by selecting one of two cards that had been placed face down, so they were unable to see which role was printed on each card. The participants knew, therefore, that they were not being assigned to either condition based on anything other than chance. The job of questioners was to produce ten questions based on their own personal interests or expertise. This meant that the dice was very much being loaded in the questioner's favour by the experimental set up. The contestants were informed that the questioner was devising some challenging questions for them. Their role was to try and answer as many of these questions as they could in the quiz show scenario. The contestants were given 30 seconds to respond to each question and the questioners only spoke to ask the questions, confirm that a response was correct, or provide the correct answer in the event of an incorrect response. Upon the conclusion of the quiz, all the participants were given a questionnaire that asked them to rate the general knowledge of the questioners and the contestants. Keep in mind that both the questioners and contestants knew full well that their roles had been randomly assigned (not based on merit) and that the questioner inherently had the upper hand because they had devised the questions. Therefore, any differences in the knowledge exhibited by the questioners and contestants were due to a situational advantage and did not reflect differences in levels of general knowledge between them. This should have been reflected in participants rating their partner's general knowledge as not being significantly different to their own, irrespective of the difference in roles. However, the results of the experiment showed that the questioners rated their general knowledge as being slightly higher than contestants. Even worse, the contestants rated their general knowledge as being much lower than the questioners. The participants had failed to take the very obviously biased situational characteristics into account in arriving at their judgements about their partner's general knowledge. They had made what came to be known as a fundamental attribution error.

Ross et al. wanted to establish if the tendency to privilege dispositional (personal) characteristics over situational variables was limited to those involved in the scenario or would also be evident in observers. Therefore, they replicated the experiment, but added two more participants to each questioner and contestant pairing who believed that they had been randomly assigned to the role of observer. The results indicated that the observers rated the questioners' general knowledge as significantly better than that of the contestants. They displayed the fundamental attribution error even though they also knew that the roles in the experiment were randomly assigned and that the questioner got to choose questions based on their own interests and expertise.

Key advice: a change of perspective can help you make better attributions for difficult behaviour

How might you guard against the fundamental attribution error? Well, in common with the literature on the spotlight effect, research is starting to suggest that changing your perspective when reviewing information can negate the fundamental attribution error. Hooper, Erdogan, Keen, Lawton and McHugh (2015) conducted a study in which participants were asked to view a video of an individual reading an essay that they had been assigned to write in an English class. The essay expressed either a pro or anti capital punishment stance. Note that the participants were made explicitly aware that the individual who composed and read the essay was not given the choice about which side of the argument they were to take. Before they viewed the video, each participant was randomly allocated to either a perspective taking training condition or a control group. The training condition consisted of 30 questions requiring participants to take different perspectives to answer abstract scenarios. A simple example of a scenario was: "I have a red brick and you have a green brick, if I were you and you were me what colour bricks would we have?" (p. 70). Participants assigned to the control group received no training prior to watching the video. Following the video, participants were given a questionnaire that asked them to infer how pro or anti capital punishment the person reading the essay was on a scale of 1–15 (1 being extremely against and 15 being extremely pro). Remember, the person in the video did not choose what side of the argument to base their essay on. The participants knew this, so they should have been returning estimates around the mid-point of the scale. Deviations from the mid-point of the scale represented the fundamental attribution error at play; the bigger the deviation, the bigger the error. The results of the experiment indicated that participants in the perspective training condition deviated less from the mid-point of the scale in giving their estimates than did the control group, irrespective of which side of the argument had been presented. The perspective training significantly reduced the incidence of the fundamental attribution error.

I realise demonstrating that people can adopt different perspectives more readily after a bit of training is all well and good, but I'm sure you'd much rather not have to self-administer a series of brain teasers any time someone's behaviour irritates you. I don't mind admitting that having a go at some of the items in the perspective taking quiz brought back uncomfortable memories of IQ tests. You know, the ones you spend hours agonising over and eventually get right, only to find out that the test was supposed to take 15 minutes! There goes my application to Mensa. However, there is a more simple method of shifting your perspective that comes from an emerging literature on the concept of self-distancing. This refers to ways that you can adopt a more detached perspective to promote rational thinking and reflection. If this is starting to sound a bit far out, rest assured that I'm not about to advocate the use of illicit drugs. This might be frowned on in meetings, particularly if you work for law enforcement, or just didn't bring enough for the other attendees.

Research suggests that switching from first to third person in the perspective you use when describing a situation can do the trick. It's similar to the perspective switching approach we covered when looking at how to negate the spotlight effect. However, self-distancing focuses more on the language you use to describe a situation, rather than just the viewpoint you take in imagining that situation per se. You can find a good review of self-distancing in Kross and Ayduk (2017). Bremner (2013) investigated the use of self-distancing on the fundamental attribution error, using the same basic attitude inference task as Hooper et al. In this instance, the experimental set up involved an individual reading an essay they had been instructed to compose in support of President Barack Obama. Participants were informed that the pro-Obama stance of the essay was due to instruction, not the author's choice. They were asked to write down their thoughts about the author of the essay and, in particular, how pro-Obama they thought the author actually was. In doing this, they were assigned to one of four groups. In the self-distancing group, participants were instructed to use the third-person perspective exclusively in their writing, i.e. use pronouns such as 'he', 'she', 'they' and their own name. In the first-person perspective group, participants were instructed to use the first-person perspective exclusively, i.e. using the pronoun 'I' to refer to themselves. In a further no instruction group, participants were not given any guidance on pronoun use and simply asked to write their thoughts on the author's actual opinion of Obama. Finally, a control group were not asked to write anything before giving their ratings. The participants were then asked to rate how pro-Obama they thought the author was using a numerical rating scale, ranging from –4 (anti-Obama) to 4 (Pro-Obama). Remember, the participants were aware that the author of the essay had its pro-Obama stance imposed on them. Therefore, ascribing a high pro-Obama attitude rating to the author would be an example of the fundamental attribution error; the higher the rating, the bigger the error. The results of the experiment indicated that participants in the third person perspective writing group rated the author of the essay as being significantly less pro-Obama than the other groups. Using the third person perspective as a way of self-distancing in accounting for the authors behaviour had made them more aware of the situational determinants at play and thus reduced the size of the fundamental attribution error.

The beauty of self-distancing is its simplicity. You can incorporate it into that silent monologue you have in your head when you're thinking about an unfolding situation or reflecting on one that has unfolded. This is referred to as self-talk (Kross & Ayduk, 2014). Yes, you heard that correctly, a psychologist just advocated that you talk to yourself, with two caveats. First, that you do it in the third person to enable you to self-distance. Second, that you do it silently, lest your group start throwing some concerned looks your way! In practice, self-talk can be a useful way of increasing your chances of managing a variety of sources of conflict within a team, such as a domineering member. In mentally trying to account for their behaviour, simply substitute a question such as, "Why do I think they are being domineering?" with, "Why does [insert your name here] think they are being domineering?" This small change could be pivotal in whether you make a personal or situational attribution for their behaviour. A situational attribution (e.g. that they might just have had a bad day prior to the meeting) reduces the odds that their behaviour will be the catalyst for conflict. If this all seems way too easy, then there is a good reason for that: it is! Recent research monitoring brain activation patterns under conditions of self-talk have identified it as being a relatively effortless task (Moser et al., 2017). It's another one of those low investment, potentially high return interventions. The take-home message is that a simple perspective shift in the way that you introspect about a potential source of conflict reduces the likelihood that you will become part of the problem, as opposed to part of its solution.

Co-ordinating team efforts: the blind leading the blind

Key advice: meeting agendas are very useful in formalising approaches to reducing potential issues with teamwork

Having just examined the propensity to blame people for their behaviour, without giving due regard to the features of the situation, it's important that we now consider how situational aspects of teamwork might contribute to its effectiveness. Students often complain that scheduling meetings, establishing team goals, co-ordinating tasks and time management can be problematical (e.g. Tucker and Abbasi, 2016). However, to what extent might these problems reflect less on the disposition of the individuals involved, as issues with the process of the team meeting situation? For example, if group discussions are just going around in circles, is this due to the lack of the appointment of a group chairperson who could have brought discussion on each item to a decision and moved things forward? What are the situational determinants of an effective team meeting? Surprisingly, research in psychology on this topic is not as extensive as you might think. This might explain why so many people relish the prospect of team meetings about as much as the prospect of catching a cold. That said, having a cold does excuse you from further meetings so it's not all bad! Nonetheless, some researchers have tried to elucidate what characteristics of meetings are conducive with them being seen to be effective by those involved. A good review can be found in Geimer, Leach, DeSimone, Rogelberg and Warr (2015). Some representative work was carried out by Leach, Rogelberg, Warr and Burnfield (2009). They conducted two international surveys of individuals from private and public-sector organisations. They used questionnaires to establish how effective participants perceived regularly attended meetings to be in terms of achieving personal, peer and organisational goals. The questionnaires sought to determine how frequently particular situational features of a meeting were in evidence. Such features included: use of an agenda; the provision of meeting room facilities; punctual start and end times; and widespread team involvement. The data indicated that the use of an agenda (circulated in advance) was particularly important in determining how effective a meeting was perceived to be. For anyone yet to encounter an agenda, it's a formal notification of a meeting, featuring its date, time and venue together with an inventory of items to be covered in the time allotted with a list of invitees and their respective roles. It's fair to say that the importance of having an agenda for team meetings is a recurring theme in the literature. Consequently, it's the use of a written agenda that I am going to focus on here. This is partly because it's good practice in and of itself, but also because it provides a way of formalising solutions to the other teamwork issues that I've identified in this chapter. Having such solutions formalised in an agenda increases the likelihood that they will be implemented.

In the opening of this chapter, we considered the issue of social loafing and established that resolving it rested upon making individual contributions identifiable via peer evaluation. Well, peer evaluation won't just happen by accident. It needs to be instigated and agreed as part of the process of teamwork. Having a written agenda provides a vehicle for this to be achieved at timely points throughout the lifespan of the group. For example, establishing the criteria by which individual contributions will be evaluated, expected standards and ground rules should be an agenda item for a preliminary group meeting.

The second teamwork issue we considered was communication within a group. Specifically, the likelihood that individuals will perceive their contributions to the group as being much more conspicuous than they actually are (the spotlight effect). The solutions for the spotlight effect revolve around reducing the extent to which a person is anchored in their own perspective by acclimatisation or adopting the viewpoints of others. An agenda for a meeting can help achieve this in two main ways. Agendas that are circulated in advance allow members to preview topics of discussion. This enables them to mentally rehearse and acclimatise to their contributions. This way, they feel less conspicuous when they speak in front of other team members. Second, if a group member thinks that something they have said needs to be actioned, they can ask for it to be an agenda item for a subsequent meeting. Generally, teams need to agree on points that require actioning, which results in that point getting more exposure and investment from other team members. Whether a group agrees or disagrees, the fact that a contribution has been discussed means it's been heard! Agenda items that are in writing can't go unnoticed as they effectively become part of the to-do list for subsequent meetings.

The third issue we considered relates to the possibility that individuals might not contribute to the decision making process for fear of upsetting the harmony of the team (groupthink). The solutions to this involve having things that enable criticality from team members being embedded into the structure and process of a meeting. Agendas can be particularly useful in this respect, as time can purposely be allocated in meetings for group members to voice concerns. This has the advantage of giving team members time to reflect on some of the points made and formulate their own views. These views can subsequently be aired in a dedicated part of the meeting where criticality is explicitly invited and welcomed. One of the main features of an agenda is that it requires someone to be nominated as the meeting chairperson. Their role is to ensure that the meeting agenda is attended to. This sits nicely with the recommendations of Janis (1982) that teams should nominate a leader whose role is to foster discussion but remain neutral in their position. The team can also use the agenda to formalise Janis's recommendation that there should be at least one member whose job it is to play the role of devil's advocate.

Interpersonal conflict was the final issue we considered before moving onto process related concerns. Here, we identified the importance of team members not responding to problematical behaviour by going straight to dispositional inferences about its cause. Having an agenda can help with this in two ways. First, agendas should be written in the third-person perspective. As we've seen, the third-person perspective is more conducive with self-distancing. This makes inferences about causes of issues more likely to take account of situational factors. Furthermore, when confronted with a challenging behaviour, having an agenda serves as a situation-based first port of call in determining what might have gone awry. For example, if someone arrives at a meeting without an expected contribution prepared, the group can check the previous meeting's paperwork to verify that the task had been allocated to them. Standards regarding conduct at meetings (e.g. that team members do not interrupt other members when they are speaking) can also be formalised in the agenda of an early meeting.

Summary

Taking the 'I' out of the team

Let's bring together some key advice on effective teamwork.

Preventing social loafing

- Individual contributions should be identifiable; people loaf less when they know they cannot hide behind group efforts.
- Team members should be accountable for their contributions. A system of peer evaluation can work well, but the whole group should be involved in the negotiations about what criteria to use and at what points during the project peer evaluation will take place.
- Try and make groups as small as practicable (if the sizes are not predetermined by your tutors). Social loafing tends to increase with group size. Also, having large groups complicates the process of co-ordinating the group effort.

Improving communication by reducing the spotlight effect

- When possible, try and mentally rehearse your planned contributions to team meetings. Getting acclimatised to articulating your points will mean you feel less conspicuous when making them. This reduces the likelihood you'll get an inflated impression about how well what you say is being attended to by your team via the spotlight effect.
- Try and imagine your position within a team from a third person perspective (as if you were another group member) rather than from your own point of view. This helps give you a more accurate

sense of your conspicuity and can aid in preventing interpersonal conflict.
- You can confirm that your contribution to a team meeting has been heard by following up with a question that requires other team members to consider the implications of what you've said.

Better group decision making: avoiding groupthink

- Nominate a chairperson for each team meeting to facilitate discussions. They should invite alternative perspectives, counterpoints and critical thinking, but refrain from contributing their own views.
- Assign at least one group member to the role of devil's advocate at each team meeting. Their sole task for that meeting is to ask things like: "What if we're not right?"; "What are the alternatives?"; "How will we respond if things don't go according to plan?"
- Invite contributions from individuals outside of the group, especially if they have expertise on the matter under consideration.

Avoiding interpersonal conflict: negating the fundamental attribution error

- In thinking about problematical behaviour, try and adopt a third-person perspective in your mental narrative on the situation. This is conducive with avoiding jumping to personal attributions that might be erroneous and escalating a problem into a conflict.
- Ensure that teamwork processes are set up such that they facilitate situational attributions. When something goes wrong, it's helpful if the team's first port of call is to check process related causes. Having written records of team meetings can help to avoid a 'he said, she said' scenario. Keep written records of meetings in the third-person perspective.
- Consider implementing a ground rule that, during meetings, discussions will be focused on problem solving, as opposed to recrimination.

Establishing effective teamwork processes

- Make the focus of the initial meeting to establish a process for working effectively as a team. An important first step is to ensure that the lines of communication are open, i.e. that each group

member has contact details for the other members. Consider having a remote discussion facility for when in-person group meetings might not be possible.
- Use a written agenda to organise the contents of meetings, this should be circulated in good time before each meeting. Any points arising from a meeting that need to be actioned should be included as items to be revisited in future agendas.
- Agree ground rules for your team early on and have them noted on the applicable meeting agenda for approval.
- Make sure discussion on the approach taken to peer evaluation is included in the agenda of an initial team meeting. The team should emerge from this discussion with clear criteria for evaluating contributions to the group along with any expected standards.

A common theme surfaces in this chapter and it's a theme that resonates with Chapter I, i.e. the problem of faulty assumptions. We assume that we will co-operate readily and give the task at hand 100% in teamwork scenarios. We assume that our contributions to a team are always communicated effectively. We assume that group harmony and cohesion always beget effective group decision making. We assume that when another team member does something unhelpful, it reflects badly on them as a person. Finally, we assume that the process of teamwork occurs organically and doesn't need an agreed-on process or documentation. The product of these assumptions is that we're often frustrated and dissatisfied by our experience of working collaboratively and are left none the wiser about why things went wrong. I freely admit that, as an undergraduate, I scoffed when I read about some of the ways that teamwork might be improved. I assumed that they were all too simple to work on something as complex as working collaboratively. I complained vociferously about working in groups as if none of the issues I experienced were anything to do with me, but tried none of the things advocated in this chapter to address these issues. Contrary to popular belief, there is an 'I' in team and it's up to each member of that team to do simple things to remove it!

References

Aggarwal, P. & O'Brien, C. L. (2008). Social loafing on group projects: Structural antecedents and effect on student satisfaction. *Journal of Marketing Education*, *30*(3), 255–264.

Bremner, R. H. (2013). Self-distancing and human reflection: Overcoming bias in judgment and emotional reasoning. Unpublished doctoral dissertation, University of Michigan, USA.

Brooks, C. M. & Ammons, J. L. (2003). Free riding in group projects and the effects of timing, frequency, and specificity of criteria in peer assessments. *Journal of Education for Business*, *78*(5), 268–272.

Burdett, J. & Hastie, B. (2009). Predicting satisfaction with group work assignments. *Journal of University Teaching and Learning Practice*, *6*(1), 61–71.

Favor, J. K. & Harvey, M. (2016). We shall not be moved: Adult learners' intransigent attitudes about group projects. Adult Education Research Conference. Retrieved from http://newprairiepress.org/aerc/2016/papers/18.

Geimer, J. L., Leach, D. J., DeSimone, J. A., Rogelberg, S. G. & Warr, P. B. (2015). Meetings at work: Perceived effectiveness and recommended improvements. *Journal of Business Research*, *68*(9), 2015–2026.

Gibbs, G. (2009). The assessment of group work: Lessons from the literature. Assessment Standards Knowledge Exchange (Centre for Excellence in Teaching and Learning in Higher Education, Oxford Brookes University). Retrieved from www.york.ac.uk/media/staffhome/learningandteaching/documents/keyfactors/The_assessment_of_group_work_lessons_from_the_literature.pdf.

Gilovich, T., Medvec, V. H. & Savitsky, K. (2000). The spotlight effect in social judgment: An egocentric bias in estimates of the salience of one's own actions and appearance. *Journal of Personality and Social Psychology*, *78*(2), 211–222.

Hassanien, A. (2006). Student experience of group work and group assessment in higher education. *Journal of Teaching in Travel & Tourism*, *6*(1), 17–39.

Hooper, N., Erdogan, A., Keen, G., Lawton, K. & McHugh, L. (2015). Perspective taking reduces the fundamental attribution error. *Journal of Contextual Behavioral Science*, *4*(2), 69–72.

Ingham, A. G., Levinger, G., Graves, J. & Peckham, V. (1974). The Ringelmann effect: Studies of group size and group performance. *Journal of Experimental Social Psychology*, *10*(4), 371–384.

Janis, I. L. (1971). Groupthink. *Psychology Today*, *5*(6), 43–46.

Janis, I. L. (1982). *Groupthink: Psychological studies of policy decisions and fiascoes* (Vol. 349). Houghton Mifflin.

Johnson, D. W., Johnson, R. T. & Smith, K. A. (2014). Cooperative learning: Improving university instruction by basing practice on validated theory. *Journal on Excellence in University Teaching*, *25*(4), 1–26.

Knight, J. (2004). Comparison of student perception and performance in individual and group assessments in practical classes. *Journal of Geography in Higher Education*, *28*(1), 63–81.

Kravitz, D. A. & Martin, B. (1986). Ringelmann rediscovered: The original article. *Journal of Personality and Social Psychology*, *50*(5), 936–941.

Kross, E. & Ayduk, O. (2017). Self-distancing: Theory, research, and current directions. In *Advances in experimental social psychology* (Vol. 55, pp. 81–136). Academic Press.

Kross, E., Bruehlman-Senecal, E., Park, J., Burson, A., Dougherty, A., Shablack, H. & Ayduk, O. (2014). Self-talk as a regulatory mechanism: How you do it matters. *Journal of Personality and Social Psychology*, *106*(2), 304–324.

Latané, B., Williams, K. & Harkins, S. (1979). Many hands make light the work: The causes and consequences of social loafing. *Journal of Personality and Social Psychology*, *37*(6), 822–832.

Leach, D. J., Rogelberg, S. G., Warr, P. B. & Burnfield, J. L. (2009). Perceived meeting effectiveness: The role of design characteristics. *Journal of Business and Psychology*, *24*(1), 65–76.

Macrae, C. N., Mitchell, J. P., McNamara, D. L., Golubickis, M., Andreou, K., Møller, S. & Christian, B. M. (2016). Noticing future me: Reducing egocentrism through mental imagery. *Personality and Social Psychology Bulletin*, *42*(7), 855–863.

Moser, J. S., Dougherty, A., Mattson, W. I., Katz, B., Moran, T. P., Guevarra, D. & Kross, E. (2017). Third-person self-talk facilitates emotion regulation without engaging cognitive control: Converging evidence from ERP and fMRI. *Scientific Reports*, *7*(1), 1–9.

Myers, S. A. & Goodboy, A. K. (2005). A study of grouphate in a course on small group communication. *Psychological Reports*, *97*(2), 381–386.

Pfaff, E. & Huddleston, P. (2003). Does it matter if I hate teamwork? What impacts student attitudes toward teamwork. *Journal of Marketing Education*, *25*(1), 37–45.

Ringelmann, M. (1913). Mechanical tilling equipment with winches and cables results of tests. *Annales de l'Institut National Agronomique*, *2*(12), 299–343.

Rose, J. D. (2011). Diverse perspectives on the groupthink theory: A literary review. *Emerging Leadership Journeys*, *4*(1), 37–57.

Ross, L. D., Amabile, T. M. & Steinmetz, J. L. (1977). Social roles, social control, and biases in social-perception processes. *Journal of Personality and Social Psychology*, *35*(7), 485–494.

Sorensen, S. M. (1981, May). Group-hate: A negative reaction to group work. Paper presented at the annual meeting of the International Communication Association, Minneapolis.

Tucker, R. & Abbasi, N. (2016). Bad attitudes: Why design students dislike teamwork. *Journal of Learning Design*, *9*(1), 1–20.

Williams, K. D. & Karau, S. J. (1991). Social loafing and social compensation: The effects of expectations of co-worker performance. *Journal of Personality and Social Psychology*, *61*(4), 570–581.

Williams, K., Harkins, S. G. & Latané, B. (1981). Identifiability as a deterrent to social loafing: Two cheering experiments. *Journal of Personality and Social Psychology*, *40*(2), 303–311.

Wilson, L., Ho, S. & Brookes, R. H. (2018). Student perceptions of teamwork within assessment tasks in undergraduate science degrees. *Assessment & Evaluation in Higher Education*, *43*(5), 786–799.

Delivering an effective presentation

It's not about you

The secret of being a bore is to tell everything.
Voltaire

1

Key advice: do not aim to transmit information, aim to promote and inspire learning

I recall seeing a picture on the internet of a sign outside of a church that read: "Do you know what hell is? Come and listen to our preacher." I thought that summed up what it's like to be stuck in a boring presentation pretty well. The archetypal presentation, and the one that you will become most familiar with as an undergraduate student, is the lecture. The primary intention of a lecture is, of course, to facilitate learning about a topic. Because of this, the lecture is a great exemplar to use in framing general advice on how to present more effectively. Be that as it may, lecturers are not invariably the best candidates for modelling good presentation practice. We've probably all been to one or two lectures that could have been entitled 'Watching Paint Dry 101' for all the interest they've inspired. Indeed, research has indicated that lectures can be anything but stimulating. For example, Sharp et al. (2017) conducted some research into the causes and consequences of academic boredom. A particularly disheartening aspect of their findings was that only 46% of the students classified their lectures as interesting or engaging most, if not all, of the time. Presumably lecturers want people to be interested in the contents of their presentation and they're not trying to be boring, so what's going on?

I think that the biggest problem in giving any presentation (lecture or otherwise) is encapsulated by my recollection of my first foray into the world of presenting. Bear with me whilst I remove my rose-tinted glasses. I was a third-year undergraduate and my supervisor invited me to talk to the current second years about my dissertation and maybe dispense a bit of advice based on my own experience. I would like to tell you that it was an auspicious start to a career as a lecturer, that I was a natural presenter and that the audience hung onto every word I said. I would like to tell you that! Unfortunately, the audience were clearly bored after five minutes and probably only refrained from showing this because the dean of school was present, the windows and doors were locked, and the smart phone had yet to be invented. The absence of a convenient distraction was particularly unfortunate for the audience because my presentation also over-ran by about double the time I had been allotted! Still, valuable lesson learned: giving effective presentations is hard!

Whatever my failings as a fledgling presenter, lack of effort on the preparation front was not among them! I started off by spending hours agonising over basic questions like: How long should I talk for? Should I give the audience breaks? What speed should I talk at? Should I stand still, or be a bit more animated? How much should I vary the tone of my voice? How should I hide my nerves? Was it OK to tell a joke? And what, pray tell, was I supposed to do with my hands, the size of which had suddenly become something of a preoccupation. Then there was the matter of my PowerPoint presentation slides. What kind of background should I use? Should I use visual and sound effects to embellish my points? What colour combinations and fonts were optimal? How many bullet points should I use on a slide? Was it better to use diagrams than text? How much text should I put on a slide? Argh! Does it have to be this complicated? No. In fact, presentations are a great candidate for the application of the US Navy's design principle of K.I.S.S. (Keep it Simple, Stupid). Before you start fretting about the above kind of questions, there is a more fundamental question you should first address to make things much easier for you (and your audience).

The problem with my presentation preparation was that I didn't, first and foremost, consider the question of the basic purpose of my role as a presenter. The answer to this question profoundly influences how you respond to more specific questions about your presentation. Let's single out the issue of how much of your allocated timeslot you should talk for to illustrate this point. If you identify (either explicitly or implicitly) that your role as a presenter is to transmit information, then you'll most likely reason that you should talk for all of your timeslot. However, in taking on this role as a presenter, your audience is relegated to passive recipients of information. Basically, they sit there whilst you talk at them! Hopefully, you'll recall from the chapter on reading and note-taking that passive engagement and memory are not good bedfellows! Therein lies the problem: the transmission of information is only half the equation; the reception of that information is equally important. If your presentation does not take account of this and simply throws heaps of information at the audience without giving them anything to do with it, they will get bored and switch off! Sure enough, research on the causes of student boredom in lectures indicates that the aspects of a lecture students find most tedious are those that do not involve active engagement with the material (Mann & Robinson, 2009). Not surprisingly, research also indicates that lectures that promote active engagement also result in better attainment in learning about the material presented (see Freeman et al., 2014 for a review).

If your goal is to avoid boring your audience and help them learn about the contents of your presentation, then you need to start by reformulating your idea of your role as a presenter. Your purpose is not to transmit as much information as possible, but rather to serve as a catalyst for learning. Your presentation should promote the same kind of active engagement in your audience that you would seek to achieve in your own reading and note-taking when learning about a topic. This chapter will help you achieve this by examining the characteristics of the way you deliver your presentation and your use of visual aids. I can't promise that the contents of this chapter will make you a prime candidate for giving the keynote address at a Royal Institution Lecture. However, if you follow some of its guidance your audience should leave the presentation venue thinking something other than: "Well, that's an hour of my life I won't ever get back!"

Presentation goals: back to the basics

I'd argue that you have four main goals in respect of promoting active engagement with your presentation. First, you must give an audience a reason to want to listen to you above and beyond the fact that they are in attendance, which may well have been compelled. Second, you must provide a clear structure or narrative in your presentation; just throwing material at the audience and hoping some of it sticks is not conducive with helping them remember what you say. Third, you need to keep the amount of information you present manageable; there are limits as to how much information an audience can absorb in the time you have with them. Finally, you must maintain audience engagement with your presentation; you want to minimise the time that their attention drifts off to things other than your efforts! To be an effective presenter you need to be proficient in achieving all these goals, so I'm going to use them to organise my advice on the delivery of a presentation. Let's start with a very simple way of giving your audience a good reason to listen to you. It involves bribery, of sorts!

Key advice: start your presentation with questions, not answers

The idea of giving an audience a reason to listen to you might sound a bit redundant. I mean, they're sitting there, right? It's even worse if you don't get to choose the topic of your presentation. I don't have any research to cite here, but I'm guessing that a presentation on the history of nudity in television and film will inherently attract more interest than one about coastal erosion (providing the former has pictures, of course). Exaggeration for the sake of emphasis apart, audiences are often very diverse in their composition. Trying to give them a reason to listen to you by second-guessing the interests of everyone present isn't feasible. Or is it? Let me ask you something: when was the last time you saw a presentation that began with a question, or questions? If you're struggling to remember, does that seem odd? If the presenter had thought about the goal of motivating you to listen to them, then it should! Recall from the chapter on reading and note-taking our coverage of research indicating that questions are a powerful catalyst for getting people to think about material. They give people a purpose for engaging with that material and a role in interrogating it. Thus, you can use questions at the outset of your presentation as a shortcut to connecting with all of your audience. Starting with questions gives them a reason to be interested in your talk, i.e. so they can discover the answer to those questions. Think of it as intellectual bribery!

The role of asking questions as a method of promoting learning goes back centuries, but as with any practice there are pitfalls. Questions are not created equal in their capacity to engage an audience, especially if the aim is to stimulate interest and promote comprehension. A full taxonomy of the kinds of questions you can ask in a presentation is well beyond the scope of this chapter, the interested reader might like to look at Tofade, Elsner and Haines (2013). However, there are a couple of distinctions that it's useful to be familiar with in thinking about how you might use questions to connect with your audience. The first distinction is that of convergent questions versus divergent questions. Convergent questions tend to involve a specific correct answer (or limited range of acceptable answers), to which little, if any, further elaboration is required. A convergent question about active engagement with material might be something like: "What does active engagement mean?" This question is gunning for a specific answer. It's only really going to distinguish between those audience members who are already familiar with the concept of active engagement and those who aren't. As soon as an audience member offers an acceptable definition, it's pretty much game over for that line of questioning. The correct answer has been given, let's all get on with our lives. Divergent questions do not have a specific correct response, or limited range of correct responses. Rather, they stimulate the recipients to think around the topic in question and produce responses that require a follow up and elaboration. An example of a divergent alternative to the previous question might be: "Suppose someone wanted to become a better presenter, what advice might you give them?" You can probably immediately see that there is no single correct or best answer to this question. Furthermore, being able to respond to it is not contingent on knowing a specific fact. It invites the audience to think about how their existing knowledge or personal experiences might be used to respond to the question. These answers will require elaboration/follow up. For example, audience members might respond to the above divergent question with a range of answers from "talk slower" to "don't include irrelevant detail". The speaker would probably want to follow up on each of these with more than just a: "that's correct/incorrect" response. Rather, they would seek to achieve elaboration on each response with a view to illustrating its connection to the concept of active engagement. Thus, divergent questions are better at stimulating interest because engaging with them is not dependent on being in possession of specific facts. They are also better at promoting comprehension because they invite follow up and elaboration that entails the application of a response to a specific goal. In effect, they get more of the audience involved in generating answers rather than just being given them. An easy way of distinguishing between convergent and divergent questions is to use their alternative nomenclature, i.e. closed versus open questions. If the question you're asking generates a specific answer that slams the door shut on that question, it's closed. If the question you're asking generates a multitude of possible answers, open to further exploration, it's open. When using questions at the commencement of your presentation, it's better to keep them open for reasons that I hope are now apparent!

In formulating questions to ask during a presentation, a useful and easily implemented method to adopt is that advocated by Dietz-Uhler and Lanter (2009). They developed a four-question technique, where each question requires that the participants use the information presented to achieve a specific goal. In doing this, the questions surreptitiously get the recipients engaging in practices conducive with deeper processing of information, which aids their memory. The first type of question (analysis) requires individuals to analyse the presented information by identifying at least one important thing they have learned from it. This can be thought of as a sly form of retrieval practice. The second question (reflection) follows the first by asking why individuals think that the thing they have learned was particularly significant. Does this question type sound like it might be activating elaborative interrogation to you? The third question (relating) asks individuals to integrate this new knowledge with something they already knew by applying what they have learned to an aspect of their lives. This resonates with the general principle of levels of processing. Being able to relate new knowledge to something that you already know is conducive with deeper processing of that material. Finally, the fourth question (generating) asks individuals to consider the implications of their learning by producing their own question about the presented material. Again, this is utilising the benefits of elaborative interrogation, but is also providing a basis for further examination of the material. In Uhler and Lanter's experiment, psychology undergraduates were asked to complete a web-based activity on one of two randomly assigned topics. They then utilised the four-questions technique either before or after the administration of a test about what they had learned. The students were also asked to indicate the extent to which they thought the four questions were effective in meeting their goals of improving analysis, reflection, relating and generation. Finally, their perception of their learning of the material having used the four-questions method and degree of enjoyment in using it was also assessed. Participants who used the four-questions method before taking the test achieved an average score of 74%. In contrast, those who used the four-questions method after taking the test obtained an average score of 59%. The results also indicated that students perceived the four-question method as effective in achieving its goals and that they enjoyed engaging with it.

In incorporating questions into your presentation, it's important to be mindful of a few considerations articulated nicely by Tofade, Elsner and Haines (2013). First, you need to sequence your questions correctly, based on your objective in asking them. For example, if the purpose of a question is to make an initial connection with the audience or to stimulate interest, then it's best placed before any expository material. If, on the other hand, the question is intended to check for comprehension or expand on an existing topic, then it's best placed after the relevant exposition. Either way, you should avoid just throwing questions at the reader without taking the time to address and explicitly conclude them before moving on. If you don't do this, it's likely that the audience will get stuck pondering a particular question and be distracted from some (or all) of the remainder of your presentation. I guess if your strongest material is at the beginning of your presentation and the rest is just filler then this might be a valid tactic, but still! Second, on a related note, do give the audience long enough to respond to your questions. In the heat of a presentation, nerves and the fact that all eyes are on you can have the effect of making seconds seem like minutes. However, enduring a deathly silence for just a few extra seconds can make all the difference to whether your questions get the chance to engage the audience. If you really can't stand the idea of uninvited silence, then invite it. Explicitly give the audience a short period of time to think of a response. If they still won't play ball, give them a prompt. If that doesn't work, rephrase the question. Try and avoid immediately answering your own questions at all costs; it defeats the point of the whole exercise. Furthermore, the audience will be discouraged from answering subsequent questions because you've just demonstrated you are happy to save them the effort! Third, as blindingly obvious as it may seem, create an environment where people want to interact with you: a smile, a nod and a thank-you goes a long way in encouraging audience involvement. These are all things that are easy to neglect when you're nervous. Don't interrupt a response from the audience, frown or be discouraging even if a contribution is not relevant. Telling someone that their answer to your question is about as helpful as a chocolate fire-guard is not conducive with encouraging others to contribute something easier for you to work with. In any case, the fault might lie with you for not asking the question clearly.

3

Key advice: your presentation needs a structure that is clearly conveyed to the audience

So, you've aroused the interest of the audience and given them a reason to listen to you. Now it's time to get stuck right in to the meat of the presentation, right? I would suggest not! Have you ever been to one of those talks where the speaker just dives into the material and you're left wondering where they are going and, more importantly, when they might stop? Not pleasant is it? It puts you on the back foot and leaves you struggling to integrate the different parts of the presentation into a coherent whole, as opposed to disparate chunks of information. Indeed, a lack of explicit structure/organisation in the form of an outline has been identified in the literature as a cause of dissatisfaction with presentations (e.g. Sharp et al., 2015). There is a very simple reason for why a lack of transparency about the organisation of information has a deleterious effect on our ability to engage with a presentation. Organisation really helps us to process and remember information. This was demonstrated nicely by another one of psychology's classic experiments. Bower, Clark, Lesgold and Winzenz (1969) performed a study in which they asked participants to remember word lists, an example of which contained 112 different minerals, e.g. Platinum, Iron, Bronze and Emerald. The experiment investigated whether the way in which the word lists were organised would affect the participants' ability to recall them. To this end, in one condition, the participants were given the word lists arranged into conceptual hierarchical structures. Taking the minerals word list as an example, at the top level of the hierarchy was the super-ordinate category of 'minerals'. Below this, in the second level of the hierarchy, 'minerals' divided into two further subordinate categories: 'metals' and 'stones'. Below this, at the third level of the hierarchy, 'metals' and 'stones' were further divided into their subordinate categories, e.g. 'stones' sub-divided into 'precious stones' and 'masonry stones'. Metals sub-divided into 'rare', 'common' and 'alloys'. Below these, the fourth level of the hierarchy featured appropriately filed members of the third level. For example, the precious stones category contained the words: 'sapphire', 'emerald', 'diamond' and 'ruby'. In the other word list presentation condition, participants were shown lists that had the appearance of a conceptual hierarchical structure, but where the words were randomly assigned to different places in that hierarchy. They had the visual appearance of being organised into a structure, but that structure did not make sense. You've probably guessed that the participants who viewed the word lists in the conceptual hierarchical structure condition recalled more words than those in the random hierarchical condition. However, the magnitude of the superiority of their performance might surprise you. They recalled three and a half times more words on their first attempt! By the third attempt, all the participants in the conceptual hierarchical structure condition recalled the entire word list; all 112 words!

As impressive as the results of Bower et al. are, you might reason that your presentations are unlikely to involve giving people word lists to recall and, therefore, wonder how the above experiment is applicable. Well, it's the principle that emerges from the experiment that is important here. Structure serves as a catalyst for thinking about the relationship between information, this facilitates memory for that information. A presenter can take advantage of this principle right from the outset of their talk by simply providing an outline of what is to come. This supports the audience in thinking about the relationship between the different parts of the presentation. Bui and McDaniel (2015) asked undergraduates to watch a 12-minute lecture recording about brakes and pumps and take notes on its contents. Prior to the lecture recording starting, participants were randomly assigned to one of three learning aid conditions. In the outline condition, participants were given a sheet of paper that contained a running list of the topics and sub-topics covered by the lecture (i.e. an outline of the contents) that they could use in their note-taking. In the illustrative diagrams condition, participants were given a depiction of how brakes and pumps worked. Finally, the control participants were simply given a blank note-pad to write their notes on. Participants in all the conditions were prohibited from pausing or rewinding the video (I'm guessing that none of them would have elected to hit the fast-forward button). So, as with a live presentation, they could not manipulate the temporal aspects of the lecture delivery. Immediately following the termination of the lecture, the experimenter took away the participants' written materials (so they never got to use their notes). They then issued a distractor word learning task for a period of 30 minutes. After this, the participants were asked to recall what they had learned in the lecture. Participants in the outline condition achieved significantly better free recall scores than those in the control condition. Giving some thought as to the structure of your presentation and making sure you clearly signpost this to the audience helps you deliver a message, rather than a mess! The other thing about structure is that thinking about it does force you to make some executive decisions about what material your presentation will entail. This brings us nicely onto the next presentation goal: keeping the amount of information you give the audience manageable.

Key advice: limit the contents of your presentation to what the audience needs to know, not everything there is to know

Recall that in the opening of this chapter I made the argument that the first step to becoming a better presenter was to view your role as a catalyst for learning, rather than the person responsible for telling the audience everything you think they need to know. Well, there is another big reason for avoiding doing the latter other than just promoting active engagement with your talk. It relates to something psychologists call cognitive load. It's important to understand this concept if you're to keep your presentation manageable for the audience. Crudely speaking, cognitive load refers to the amount of mental effort you must expend to understand something. Have you ever attended a presentation (or five) where the speaker seems less intent on presenting information to the audience as pummelling them into submission with it? Bullet point after interminable point until the main point being made (if there ever was one) is completely lost! If you recognise this scenario, then you've been the victim of a presenter who has, for whatever reason, forgotten that we all have limits to the amount of information we can process at any one time.

The theory of cognitive load has its origins in work on problem solving in mathematics (Sweller, 1988). Stay with me on this one, it's very relevant to the extent to which your audience can make sense of your presentations, even if their topic isn't advanced algebra! Broadly speaking, the theory postulates that information exists on a continuum from low interactivity to high interactivity. Information low in interactivity contains individual concepts that can be understood independently. Information high in interactivity entails individual concepts that can only really be completely understood in terms of how they relate to one another. No prizes for guessing which one takes more effort. Equally, no prizes for guessing what end of the continuum much of the information one would find in a degree-level presentation inhabits! The level of cognitive load that the information itself places on the user is called intrinsic cognitive load. Central to the idea of the cognitive load theory is the mechanism of our working memory (Baddeley & Hitch, 1974). This is often referred to in lay terms as short-term memory. You can think of working memory as a kind of buffer that temporarily stores information for processing. Working memory has a limited capacity, you may have heard of 'the magic number seven' expression before. This refers to some classic research by Miller (1956) on the average number of units of information that can be held in the working memory for processing at any one time. This represents a challenge for the audience of presentations, as they are not regulating their exposure to the information as they would if they were studying independently. Instead, the audience is at the mercy of the speaker to be cognisant of the amount of information they are giving their working memory to deal with within a short timeframe. The more the presenter gives the audience's working memory to deal with, the higher the intrinsic cognitive load associated with processing the information. High intrinsic cognitive load increases the likelihood that the audience will get overburdened and lose track of the point being made.

A presenter can reduce the intrinsic cognitive load associated with the information they present by reducing the burden they are placing on the audience's working memory. They can achieve this by cutting back on the number of pieces of information that the audience has to process at the same time. This is most readily achieved by a presenter limiting the scope of their presentation and then being specific about the aims for each component of their presentation. For example, in the above section of text my aim was to explain why your presentations should avoid overloading your audience with information, which makes it hard for them to discern your main message from unnecessary detail. The exposition I gave you on cognitive load and working memory was oriented to achieve this; no less, no more. It won't surprise you to learn that each of these concepts has a bucket load (that's a legitimate scientific term, by the way) of literature associated with them. They are much more involved than I have conveyed here. I could have told you how working memory emerged from the multi-store model of memory, originally proposed by Atkinson and Shiffrin (1968). I could have told you about each of its components: the central executive, the visio-spatial scratch pad, the phonological loop and the episodic buffer. I could have told you about research on manipulating the capacity of working memory. Would any of this have contributed to me achieving my aim in delivering the intended message? No. In fact, I'd wager that by the time I'd got done with that little lot, you'd probably have forgotten the point of me even bringing up the concepts of cognitive load and working memory. Sure enough, there is research on the determinants of an audience's perception of the success of a lecture indicating that a presenter's ability to identify the key points is of paramount importance (e.g. Copeland, Longworth, Hewson & Stoller, 2000). The message of such research is clear: keeping things manageable for the audience involves constraining the information you give them to what they need to know, not all there is to know!

5

Key advice: a bit of variety does wonders in keeping an audience's attention

The last objective of a presentation is to keep your audience engaged with your talk, which leads us to that old chestnut of attention span and its implications for you as a presenter. You'll no doubt have heard lots of rather unflattering comparisons between the average human attention span and that of the common goldfish. You might even nod vigorously in sympathy when a colleague or friend complains about their short attention span, right before they spend an entire day watching "just one more episode" of *House of Cards*. It does seem to be somewhat axiomatic in both lay and educational circles that attention functions a bit like a torch with a rapidly discharging battery. You point it at something and the light illuminates the subject brilliantly at first, but not for long. Indeed, Wilson and Korn (2007) noted that educational materials often provide guidance to the effect that attention begins to decline after ten to 15 minutes and goes steadily south after that. So, is the appropriate advice for budding presenters to say whatever you've got to say in 15 minutes and then exit stage left pretty damn quickly? Would you be justified in marching up to one of your tutors and using this nugget of information to argue that you couldn't possibly be reasonably expected to sit through a two-hour lecture? Nope! Sorry! I don't want to get you too bogged down in the literature, but the basis for the 10–15-minute attention span estimate is dubious. You can find a really good review of why in Bradbury (2016). For the purposes of this chapter, it suffices to say that the 10–15-minute estimate comes from studies that have had problematical ways of measuring attention. The frequently cited work of Hartley and Davies (1978) wasn't even addressing attention per se, but rather note-taking behaviour in lectures. This might not be so bad if note-taking behaviour was a valid proxy for attention, but there is no evidence that this is the case. Differences in note-taking behaviour are more likely to reflect differences in individual students' note-taking practices. Oh, and their perception of whether they think anything being imparted at that point in the lecture merits being noted. Indeed, a lack of note-taking might be indicative of a student attending particularly closely to something the presenter is saying. Researchers have also tried to quantify audience attention using measures of memory, which are not satisfactory owing to the conflation of session length and volume of information. Longer sessions generally involve the presentation of more information. Therefore, poorer recall performance could as easily be a reflection on limitations associated with memory as those associated with attention. Researchers have also previously monitored attention levels of audience members via direct observation, but this is not exactly a precise science. For example, how does one measure breaks in attention within an audience: is that person fidgeting, or do they just have a rash? Probably best not to give that one too much thought! Maybe give the seat they are in a wide berth for a while just to be on the safe side! Of course, the biggest problem associated with direct observation studies is resisting the temptation to do a lame David Attenborough impression: "Here we see the common undergraduate, dutifully pretending to listen to the lecture whilst using university Wi-Fi to browse Amazon.com."

Contemporary research has attempted to side-step some of the above issues by using technology to measure audience members' self-reported levels of attention. Bunce, Flens and Neiles (2010) asked undergraduates in an introductory chemistry course to self-report lapses in attention using three button clickers. Each button on these clickers corresponded to a period of inattention (one minute or less, 3–5 minutes and five minutes or more, respectively). Students were asked to press the appropriate button whenever they became aware that their focus had drifted off the content of the lecture. This gave the researchers a measure of the frequency, duration, timing and pattern of lapses in attention. They manipulated the approach used in the presentation of the course content between lecturing, demonstration and asking questions (which the students responded to with the clickers). This enabled them to compare audience attention levels for these three approaches whilst each approach was being used.

Several interesting findings emerged from this study. First, there was not a 10–15-minute window at the outset of the lecture where the audience was consistently highly attentive. In fact, the audience fluctuated between periods of attention and inattention. These fluctuations occurred as early as 30 seconds into the lecture (that's the bad news). However, before you throw away everything but the opening greeting of your presentation, here's the good news. The most common duration of an attention lapse was less than one minute, so it's not simply the case that an audience disengage with the content of a presentation and then never come back. In fact, the data was more consistent with people actively trying to re-engage with content once they realised their mind had wandered. Further good news comes from the finding that attention levels were affected by the type of presentation approach being used. Surprise, surprise, the approaches that utilised demonstrations and questions generated fewer lapses in attention than the lecturing parts of the class. Moreover, the results indicated that using demonstrations or questions had a positive knock-on effect on attention levels for the lecture segments that immediately followed them. It's like they were serving as attentional palate cleansers. Overall, results such as these indicate that it's entirely reasonable to expect people to pay attention for more than 15 minutes. However, there are approaches to giving a presentation that are more conducive to greater levels of attention, i.e. those that don't involve talking at the audience the entire time. The research indicates that you should consider interspersing talking to the audience with approaches (such as asking questions) that require their engagement to periodically recharge their attention for subsequent content. The lesson for you, as a budding presenter, is that audience attention is less like a torch with a rapidly discharging battery and more like a kinetic watch. It'll work well enough for you providing you give it the occasional shake.

Death (of bad presentations) by PowerPoint

6

Key advice: to create effective slideshows, you must first understand their purpose

I feel that I should start the second half of this chapter by relaying to you a conversation I once overheard between two colleagues following a presentation.

PROFESSOR A: "Was that slideshow hard to create?"
PROFESSOR B: "No, why?"
PROFESSOR A: "Because it was f***ing hard to sit through."

With that terse, but indisputably very clear, feedback in mind we move on to the thorny subject of how to use slideshows in your presentations. By slideshows, I mean the presentation of text, graphics, animations and sounds etc. via the use of projection to a large screen, usually located behind the speaker. I will be referring to PowerPoint as an exemplar of the software used to create slideshows throughout this section of the chapter, simply because it's the market leader (Thielsch & Perabo, 2012). Accordingly, it's the software named in much of the research. However, users of other presentation creation software should not feel excluded. The guidance offered here refers to the principles underpinning the effective use of multimedia in presentations per se, so is applicable to any presentation software. The following is a brief guide to what psychological research has to say on how to produce more effective presentation slideshows. It's not a step-by-step guide on how to use a specific piece of presentation software.

Let's start by considering why it can be a good idea to use slideshows in giving a presentation. You will recall that we've discussed the idea of intrinsic cognitive load, which comes from the nature of the information being presented itself. You might have wondered whether there is also extraneous cognitive load, which comes from the way information is presented. Indeed there is! Sweller (2005) made exactly that distinction. Given this, you might think that expecting an audience to attend to a slideshow whilst they listen to the speaker talking serves only to compound the extraneous cognitive load associated with the presentation. Why would a presenter want to do this? Why not just dispense with the slideshow and, in doing so, reduce the extraneous cognitive load placed on the audience? Well, that would seem to be sound logic. However, it transpires that adding sources of information to a presentation can either increase or decrease cognitive load depending on the interaction between them. To explain this, we need to briefly visit another one of the classics of psychology: dual code theory, postulated by Paivio (1971). Simply stated, dual code theory proposes that the mind represents (codes) information in two ways – verbally or via the use of visual imagery – and that there are memory stores associated with each type of memory – verbal memory and image-based memory. Verbal and image-based codes and their respective memory stores are discreet entities and can code information independently, but they also interact with each other. Dual code theory posits that information that is processed verbally and visually is more likely to be retained in memory. Research has often shown this in experiments that have demonstrated superior recall for concrete items that are easy to picture (e.g. a table) than abstract words (such as fairness). It's also been demonstrated by research that has manipulated the way that information is coded and demonstrated an additive effect of using both visual and verbal coding together over using either of them independently. Evidence of this nature has been found in the context of presentations by Mayer (2009). This series of experiments involved presenting students with educational materials via narration and animation versus narration alone, or via text and illustration versus text alone. Following this, the students were asked to solve problems based on the information that had been conveyed to them. Students performed significantly better when both visual and verbal information was available. It's this additive effect of verbal and visual coding that constitutes a principal reason why slideshows (PowerPoint or otherwise) can be an effective ally in presentations. However, the operative word in that last sentence is 'can'.

If facilitating the processing of information was as simple as just presenting material verbally and visually then, given the pervasiveness of PowerPoint presentations, we should have a lot of happy audiences. Also, software like PowerPoint would be universally lauded as a panacea for bad presentations. You probably won't be surprised to find out that this is not the case. Some commentators have even gone as far as to call PowerPoint evil (e.g. Tufte, 2003). So, what's going on? Well, it transpires that just the presence of verbal and visual information is not enough; it's the way these two sources of information are integrated that matters. Unfortunately, it's this integration that presents the designer of the slideshow with ample opportunity to screw things up! For example, have you ever sat through a presentation where the person up front did nothing but read verbatim off their slides? This practice is affectionately, or maybe that should be non-affectionately, referred to as PowerPoint karaoke. Frustrating isn't it? Sure, the speaker's verbalisation is accompanied by visual sensory input in terms of the words appearing on the screen, but these words require more verbal than visual coding. Consequently, your verbal processing is getting double the workload whilst your visual processing is largely left twiddling its fingers.

So, the proper purpose of slideshows is to reduce the intrinsic cognitive load of a presentation by taking advantage of dual coding. How do we design slides such that they achieve this objective and don't just become a source of extrinsic cognitive load? A body of research in multimedia learning has emerged over the last 20 years to respond to this question and elucidate how best to integrate verbal and visual information (e.g. Mayer, 2014). The outcome of such research is a series of principles that provide guidance on multimedia design conducive with reducing cognitive load. However, just throwing such principles at you at this point would be akin to providing a solution to a problem that hasn't yet been properly defined. If I'm going to give you advice with the biggest bang for your buck, then we first need to determine what audiences have identified as the most common and annoying problems with slideshows. We can then target advice at these issues specifically. Happily, I know of just the research that will enable us to do this!

7

Key advice: knowing about mistakes in slideshow design isn't the same as knowing how to fix them

Kosslyn, Kievit, Russell and Shephard (2012) noted that it's not hard to find criticisms of PowerPoint but, for all the grumbling, the quality of slideshows remains highly variable. Kosslyn et al. suggested that a reason for the continuing issues with PowerPoint was that the consequences of bad presentation design is obvious to people (e.g. annoyance at not being able to take in the contents of a busy slide). However, the psychological principle (e.g. relevance) that had been violated to create the fault in the design of the offending slide (i.e. too much information crammed into one slide) was not as obvious. Of course, if individuals don't understand the principle behind why an aspect of a slideshow's design is annoying, it's hard for them to correctly identify the specific design fault and effectively remedy it. Kosslyn et al. went on to argue that research should address this issue by elucidating principles of good practice when designing slides. Furthermore, these principles should be informed by research on the way that humans process information. The absence of such research produces a scenario whereby the bad presenter blames their tools and the hapless presentation software takes the fall for the ignorance of its user.

Kosslyn et al. (2012) obtained a large cross-section of PowerPoint presentations from the academic, business, governmental and educational sectors. They went about developing criteria against which to evaluate these presentations by specifying the necessary mental tasks that an audience member needs to achieve to understand a presentation's contents. First, they need to be able to encode the information. Second, they need to integrate the information into their working memory. Third, they need to be able to extract meaning from the integrated information by comparing it to material stored in their long-term memory. Kosslyn et al. then set about applying existing literature from cognitive psychology on these three tasks to postulate associated principles from which rules of good practice could be specified. For example, encoding information is governed by principles relating to the discriminability of the stimulus, i.e. patterns need to stand out from their immediate surroundings. In total, eight principles were specified (several for each task) that generated associated rules of good practice and corresponding violations. Sticking with the example of the encoding task related principle of discriminability, one rule would be that the colour of the text used needs to be distinct from the background of the slide. The associated violation of this rule would be that the text does not adequately stand out from the background of the slide. This process gave the researchers a total of 137 violations to assess a sample of 140 PowerPoint presentations in relation to in their first study. Remember this the next time you complain about having to sit through a single presentation! The researchers monitored the presentations for violations and made a note of which rules were being violated. If one or more violations were committed for a principle, then it got a score of one. A clean bill of health for a principle was represented as a zero. The results indicated that, on average, presentations contained violations of rules in six of the eight principles. Before you think that the experimenters might have been nit-picking, the kind of errors were fundamental. Top of the tree was our friend discriminability, i.e. people were producing slides with visual features too similar to be easily distinguished. To make matters worse, there was no difference in the number of violations between the different categories of presentations. The academic presentations weren't any better than those from the other sectors. Admittedly, that's a bit embarrassing! The experimenters concluded that the psychological principles underpinning good presentations were either not self-evident, or simply being ignored.

In their second study, Kosslyn et al. sought to examine whether the general public would be sensitive to the types of violations that they had just identified. Participants were asked to audit their personal experience of seeing presentations in relation to these violations via a questionnaire. Where they had encountered a violation they were also asked, using a Likert scale response, how frequently they had previously observed it and the extent to which it had bothered them. Over 60% of the participants indicated that they had witnessed at least some instances of violations for each of the seven principles included in the questionnaire, and that they had found these to be at least somewhat annoying. We'll return to this data shortly as the basis of the guidelines for the advice on preparing a slideshow. However, before we do, it's also worth briefly referring to the third experiment that Kosslyn and his colleagues performed. Study two demonstrated that, when prompted, participants recognised and articulated annoyance about specific faults with slideshows. However, retrospectively recognising a fault with a slide when it has been spelled out for you is not the same as identifying a fault and being able to explain why it has occurred yourself. This is what the third study addressed.

To examine if participants could identify bad slide design practice of their own accord, the experimenters presented them with a series of pairs of slides that appeared simultaneously on a screen. Each slide pair corresponded to one of the presentation principles previously identified (e.g. discriminability). One of the slides exhibited a violation (such as a clash between the slide's background image and the text). The other slide featured identical contents, but not the offending violation. Each pair of slides was accompanied by a corresponding question, e.g. which of these two slides does a better job of presenting the text legibly? The participants' task was to select the slide from the pairing that represented good practice and then explain the reason for their selection. Surprisingly, on average, participants chose the slides containing a violation 20% of the time. Furthermore, even on the occasions when they identified the slide indicative of good practice, they were unable to correctly account for the reason it was the correct choice one-sixth of the time! You might be inclined to think that those numbers aren't so bad. After all, the participants were right most of the time. However, consider first the implications of a single, but rudimentary error. Let's go with a violation under the principle of relevance, whereby the presenter has crammed the equivalent of a medium sized novel's worth of text into each of their slides. It's only one error, derived from one principle. However, do you want to sit through their slideshow? Me neither! Second, although the absolute number of errors might not have been as catastrophic as you may have expected, they tended to be distributed across the different principles. People were making errors across the board. When looking at the data concerning the percentage of participants that had made at least one error with respect to a specific principle, Kosslyn et al. found that there were no principles that attracted zero errors. Indeed, the percentage of participants who had made at least one error with respect to a specific principle went as high as 97%. Similarly, there were no principles that were free of errors in the event of correct slide selection; as many as 85% of participants made at least one error with respect to a principle in this regard. The results of this experiment go a long way to explaining why some slideshows can be so bad: people are often unable to identify good practice in slide design. It also explains why people might be able to distinguish between a slide containing a violation and its corrected counterpart, yet still commit that violation in their own authorship of slides. Basically, they don't understand why the fault has arisen and, therefore, what they can do to avoid it. That's where the remainder of this chapter comes in.

The seven deadly sins of slideshows (and how to atone for them)

In trying to help you produce better slideshows, you'll be relieved to know that I'm not about to cover all 137 violations listed by Kosslyn and colleagues with their associated remedies. Rather, I'm going to use the data they obtained in the second of their studies to identify the most frequently occurring and most annoying issues. To do this, I simply cross-referenced the top five most prevalent and top five most annoying violations identified in Kosslyn et al.'s research. Three of the top five most annoying violations also happened to be in the top five most frequent violations (it figures!). This leaves four violations that were exclusive to either the most frequent or most annoying lists. I'm going to cover all seven of them as the sins you need to avoid if you want to prevent your slideshow inducing a mass outbreak of insomnia, head-scratching, face-palming, or combination of all of the above. Given that I've already reviewed the work that motivates why I'm focusing on these seven sins, the closing part of this chapter is going to major on practical advice rather than theory. The advice contained here will be articulated in writing rather than visually. For a comprehensive (and visual) guide to detailed do's and don'ts of slideshows, the reader is referred to the excellent book *Clear and to the point* (Kosslyn, 2007).

Key advice: eliminate extraneous content. Each of your slides needs a specific purpose that determine its contents

Top of the lists of most frequent and most annoying faults with slideshows is when a presenter obscures part/all of their presentation with unnecessary detail. Irrelevant (extraneous) detail increases the intrinsic cognitive load of your slides, making it harder for the reader to extract the important message. Research on multimedia design advocates that you increase relevance (or coherence as they refer to it) simply by removing extraneous information. However, how do you best go about achieving this? It's unlikely that extraneous content finds its way into slides because presenters are trying to make life hard for the audience. Such unnecessary information more likely reflects a presenter getting side-tracked by something of tangential relevance that happens to be interesting. Of course, if such material is interesting enough to side-track the presenter, then it's probably going to have the same effect on the audience (Mayer, Griffith, Jurkowitz & Rothman, 2008). A consequence of not being sufficiently focused in the information you include in your presentation is that it can impede your progress through your slideshow.

9

Key advice: don't take too long to deliver your message

Getting side-tracked by extraneous information often leads to another violation that made the top five in the most annoying presentation faults list, i.e. that the presenter got through the presentation too slowly. So, what can you do to help you filter out the unnecessary (if interesting) detail and maintain the momentum of your presentation. Well, the key here is to be explicit about the specific purpose of each part of your slideshow. This is where having good titles for your slides come in very handy. Frequently, presenters use slides with either no title or a broad phrase. It's wise to think of a slide title as the remit for the slide; the more specific you make it, the less inclined you will be to drift off topic. Doing this also reduces the likelihood that the audience will struggle to see the main point of your slide. Alley, Schreiber, Ramsdell and Muffo (2006) advocate using the Assertion/Evidence approach, whereby a slide title makes an assertion that the contents of the slide must then back up. For example, an assertion/evidence-based title about good practice in producing titles for your slides might be: "Using assertion/evidence-based slide titles keeps the slide contents relevant." That title requires that you address it in the body of the slide and provides a strict filter for its contents. Similarly, it also cues and empowers the audience to examine the contents of the slide with a purpose, i.e. to see how it substantiates the assertion in the slide title. You may remember from the reading and note-taking chapter that reading with a purpose is a very helpful thing to do as part of active learning. Ambiguity begets ambiguity. Give each slide in your presentation a very specific purpose, then audit anything you're contemplating inserting with respect to that purpose. If it ain't contributing very directly to the slide's remit, bin it!

10

Key advice: ensure you give enough exposition; don't assume knowledge of important terms and concepts

The presence of too much information can make it difficult for the audience to see the wood for the trees, but too little information is equally problematical in getting your main point across. Perhaps unsurprisingly, the violation of 'not enough exposition' occupied the number one slot in the most annoying presentation errors list from Kosslyn et al.'s research. Mercifully, it did not also feature in the top five most prevalent errors! Nonetheless, we've all been to at least one presentation that has made us wonder whether we were appropriately qualified to be there! This often occurs because of something we mentioned right back in the first chapter: the hindsight bias. If you recall, this refers to the tendency to view something that has been learned as obvious. This is a real problem in the context of presentations. If the person up front thinks that something is obvious, what do you reckon this does to the chances that they will give it enough exposition for an audience not at their level of knowledge? They'd probably deem such exposition as patronising and, after all, the speaker is supposed to be an expert, right? Surely experts need to display a commensurate level of knowledge in their presentation? I refer you to a theme espoused right at the start of this chapter: the presentation is not about the presenter; it's about the audience. If you want an audience to understand the contents of your presentation, you need to lay down the appropriate knowledge foundations.

The fundamental mistake presenters often make in respect of laying down the appropriate knowledge foundations is to erroneously assume audience familiarity with technical terms and concepts. In correcting this error, there is a useful lesson to be garnered from the multimedia design literature on retraining (e.g. Mayer, Mathias & Wetzell, 2002) called pre-training. Pre-training simply involves familiarising the audience with key technical terms and concepts at the beginning of the presentation. A simple and effective way of achieving this is to use a slide containing a glossary (of sorts) of any key information that serves as a prerequisite for understanding the rest of your slideshow contents. If the audience reaction to this slide indicates you've not pitched your presentation at the right level, it's better to find out at this point (where you can still do something about it) than after your talk is over! Indeed, Apperson, Laws and Scepansky (2008) conducted a questionnaire-based study of students' preferred PowerPoint practices and found that lecturers putting up slides defining key terms and definitions achieved the third highest preference score. This approach is particularly useful with subject-specific terminology or abbreviations. These are often the first things that a knowledgeable presenter throws at an audience, oblivious to the fact that they confuse the heck out of the uninitiated! So, avoid undefined concepts, terminology or abbreviations in your B2B MTG PPTs unless you want your audience thinking WTF!

11

Key advice: exercise caution in using humour and pictures in your presentation

Thus far, the sins we've addressed have predominantly related to the amount of information presented. The remaining slideshow violations have more to do with the way that information is presented. According to Kosslyn et al.'s research, audiences frequently felt that presenters did not inject any humour or illustrations into their slideshows to lighten complex material. Let's deal with the humour element of this complaint first. Arguments have been made within academia that a speaker's delivery should be more akin to a performance than a presentation (e.g. Short & Martin, 2011). Unfortunately, such research has failed to differentiate the contribution of humour from other factors such as audience interaction, mode of presentation, use of personal references, etc. To be fair, it's not even clear if this is possible. Humour is inherently subjective and context bound. For every presentation enhanced by the wittiness of the person up front, there are three more that have been made awkward by someone trying too hard to be funny only to be met with the proverbial tumbleweed blowing across the room. I'm sorry, but I think trying to teach you how to make a slideshow funnier is a non-starter. However, I can address the superordinate thing that is likely responsible for making humour effective. Unlike humour, this can be applied indiscriminately. I refer to the personalisation principle. This signifies the finding that multimedia presentations that are in an informal, conversational style tend to be more conducive to active learning than those given in a formal style. Studies have suggested that making use of this principle can be as simple as inserting possessive adjectives such as the word 'your' into a presentation. For example, say: "extraneous information increases your cognitive load" rather than: "extraneous information increases cognitive load". You can see a review of this kind of research in Ginns, Martin and Marsh (2013).

Being cognisant of the performance aspects of a presentation by, for example, not standing on the spot or hiding behind a lectern is wise. Varying the tone and volume of your voice (when appropriate) makes your audience less likely to view you as a robot. No one roots for robots. Hey, that would make a great car bumper sticker! I should probably get some sleep!

Having addressed the incorporation of humour into your slideshow, let's move on to the use of pictures/illustrations. We've already covered the potential utility of combining text and pictures in reducing cognitive load as part of the rationale for using a slideshow as the multimedia principle (e.g. Mayer, 2014). However, images do not invariably have beneficial effects within presentations, so it's worth providing some broad guidance about using them effectively. The first thing to say is that images are not helpful if the audience cannot see their relevance to the point being made. There is evidence that irrelevant pictures have a deleterious effect on both memory for, and satisfaction with, a presentation's contents (e.g. Bartsch & Cobern, 2003). Just throwing pictures at a presentation in the hope that they will lighten it up will likely only increase the intrinsic cognitive load of your material. If the picture isn't helping, then it's just one more superfluous thing that the audience must process. So, is there a quick and dirty way of filtering pictures for relevance? Well, using the evidence assertion approach as a means of reducing irrelevant content can be applied to pictures as well as text. Garner and Alley (2013) implemented this approach such that the assertion (message) of a slide was presented as a sentence in the slide title. The body of the slide was occupied with a visual depiction of the evidence (support) for that assertion. The role of the presenter was to elaborate on the pictorial contents of the slide. Using this format reduces cognitive load by making use of the visual and verbal coding of information (i.e. dual coding).

The multimedia design literature (e.g. Mayer, 2014) offers some advice on how to exploit dual coding by supporting the audience in generating connections between verbal and visual information. First, presenting visual images with just a verbal narration is more effective than supplementing the image with extensive text descriptions and narration. This is referred to as the redundancy principle. Second, the visual and verbal information must be close together. This is called the contiguity principle. Taken together, these two principles provide a very neat way of assessing the worth of a picture in your slideshow. Simply ask yourself two questions. First, does the picture with a verbal narrative work without the need to festoon it with lots of associated text? Second, can the picture be used without distancing more important text exposition from the assertion being made? If the answer to either or both these questions is no, then consider sticking with text and narration. A picture is supposed to paint 1,000 words, not duplicate them. If it's not making explaining something easier, kindly step away from Google Images!

12

Key advice: your slides should generate a narrative, not serve as a script

Advocating that you avoid the duplication of effort in using pictures and text, leads us onto another sin that featured in both the top five most frequent and annoying presentation error lists. This error involves the presenter reading their presentation word for word from their slides (aka PowerPoint Karaoke). If the potential advantage of using slideshows in presentations comes from utilising visual and verbal codes, then generating two corresponding verbal codes for the audience to process somewhat defeats the object! It creates the impression that the speaker is unprepared. Moreover, it does beg the question of why the speaker dragged the audience to a venue only to watch them read from their slides. They could have simply posted the slides on the internet for them to read in the comfort of their own homes! There are several things you can do to help ensure that you don't fall into the PowerPoint Karaoke trap. First, and most obviously, start with the thing that empowers PowerPoint Karaoke: the content of the slides you're using. You should view your slides as the catalyst for verbal explanation, not a script. As Garner et al. (2014) point out, the more words you cram into a slide, the more you will be tempted to read from it. That's to say nothing of the fact that you'll have to use a font size so small that no one in the back row will be able to read your slides without the loan of a telescope from NASA. The simplest way of avoiding this is to restrict yourself to using a large font. If you specify a minimum 28-point font size, you physically can't cram a script into a slide. This will force you to use bullet points to make assertions that require elaboration. Having done that, your job is then to rehearse your talk using these bullet points to ensure they are effective as prompts for you to provide the relevant exposition verbally. Going beyond the contents of slides to provide examples, elaborate on points and provide the basis for discussion, topped the list of student preferences in the Apperson et al. study. Chances are, doing this will be very uncomfortable for you at first. Cast your minds back to Chapter I where we covered the illusion of knowing, which is caused by having the question and answers available to you when reviewing material. Well, slides with proper bullet points don't provide all the answers; that's up to you! Good slides obviate the illusion of knowing and serve as a litmus test for whether you really know what you're talking about. If you can't expand on a bullet point without recourse to a script, then you're not sufficiently familiar with the material. If you're reading from a script, you're neither looking at the audience, nor projecting your voice in their direction. You're also eroding their good-will towards you. Watching someone read from a script rightly invites questions about the presenter's level of knowledge and thus their suitability to give the presentation in the first place. What you say to an audience doesn't have to be perfect, but it should never be scripted. Don't be frightened of making a few bumbles. Remember the spotlight effect: your slip ups are far less conspicuous than you think!

Even when a presenter is using their slideshow to highlight points rather than project a script, it's still eminently possible for them to over-egg the pudding. Another sin that made both the top five most frequent and annoying presentation error lists were slides that contained too much information to absorb before the next slide was presented. A simple cause of this occurs when the presenter festoons a slide with too many individual bullet points and overloads the audience's working memory capacity. Recall that the average number of units that an individual can retain in their working memory is seven, plus or minus two. So, a slide with seven bullet points is hardly under-burdening the audience. Consider setting a limit on the number of bullet points used on any slide to a maximum of five (including the title).

Key advice: get the audience to make use of the information you present

Of course, excessive use of bullet points is not the only impediment to an audience being able to absorb the contents of one slide before the next one is put up. Problems of this nature can also occur when the speaker forgets that the conditions they enjoyed when swotting up for their presentation are very different from those experienced by their audience! For example, the presenter could use strategies to foster active engagement with the material (e.g. elaborative interrogation and self-testing) at their leisure when they were learning about it. However, they often don't afford their audience the same opportunities in giving their presentation, even though slideshow creation software offers ample scope to do this (Berk, 2011). One of the things I advocated in the first half of this chapter was to ask the audience questions as a means of giving them an incentive to listen to you. Questions can also be placed on slides following the exposition of content to help the audience actively engage with the material being presented. Gier and Kreiner (2009) found that PowerPoint presentations featuring interpolated content-based questions resulted in higher levels of student performance on quizzes based on that topic and in subsequent examinations. Similar results were obtained by Szpunar, Khan and Schacter (2013). The advent of free polling software combined with the pervasiveness of mobile phone ownership also creates opportunities for an entire audience to respond to content-based quizzes. Using polling software also gives the presenter an informed way of gauging whether the audience is following them. You might think that the incorporation of such software into your presentation will render you more of a hostage to technology than your slideshow paraphernalia already makes you. If so, then a simple slide with an exercise that asks the audience to apply what they have learned can do the trick. It all comes back to that basic principle of getting the audience involved with the contents of your presentation. Try and ensure that your slideshow challenges your audience to do something with the material you're presenting.

14

Key advice: don't use presentation effects unless they have a useful and consistent meaning

Not giving an audience enough opportunity to process the message of a slide before moving onto the next one can be a problem. However, sometimes the issue is more related to a failure to highlight the take-home message of a slide. This is reflected in a fault that appeared in the most frequent errors list of Kosslyn et al.'s research, i.e. the presenter did not use a pointer or otherwise direct audience attention to important details. A common scenario is that in displaying slides that contain several different elements (e.g. text-based bullet points) the presenter displays all of the slide simultaneously. Since attention is naturally drawn to things that appear different, visually equivalent text is assumed to be equally important. Therefore, the audience examines the contents of the whole slide from beginning to end, rather than direct their attention to which aspect of the slide the presenter is currently talking about. This is not ideal, as the lack of contiguity between the visual and verbal codes of a component of a slide make it harder for the audience to process that information. An easy way around this is to use animation to present individual components of a slide successively and then remove (or mute) them as you move on to the next component. Multimedia research refers to such strategies as signalling (Mayer, 2014). Used deliberately and appropriately, signalling can be a powerful way of making sure the attention of your audience is directed to the most important aspects of your slides. At the very least, it's a good thing to know about so you can avoid inadvertently directing the audience to less important parts of your slides via arbitrary use of font style, colour or size. As an example, how often have you made the heading of each of your slides larger than the content? Do your headings always contain the most important message of your slides? If they don't, your use of signalling is not optimal.

Signalling works because of what Kosslyn et al. refer to as the principle of informative change. This states that people make inferences about the significance of changes in the visual properties of how something is presented to them. These inferences can be helpful or harmful to your message, depending on how appropriate they are and the consistency with which they are used. As an example, let's say that you have consistently used an animation to introduce new elements on your slides. If you arbitrarily change that animation, your audience is likely to assume that you've done this for a reason. They will then try and figure out this reason at the expense of concentrating on the content you're delivering. So, before you crack out the crazy animations, exotic fonts, and slideshow sound effects, ask yourself three things. First, am I drawing attention to the right part of my slide? Second, is the significance of the effect I'm using obvious and appropriate to the meaning of the information I'm conveying? Third, am I being consistent in its use, i.e. does it signal the same thing each time it appears? As is the general rule with presentations, simpler is often better. Just because you can make that text glow neon, rotate 360 degrees and exit screen left to the sound of applause doesn't mean you should! If nothing else, heeding this advice will save you hours in front of PowerPoint, tearing your hair out in the process of getting your slideshow animations to start and end on cue! Trust me, I've been there!

Summary

Prospering with presentations

From the outset of this chapter, I've argued that the primary purpose of a presentation is to catalyse learning for the audience. Effective presenters are those who orient the delivery of their presentation and their visual aids in a manner most conducive to promoting learning. Let's summarise the key advice contained within this chapter on how you can achieve this.

Satisfying the goals of a presentation

- Give your audience a reason to engage with your presentation. You can motivate people to attend to you by giving the information you present an obvious use from the outset. For example, try opening your session by challenging the audience with a question that you can frame the contents of your presentation as the answer to.
- Provide a clear structure and narrative in your presentation. Presentations that just throw information at the audience and lack a discernible and logical structure are hard to absorb. Start with an outline slide where you explicitly state the contents of your presentation and the way they will be organised into a narrative. Signpost where you are in relation to your outline throughout your presentation.
- Keep the amount of information you present manageable. Try thinking of a key objective for each part of your presentation and audit the information you include purely in terms of how concisely it supports that objective. Avoid including material for the purposes of intellectual vanity.
- Maintain audience engagement. Audience concentration tends to drift when they become habituated to presentations where their involvement is neither required, nor invited. Try interspersing your presentation with activities that require the audience to do something with its contents e.g. a demonstration, Q&A, or quiz.

Improving your slideshows

- Make sure each of your slides has a clear main point; avoid tangentially relevant information. Try making the main point of your slides explicit in their titles. This helps you focus on spending the body of your slides addressing the main point being made, rather than getting side-tracked by the minutiae.

- Make sure you give your audience enough exposition of important concepts and terminology. Try using an initial slide as a glossary of concepts/terms/abbreviations required to understand the contents of your presentation. This will enable you to check your assumptions about the level of your audience's knowledge and fill in any gaps.
- Personalise your presentation. An easy (if rather superficial) way of achieving this is to use personal pronouns such as 'you' and 'your' in the language of your presentation. Pictures can be very helpful in conveying information, but restrict their use to where they are relevant, not simply duplicating text and can be presented contiguously with related expository material.
- Ensure that your slides serve as narrative generators, not scripts! Do not just read off your slides. Design text-based slide contents as your prompts for verbal explanation, then rehearse your talk using them. If you cannot achieve this, then you're not yet familiar enough with the subject matter covered in the applicable slide and need to refer to your reading. If you're confident in your knowledge, but a little rusty in your articulation, a few practice runs will help you rectify that.
- Ensure that your slides give the audience the opportunity to absorb their main messages. Try limiting the number of individual elements on a slide to a maximum of five (including the title). Interpolate slides with activities that require the audience to do something with the information they have been given. For example, ask them to apply the contents of a slide in the resolution of a relevant problem.
- Ensure that you use visual cues appropriately to direct the audience's attention. Try selectively revealing elements of a slide as you come to them, then conceal them when you move onto the next element. Use text effects and animations sparingly, appropriately and consistently so they convey meaning. Do not use such features randomly or arbitrarily.

Most, if not all, of us can think of a time when we have had to sit through a presentation that has made us wonder if we had perhaps wronged the presenter in a previous life and were now getting our comeuppance. Unfortunately, research from the likes of Stephen Kosslyn and his colleagues suggests that the principles of good presentation practice are not intuitive. Furthermore, being able to identify and grumble about presentation flaws doesn't necessarily mean we're empowered to fix them. The purpose of this chapter has been to elucidate some key advice on giving effective presentations. Implementing this advice is not going to make presentations a piece of cake for you overnight. However, making life easier for you is not the objective. Applying the advice given in this chapter will quickly make life easier for your audience and that is, ultimately, what makes for an effective presentation.

References

Alley, M., Schreiber, M., Ramsdell, K. & Muffo, J. (2006). How the design of headlines in presentation slides affects audience retention. *Technical Communication, 53*(2), 225–234.

Apperson, J. M., Laws, E. L. & Scepansky, J. A. (2008). An assessment of student preferences for PowerPoint presentation structure in undergraduate courses. *Computers & Education, 50*(1), 148–153.

Atkinson, R. C. & Shiffrin, R. M. (1968). Human memory: A proposed system and its control processes. In *Psychology of learning and motivation* (Vol. 2, pp. 89–195). Academic Press.

Baddeley, A. D. & Hitch, G. (1974). Working memory. In *Psychology of learning and motivation* (Vol. 8, pp. 47–89). Academic Press.

Bartsch, R. A. & Cobern, K. M. (2003). Effectiveness of PowerPoint presentations in lectures. *Computers & Education, 41*(1), 77–86.

Berk, R. A. (2011). Research on PowerPoint: From basic features to multimedia. *International Journal of Technology in Teaching & Learning, 7*(1), 24–35.

Bower, G. H., Clark, M. C., Lesgold, A. M. & Winzenz, D. (1969). Hierarchical retrieval schemes in recall of categorized word lists. *Journal of Verbal Learning and Verbal Behavior, 8*(3), 323–343.

Bradbury, N. A. (2016). Attention span during lectures: 8 seconds, 10 minutes, or more? *Adv Physiol Educ, 40*(4), 509–513.

Bui, D. C. & McDaniel, M. A. (2015). Enhancing learning during lecture note-taking using outlines and illustrative diagrams. *Journal of Applied Research in Memory and Cognition, 4*(2), 129–135.

Bunce, D. M., Flens, E. A. & Neiles, K. Y. (2010). How long can students pay attention in class? A study of student attention decline using clickers. *Journal of Chemical Education, 8*.

Copeland, H. L., Longworth, D. L., Hewson, M. G. & Stoller, J. K. (2000). Successful lecturing: A prospective study to validate attributes of the effective medical lecture. *Journal of General Internal Medicine, 15*(6), 366–371.

Dietz-Uhler, B. & Lanter, J. R. (2009). Using the four-questions technique to enhance learning. *Teaching of Psychology*, *36*(1), 38–41.

Freeman, S., Eddy, S. L., McDonough, M., Smith, M. K., Okoroafor, N., Jordt, H. & Wenderoth, M. P. (2014). Active learning increases student performance in science, engineering, and mathematics. *Proceedings of the National Academy of Sciences*, *111*(23), 8410–8415.

Garner, J., & Alley, M. (2013). How the design of presentation slides affects audience comprehension: A case for the assertion-evidence approach. *International Journal of Engineering Education*, *29*(6), 1564–1579.

Gier, V. S. & Kreiner, D. S. (2009). Incorporating active learning with PowerPoint-based lectures using content-based questions. *Teaching of Psychology*, *36*(2), 134–139.

Ginns, P., Martin, A. J. & Marsh, H. W. (2013). Designing instructional text in a conversational style: A meta-analysis. *Educational Psychology Review*, *25*(4), 445–472.

Hartley, J. & Davies, I. K. (1978). Note-taking: A critical review. *Programmed Learning and Educational Technology*, *15*(3), 207–224.

Kosslyn, S. M. (2007). *Clear and to the point: 8 psychological principles for compelling PowerPoint presentations*. Oxford University Press.

Kosslyn, S. M., Kievit, R. A., Russell, A. G. & Shephard, J. M. (2012). PowerPoint® presentation flaws and failures: A psychological analysis. *Frontiers in Psychology*, *3*, 1–22.

Mann, S. & Robinson, A. (2009). Boredom in the lecture theatre: An investigation into the contributors, moderators and outcomes of boredom amongst university students. *British Educational Research Journal*, *35*(2), 243–258.

Mayer, R. E. (2009). *Multimedia learning* (2nd edn). New York: Cambridge University Press.

Mayer, R. E. (2014). Research based principles for designing multimedia instruction. In V. A. Benassi, C. E. Overson & C. M. Hakala (Eds.), *Applying science of learning in education: Infusing psychological science into the curriculum*. Retrieved from http://teachpsych.org/ebooks/asle2014/index.php.

Mayer, R. E., Griffith, E., Jurkowitz, I. T. & Rothman, D. (2008). Increased interestingness of extraneous details in a multimedia science presentation leads to decreased learning. *Journal of Experimental Psychology: Applied*, *14*(4), 329–339.

Mayer, R. E., Mathias, A. & Wetzell, K. (2002). Fostering understanding of multimedia messages through pre-training: Evidence for a two-stage theory of mental model construction. *Journal of Experimental Psychology: Applied*, *8*(3), 147–154.

Miller, G. A. (1956). The magical number seven, plus or minus two: Some limits on our capacity for processing information. *Psychological Review*, *63*(2), 81–97.

Paivio, A. (1971). Imagery and language. In *Imagery* (pp. 7–32). Academic Press.

Sharp, J. G., Hemmings, B., Kay, R., Murphy, B. & Elliott, S. (2017). Academic boredom among students in higher education: A mixed-methods exploration of characteristics, contributors and consequences. *Journal of Further and Higher Education*, *41*(5), 657–677.

Short, F. & Martin, J. (2011). Presentation vs. performance: Effects of lecturing style in higher education on student preference and student learning. *Psychology Teaching Review*, *17*(2), 71–82.

Sweller, J. (1988). Cognitive load during problem solving: Effects on learning. *Cognitive Science*, *12*(2), 257–285.

Sweller, J. (2005). Implications of cognitive load theory for multimedia learning. In R. E. Mayer (Ed.), *The Cambridge handbook of multimedia learning* (pp. 19–30). Cambridge University Press.

Szpunar, K. K., Khan, N. Y. & Schacter, D. L. (2013). Interpolated memory tests reduce mind wandering and improve learning of online lectures. *Proceedings of the National Academy of Sciences*, *110*(16), 6313–6317.

Thielsch, M. T. & Perabo, I. (2012). Use and evaluation of presentation software. *Technical Communication*, *59*(2), 112–123.

Tofade, T., Elsner, J. & Haines, S. T. (2013). Best practice strategies for effective use of questions as a teaching tool. *American Journal of Pharmaceutical Education*, *77*(7), 1–9.

Tufte, E. (2003). PowerPoint is evil. *Wired Magazine*, September. Retrieved from www.wired.com/2003/09/ppt2/.

Wilson, K. & Korn, J. H. (2007). Attention during lectures: Beyond ten minutes. *Teaching of Psychology*, *34*(2), 85–89.

Revision

Cleaning up a dirty word

For the things we have to learn before we can do them,
we learn by doing them.

Aristotle

1

Key advice: your intention to learn matters less than how you do it

Hold it right there! If you've skipped right to this chapter hoping that you can use its contents to circumvent reading the rest of the book, you might want to think again! The most fundamental mistake you can make in your approach to revision is to think of it as being disassociated from the process of learning. There is no revision silver bullet that can offset a lack of prior engagement with your course materials. Revision is all about consolidating what you have been learning. Effective revision requires that you understand the importance of metacognition for your studies (Chapter I). It entails knowing how to avoid succumbing to procrastination (Chapter II). It involves knowing how to read and take notes effectively (Chapter III) and so forth. If you've not already been going about your studies in an efficient manner, you're making revising a much harder and more frustrating task. The advice imparted in the previous chapters of this book is directly applicable to revision and should be your first port of call before reading any further.

You might be inclined to think that continuing to extol the benefits of effective study practice at this late stage is a bit surplus to requirements. Surely, examinations bolster the strength of your impetus to learn and this will offset any remaining shortcomings in your studying methods? Admittedly, this sounds good intuitively, but this idea was dispelled long ago by one of the classic studies in memory research (Hyde & Jenkins, 1969). They performed a version of Craik and Tulving's (1975) levels of processing experiment, discussed back in Chapter III. Participants were asked to commit a list of words to memory under one of two processing conditions. Participants assigned to the visual (shallow) processing condition were asked to assess whether each word on the list contained the letter 'e'. Participants assigned to the semantic (deep) processing condition were asked to rate each word on the list according to its pleasantness. Here's the twist: only half of the participants in each of the two processing conditions were told they should learn the word list because their ability to recall them was going to be tested. This half of the participants was looking at the word list with the intention to learn its contents. The other half of the participants were given no instructions to learn the list, or warning of the forthcoming test. They were looking at the word list incidentally; there was no explicit intention to learn and no expectation that learning would be tested. The results were clear: the intention to learn did not significantly affect recall performance. What mattered to the ability of the participants to recall the words on the list was whether they processed them using visual (shallow) or semantic (deep) processing. As expected, the performance of those assigned to the semantic (deep) processing condition was superior. The lesson for you is clear: exams may well bolster the strength of your intention to learn, but it's the approach you take in your learning that matters. Ineffective approaches don't become effective just because you're using them in earnest. In contrast, effective approaches remain effective even when you're looking at material in a more incidental fashion. With that in mind, the purpose of this chapter is to provide some practical advice on how you can orient your revision practices to consolidate and best deploy what you have previously learned about studying effectively. I'm afraid that none of the advice in this chapter will make your revision easier to implement. However, after reading this chapter I hope I will have convinced you that easy and effective are not synonymous when it comes to revision (and learning generally).

Jamais vu: it's what happens when you cram

You've most likely been there: 11 pm before the night of the big exam, running through the cramming checklist. Vast array of reading materials? Check. Constant supply of strong coffee? Check. Nagging feeling that despite having been in this scenario many times before, it somehow seems like a fresh ordeal every time? Check. Sure enough, the literature indicates that students frequently use the revision strategy of cramming (e.g. McIntyre & Munson, 2008). Think back to the last exam you crammed for. Did you pass? Maybe you even got a good mark? It might surprise you to learn that there is evidence that cramming is not necessarily a completely ineffectual study strategy, at least for the short-term retention of material (e.g. Simon & Bjork, 2001). So, maybe cramming isn't such a bad thing? Perhaps you should just put up with the transient stress and hardship and stick with what you know? However, before you do that, I have two questions for you. First, how much of the material you crammed can you still remember? Second, have you ever really tried another approach?

2

Key advice: spacing out your revision is more effective than cramming

Research on cramming goes back over a century to the seminal work of one of the pioneers of psychology, Hermann Ebbinghaus. Relax, I'm not about to occupy the next 20 pages giving a full historical account of this area of research. For our purposes, picking out a few highlights will do. Ebbinghaus (1885) was the first person to compare the rehearsal of information occurring over spaced out intervals (distributed practice) and the rehearsal of information without such intervals (massed learning, also known as cramming). He demonstrated memory for items that were rehearsed via distributed practice was superior to memory for items rehearsed via massed learning. This finding was to become one of the most robust and well-established in all of cognitive psychology and is referred to as the spacing effect (for a review, see Küpper-Tetzel, 2014).

Researchers were keen to capitalise on the spacing effect and examine if it would also work alongside the use of study methods other than just the rehearsal of information. Could the spacing effect also enhance the benefits of the testing effect (i.e. retrieval practice) in studying? This possibility raised an additional question: what was the optimal spacing between each instance of retrieval practice? Was it better to keep them equally spaced or successively increase them? Landauer and Bjork (1978) addressed this question in what was to become a landmark study into the spacing of retrieval practice. In a first experiment, participants were shown cards bearing fictitious names (i.e. first and last name pairings) in a study trial. There would be three further presentations of each of the pairings in repeated test trials. In these test trials one of the names from each pair would be missing on the card, so the participants had to recall the missing name. In doing this they were using retrieval practice to commit the name pairings to memory. The test trials were interspersed with the presentation of other name pairings. The experimenters manipulated the intervals between the initial study trial and the repeated tests by varying the number of other name pairings they were interspersed with. Participants assigned to a control condition were not given the opportunity to practice retrieving any of the name pairs. In the equally spaced retrieval condition the participants would see the first test trial after the presentation of five other pairings, then once more after five further pairings and then a final time after another five pairings. In contrast, participants in the expanding retrieval practice condition saw the first test trial after the presentation of one other pairing, then once more after four further pairings and then a final time after another ten pairings. Therefore, the total time over which the retrieval opportunities occurred was the same for both retrieval practice conditions. Only the distribution of the retrieval opportunities was varied: equally spaced versus increasing. After a period of 30 minutes, the participants' memory for the first and last name pairings was assessed with a final test. As one would hope, the participants in both the equal and expanding retrieval practice groups remembered significantly more first and last name pairs than those in the control group. However, the participants in the expanding interval retrieval condition also exhibited better recall of the name pairings than those in the equally spaced retrieval condition. A second experiment by Landauer and Bjork replicated this finding with stimuli that involved name and face pairings.

In the following decades, the literature provided pretty much unanimous support for the use of spaced retrieval practice as a study method (e.g. see Cepeda, Pashler, Vul, Wixted & Rohrer, 2006 for a review). However, research comparing expanding versus equal interval retrieval practice was more equivocal. For example, Karpicke and Roediger III (2007) replicated the basic experimental set up of Landauer and Bjork (1978) but used vocabulary pairs, rather than first/last name and name/face pairs. They also incorporated two retention periods before administering the final test: ten minutes and two days. Their findings also indicated that participants in the expanding interval retrieval condition remembered more pairs than those in the equally spaced retrieval condition. However, this only applied to participants who were given the final test ten minutes after the last retrieval practice. When participants were given a test two days after the final retrieval practice, the individuals in the equal interval retrieval condition remembered more pairs than those in the expanding interval retrieval condition.

You'll have, no doubt, noticed that the above two experiments both involved memory for pairs of stimuli. Admittedly, this is not especially representative of much of the material you'll have to remember for examinations. However, research has also examined recall of factual information contained within text. For example, Karpicke and Roediger (2010) asked participants to read passages of text and then gave them three retrieval practice opportunities, or no retrieval practice. For those who could practice retrieving the contents of the text, the experimenters manipulated whether this practice occurred on an equal or expanding interval basis. They also manipulated whether the participants got feedback on their performance after each attempt. Four minutes after the final retrieval practice, participants were asked to write down as much of the text as they could remember. They also attempted to recall the contents of the text again one week later. The results indicated that spaced retrieval practice resulted in significantly better factual recall than simply reviewing the text once before taking the test. No surprises there! Participants who had received feedback on the results of their retrieval practices exhibited better memory for the text than those who did not receive feedback. Again, no big surprises. However, there were no significant differences in the recall performance of the participants in the equal spaced and expanding interval retrieval practice conditions. Both approaches enhanced the long-term retention of the text.

3

Key advice: increasing the intervals over which you try and retain information can help you revise similar material

So, should you dispense with the idea of spacing your revision sessions out at increasing intervals? Well, maybe not. Your memory for the things you study is affected by more than just the passage of time that passes between studying and the exam. It's also highly influenced by what you do during this period. Have you ever had the following experience? You're studying one aspect of a topic and then move onto a related aspect, before realising that you can't remember a damned thing of what you were looking at first? If so, you've just demonstrated something called retrospective interference. Your current learning has interfered with your ability to remember something you were previously learning. Storm, Bjork and Storm (2010) theorised that the reason expanded interval retrieval practice wasn't consistently proving superior to its equal interval counterpart was because experiments weren't accounting for the effects of interference. In a typical study, the interval between each retrieval practice was filled with a distraction task that was completely unrelated (e.g. reading or viewing unrelated content). Storm et al. reasoned that if the intervals between each retrieval practice contained a task that would interfere with the material being studied, then that material would become more vulnerable to forgetting. Under these circumstances, they argued that the benefits of expanded interval retrieval practice would become apparent. Storm et al. set out to test this hypothesis by first conducting an experiment to see if they could replicate the findings of Karpicke and Roediger (2010). They used a similar experimental set up in which participants were asked to study a passage of text under either equally spaced or expanding interval retrieval practice conditions. In the intervals between retrieval practice, the participants read a passage of text on an unrelated topic. They were then given a final test to assess their recall of the material one week later. Consistent with the findings of Karpicke and Roediger (2010) Storm et al. found no differences in the recall of information between participants in the equal and expanding interval retrieval practice conditions. However, they then repeated the initial experiment, but this time they changed what the participants read in the intervals between their retrieval practice. In this experiment, they would be reading a similar topic in the intervals as the one they were studying. This increase in similarity between the topics used for study and during the intervals increased the likelihood of retrospective interference occurring. In other words, the study material was now more vulnerable to being forgotten. Storm et al. found that participants in the expanding interval retrieval practice condition recalled around twice as much of the studied material as those in the equal interval retrieval practice condition. They concluded that expanded interval retrieval practice, rather than being advantageous in all conditions, pays dividends when studied material is at greater risk of interference from other sources.

The principal take-home message for your revision practice thus far is that it's more effective to space your study out than to cram. It's not that cramming doesn't work per se; it just doesn't work as well as spacing. The other downside to cramming is that the information committed to memory often has a short lifespan, so it's not an ideal approach if the goal is to retain that information past the exam! It's the perceived short-term effectiveness and simplicity of cramming that lulls people into thinking it is a good revision option. However, as we've frequently noted in this book, perception and reality are often not one and the same thing. Our tendency to look favourably on cramming might also reflect the fact that when we do it, it's likely because we've just left it too late to revise any other way. It would be corrosive to our confidence going into an exam to think of cramming in a negative light as we're walking into the exam room having used it to revise! Psychologists call this post-hoc rationalisation. Studies such as Toppino and Cohen (2010) indicate that when given the option to choose between cramming versus spaced study, people tend to opt for the latter. The lesson for you is that you need to give yourself the option of taking advantage of using the spacing effect by planning your revision in advance. A quick recap of some of the advice on avoiding procrastination in Chapter II might be in order.

In planning the spacing of your revision, don't fret over trying to figure out the optimal interval length between your revision sessions. Research such as that by Cepeda, Vul, Rohrer, Wixted and Pashler (2008) indicates there isn't a single optimal figure. Simple guidelines on scheduling your revision intervals are sufficient. In terms of the number of intervals you use, too few is more of a problem than too many. If you have 12 hours to dedicate to a topic and three weeks before the exam, it's better to use six two-hour sessions than two six-hour sessions. In terms of the timing between your intervals, obviously don't make things too easy to recall. That feeling of confidence in your memory you get in reviewing material one minute after you've read it is likely an illusion of knowing (an old friend from Chapter I). Incorporate retrieval practice into your spaced studying and give yourself feedback on your performance. The positive effects of retrieval practice on learning are additive with those of spacing. Using retrieval practice also gives you evidence upon which you can judge your revision progress. Finally, when studying a series of topics that are similar, or feature overlap, it's a good idea to increase the spacing of the intervals between your revision sessions. Doing this helps to negate memory interference between similar material. Again, don't obsess over the size of increase in the spacing between study intervals. Think in terms of moving from minutes, to hours to days, using your performance on retrieval practice as the basis for your progression.

Harnessing context: it's all relative, relatively

Key advice: interleaving your studying can help you distinguish and remember similar material

Thus far we have looked at how you might distribute the time you have available for your revision. However, the literature on expanded interval practice and interference alludes to another one of your revision considerations: how you distribute the subject matter of your revision. Any topic can be broken down into sub-topics, terms, concepts, principles, etc. For example, if we were revising for a paper on the topic of memory enhancement techniques we might encounter concepts such as: elaboration; retrieval practice; distributed practice and summarisation. Broadly speaking we could expose ourselves to these concepts in one of two ways: blocking or interleaving. With the blocking approach our exposure to each concept would be grouped together. For example, we would focus on learning the definition of elaboration, then an example of its use, then a representative piece of evidence concerning its effectiveness. After we had done this for the concept of elaboration, we would use the same approach for each of the remaining concepts of retrieval practice, distributed practice and summarisation in turn. The alternative to this would be to use the interleaved approach, where our exposure is not grouped by the concepts, but rather by sub-topics, questions or themes. Taking an interleaved approach to our memory enhancement topic would involve us alternating between the concepts. For example, we might start by learning about the definitions of elaboration, retrieval practice, distributed practice and summarisation. After we had done this, we would then repeat the process by moving across the concepts to learn about examples of each of them. Then, finally, we would look at the evidence for the effectiveness of each of the concepts in turn. Literature on the relative efficacy of the blocked versus interleaved approach to studying is a fairly recent development in cognitive psychology. However, research is beginning to suggest that interleaving your revision might be a useful strategy, particularly when learning about similar concepts, terms, principles or skills.

A representative example of evidence for interleaving was provided by Kornell and Bjork (2008). In this research, students were given the challenging task of learning to distinguish between the subtly different styles of a series of artists. In one of their experiments, participants were shown six examples of paintings from six artists, with each example baring the name of its creator. They achieved this using either blocked or interleaved presentation. Participants assigned to the blocked presentation condition would see all six examples from the first painter, before moving onto the six examples from the next painter and so on. In contrast, participants in the interleaved group would see the first example from the first painter, then the first example from the second painter and so on. They would repeat this process until they had been exposed to all six examples of the work from each of the six artists. This learning phase of the experiment was followed by a distraction task involving mental arithmetic. The experiment concluded with the test phase in which participants were shown previously unseen examples of work from each artist and asked to identify who was responsible for it. Participants who were exposed to the example pictures via interleaved presentation were better at identifying which artist was responsible for the previously unseen pictures used in the test phase of the experiment.

At first glance, Kornell and Bjork's experiment might seem a little esoteric, or only applicable to students of fine art. However, using works of art was a clever way to demonstrate the application of memory to the process of learning by examples. Psychologists call this inductive learning and it's a big part of the process of education, especially in distinguishing between things that seem similar at first glance. The participants in the above study had not previously seen the pictures featured in the test phase of the experiment. Therefore, they couldn't simply retrieve a memory of the corresponding picture from when they were viewing the paintings in the experiment's learning phase. To identify the artist responsible for each painting, they had to view each artist as a category and their work a member of that category. Any category has distinctive and stable features that define what belongs in it. In the context of painting, it's the style of the artist (e.g. their choice of colours, the boldness of their brush strokes, etc.) that constitute those features. In viewing examples of the work of each artist, participants were learning to distinguish between their work, i.e. differentiate between different categories of information. This is where interleaving is thought to exert its effect. If you have several similar sources of information, comparing and contrasting each source makes it easier to see the differences. Interleaving makes this process easier by alternating between examples taken from each of the sources of information.

You may have noticed the overlap between the interleaving and spacing approaches. Any effort to use interleaving inherently also involves spacing. If you have three concepts to learn and wanted to use interleaving, you would likely alternate between them by moving from the first, to the second, to the third and then repeat this process. In this scenario, each of your exposures to any of the three concepts will be naturally spaced out by the time you allot to studying the other two concepts. In contrast, blocked presentation doesn't, by default, benefit from the spacing effect. You might, therefore, wonder whether interleaving has any benefits over and above those of the spacing effect. Research has addressed this by comparing learning under blocked versus interleaved conditions whilst controlling for the effects of spacing. For example, Kang and Pashler (2012) used the same artist identification experimental approach as Kornell and Bjork. However, in their blocked exposure condition, the presentation of each example from a given artist was interspersed with an unrelated cartoon drawing. This manipulation meant that the participants in the blocked and interleaved presentation conditions all benefited from the spacing effect. Thus, any differences in performance between these two conditions must be due to the additional effect of interleaving. Sure enough, in the test phase of the experiment, students who had studied the work of the artists in the interleaved condition correctly matched them with previously unseen examples of their work more often than students in the blocked condition.

Although, it's a relatively recent area of study, research on interleaving is producing consistently positive results (see Carvalho & Goldstone, 2014). It's certainly worth experimenting with this approach when revising, but there are some caveats as to when you can use it to optimal effect. Interleaving seems to bias attention towards looking for differences. Therefore, it's most effective when you're studying concepts that are similar, i.e. that require more effort to distinguish from each other. It's also effective under conditions where you are actively involved in assigning information to a category. Conversely, blocking seems to bias attention towards looking for similarities, so it's more suited to situations where concepts can be more easily distinguished, or when category membership has been pre-determined (Carvalho & Goldstone, 2015). As with the spacing method, it's a good idea to use retrieval practice as a measure of your learning when using the interleaving approach. A word of warning, when you first start using interleaving it might seem less effective, counter-intuitive or more effort than it's worth. Indeed, research such as Rohrer and Taylor (2007) illustrated that participants using interleaving achieved lower scores in practice tests, but then went on to obtain better final test scores. As Soderstrom and Bjork (2015) point out, this reflects the fact that people often misinterpret mistakes made during practice or acquisition as signs of an ineffective approach to learning. Actually, such mistakes are helpful to learning because they put a dent in short term measures of performance. In doing this they identify a problem to be resolved. It's the academic equivalent of the old stage show adage that if the dress rehearsal goes badly, the opening night goes well. Despite this, research has also shown that people have persisted in reporting the grouped presentation of stimulus to be more effective than interleaving even though their final test results suggest otherwise (e.g. Kornell & Bjork, 2008). This is likely due to ease of implementation being confused with effectiveness. Sure, it's more difficult to space out your revision, interleave similar topics and use retrieval practice to assess your progress than just cram, block topics together and hope for the best at the exam. However, when it comes to your choice of revision methods, think in terms of a visit to the gym: you need to sweat a bit for it to really work! Methods like spacing, interleaving and practice retrieval create what Bjork and Bjork (2011) refer to as desirable difficulty; they trade a bit of short-term pain for a good amount of long-term gain.

5

Key advice: recreating the most salient feature of the exam room in your study environment can help with your memory

Thus far, we've looked at how you can manipulate when you study and what you study to enhance your revision practices, but what about where you study? The research on interleaving is an example of the importance of the relationship between what is currently being studied and what preceded it (i.e. the stimuli context) for memory. However, research on memory has also examined the effect of the environmental context in which information is studied. So, we should examine if such research has any implications for the set-up of your revision environment. Godden and Baddeley (1975) conducted a landmark study into the effect of environmental context on memory. The impetus for their experiment came not from psychology, but from a bio-technology based study into working underwater. During this research, it transpired that divers reported having difficulty in recalling things they had learned whilst underwater when they were back on dry land (Egstrom, Weltman, Baddeley, Cuccaro & Willis, 1972). Egstrom et al. suggested this was more likely to be due to the discrepancy between the environments that learning and recall were occurring in, than the underwater conditions just not being conducive to learning per se. Godden and Baddeley argued that learning information underwater or on dry land was an ideal basis upon which to examine the impact of context on memory because the difference between the two environments is so pronounced. They conducted a simple experiment in which they asked divers to memorise word lists and manipulated the congruence of the conditions under which learning and recall occurred. The divers were asked to memorise word lists both on dry land and underwater. They then subsequently attempted to recall these word lists in two conditions. In the congruent condition, the learning and recall occurred in the same environment (e.g. learning and recall both occurred underwater or on land). In the incongruent condition learning and recall happened in different environments (e.g. learning occurred underwater and recall occurred on land or vice versa). The results indicated that the location that the word lists were learned in were not, in and of themselves, important. What mattered was the congruence between the learning and test environments. The divers who learned the lists underwater recalled more words when tested underwater than they did when they were tested on land and vice versa.

The Godden and Baddeley experiment provided a striking demonstration of what psychologists refer to as context dependent memory, which occurs when environmental features are encoded along with the desired information. These features then serve as memory prompts when the individual encounters them at some point in the future. Context dependent memory has been investigated and demonstrated extensively over the last 40-plus years (see Isarida & Isarida, 2014 for a review). Of course, you're wondering about the implications of this line of research for your revision. Does it mean that from now on you should only revise in the same environment that you will sit the exam in? Fortunately, no. Following the Godden and Baddeley study, evidence for the importance of reinstating the entire learning environment when testing memory in order to promote optimal performance was equivocal. Subsequent research revealed that environmental memory prompts take a backseat when the information being studied contains better cues, e.g. when it's meaningful content, studied for longer periods (Isarida, Isarida & Sakai, 2012) and where the immediate environment can be supressed (Smith & Vela, 2001). Put crudely, when you study or take exams, your study materials are much more salient than the environment you're in (assuming you don't study in a circus) and a much better source of memory cues than that environment.

You're relieved, I'm sure, to know that there is nothing to be gained by moving the entire contents of your study into a university exam room to make your learning and test conditions congruent. One lost job for the removal trade, I guess! However, that doesn't mean there is nothing to be gained from the work on context dependent memory. You can benefit from making sure your study environment and the exam room are congruent in some key respects. One important contextual variable that you might want to try and ensure is equated between your study and test environment is ambient noise. Grant et al. (1998) conducted research in which students were asked to study an academic text before taking both a short answer paper and multiple-choice test on their comprehension of the material. The experimenters manipulated whether each participant studied the text in quiet or noisy conditions. The noisy condition of the experiment was produced by playback of a tape recording of the ambient noise at lunchtime within the university cafeteria. Participants then took the tests under noise conditions that were either congruent or incongruent with what they experienced when studying the material. The results indicated that the noise conditions (noisy versus quiet) did not affect test performance in and of themselves. As with the Godden and Baddeley study, what mattered was the congruence between the learning and test environments. Participants who were exposed to background noise when studying, but not when tested (or vice versa) achieved lower test scores than those who were exposed to the same noise conditions when studying and being tested. So, there you have it: research justification for telling anyone you live with to keep quiet when you're studying. If they don't, try gaffer tape! OK, maybe not, but don't try and drown out ambient noise with music. It's not that listening to music when studying would necessarily be a bad thing, if you could also listen to it whilst taking an exam. Unfortunately, taking a stereo into an exam hall is generally frowned upon! This might explain why Gurung (2005) found listening to music as being one of the study habits that negatively correlated with exam performance.

6

Key advice: the benefits of self-testing effect work across different test formats

Thus far, we've looked at the importance of context in terms of the relationship between the different topics you might have to study. We've also looked at context in terms of the relationship between the environments that your studying and examinations take place in. However, what about the contextual relationship between the way you study and the format of the exam you're taking. For example, one of the things that I've advocated extensively in this book is the use of retrieval practice. Does it matter if the format you use for testing your retrieval matches the format of the examination you're taking? Endres and Renkl (2015) examined this very question as part of an attempt to uncover the workings of the testing effect. In their experiment, participants were asked to read three academic pieces of text. Each of these texts was then studied in one of three ways. In a free recall retrieval practice format, the participants were simply asked to write down the contents of the text they had just read from memory. In a short answer retrieval practice format, participants were given a series of short questions about specific aspects of the text. Finally, in a re-study condition, participants simply reread the text without taking any form of quiz. After studying each text, the participants were asked to rate how much mental effort they felt it took to study the material (from 0 to 100%). A week later, they were tested using both the free recall and short answer methods for each of the texts they had studied. The results indicated that both formats of retrieval practice produced superior recall of the texts over simply re-studying (i.e. the testing effect). They also indicated the size of the testing effect was not significantly different between the free recall and short answer retrieval practice formats. Finally, the results revealed that the testing effect did not depend upon congruence between the format of the retrieval practice test and the final test. This seems to be the consensus of the literature on the testing effect (e.g. Karpicke, 2017). Therefore, you shouldn't worry unduly about matching the format of your retrieval practice to that of your exam, nor should you obsess over the type of retrieval practice you use. They key thing seems to be that you use retrieval practice, give yourself feedback on your performance and use that information to ensure you're not making things too easy for yourself.

Master the ordeal by re-creating it

7

Key advice: you must prepare for any additional demands that the format of your exam will make of you over and above factual recall

As we've noted, the consistency between the format of your retrieval practice and your final examination doesn't appear to be critical in your ability to recall subject matter. However, this is not to say that you can disregard the type of exam you are revising for in your approach to revision. Examination formats can test more than simply whether you know your onions! A limitation of the research on retrieval practice is that the final tests used in that research often feature short answer, multiple choice or fill in the blank questions. Rarely are participants asked to write an essay. Not using essays in experimentation is entirely understandable. After all, would you volunteer for a study that involved composing an essay that didn't offer you a princely sum of money in return? Neither would I! Quizzes are much easier ways to quantify learning via a numerical score. Essays are graded too, of course. However, the grade awarded to an essay reflects more than just the demonstration of knowledge; it also reflects the application of that knowledge and the way it's articulated. Therefore, it's important to go into an essay-based exam accustomed to meeting the demands it places on you over and above subject knowledge. Yes, I'm afraid this does mean what you think it means: you're going to have to get some practice in!

There are several very good reasons why practice essay writing will help you develop an understanding of your state of readiness for essay-based exams, nicely articulated by Curcio, Jones and Washington (2007). First, practice essays help you think about what the essay question might be, assuming it's unseen. Thinking of hypothetical exam questions invites you to consider how you might use your knowledge in responding to those questions. Doing this reduces the odds of you being blind-sided by an unexpected question come the examination. Of course, you might not correctly anticipate the examination essay question, but that doesn't matter. Practising planning a response to hypothetical essay questions is valuable in and of itself. You're going to have to plan what you write at the beginning of an essay-based exam whether you've correctly anticipated the question or not. It's just a bit easier if you've guessed correctly!

Of course, if you know what the essay title is in advance of the exam, then that takes the guess work out of the equation. However, this doesn't negate the need to plan how you're going to address the question. Expectations for the quality of the responses to seen exams are often higher than those for unseen exams as, well, it's not like you didn't know what was coming!

Of course, the mark you will get for your essay depends on more than just your planning, it's also determined by the quality of the execution of your plan. Therefore, you should be examining your essay writing performance. That's where the second benefit of essay practice comes in: it helps your work develop in relation to criteria other than just outright knowledge. Retrieval practice will help you gauge whether you have developed the requisite knowledge for an essay question, but it won't indicate whether your essay composition is up to scratch. To achieve this, you need to have a go at a hypothetical essay question and then review your efforts with a copy of the exam essay marking criteria to hand. If you've developed a plan to address an essay title, composing a practice essay based on your plan is an ideal litmus test of its effectiveness.

The third and fourth benefits of practising exam essays occur when you apply essay marking criteria to your efforts. Evaluating your performance empowers you to identify your strengths and weaknesses. For example, you might find out that you tend to neglect developing a narrative in your exam essays in favour of throwing more information at the page. Of course, if you know where your weaknesses lie, you can address them. Curcio et al. found that students who had undergone an essay writing practice intervention prior to a final essay-based examination obtained higher grades than their unpractised counterparts. This was a fortunate outcome, given that the participants in this research were studying law. Had they not benefited from all that additional essay writing practice, the experimenters might have faced a lawsuit for false advertising.

8

Key advice: replicate the constraints of the examination you're taking in practising for that exam

The general format of an exam (e.g. short answer/MCQ/essay) is not the only thing you need to be cognisant of when revising. Within each format of exam, there will be additional conditions that you should also take account of. The duration of the exam is an obvious candidate here. Being able to produce a wonderful practice essay in two hours is all well and good. Unless, that is, the exam is scheduled for an hour! Perhaps you've been composing your practice short answers on a PC. That's OK, assuming you can use a PC in the examination, or can hand-write as fast and accurately as you type. You might be revising for a multiple-choice test with your source materials open. This is all well and good if the exam is an open book format, but it's going to render your revision very vulnerable to erroneous judgments of learning if you can't take materials into the examination room with you. They key message here is that you should replicate the constraints of the examination you're taking in practising for that exam.

Summary

Making revision count, by making your life a little harder

Let's summarise the key advice contained within this chapter on how you can make your revision more effective.

- First, and most importantly, don't think of revision as a substitute for engaging with your lectures and course materials in a timely fashion. Revision is about consolidating what you have been learning previously; it's not supposed to be the point at which you start learning!
- The strength of your intention to learn may be greater as your exams approach, but intention to learn is not the principal determinant of how effectively you learn. It's your approach to studying that matters most. You should always implement the advice from earlier chapters in your revision.
- Avoid cramming. It may feel like it works OK, but spacing your revision out works better. This is particularly true when it comes to retaining knowledge for longer periods. The positive effects of spacing and retrieval practice are additive, so incorporate them both into your approach to revision.
- Don't obsess over the duration of the intervals between each of your spaced revision sessions. As a rule, over a given period of time, it's better to have a larger number of shorter sessions than fewer longer sessions. Also, longer intervals between revision sessions tend to be associated with lengthier retention of knowledge. You can use your performance on retrieval practice

exercises as guidance on how big the intervals between your study sessions should be.

- Where you find yourself studying topics/concepts that are similar it's a good idea to consider expanding the length of the intervals between each of your study sessions. This expanding interval approach seems to be useful in helping prevent what you are currently learning interfere with what you have just learned. As with equally spaced interval studying, use your performance on retrieval practice exercises as guidance on how much you increase the intervals between your study sessions by.
- Where you find yourself studying topics/concepts that are similar, it's also a good idea to try alternating between them within each of your revision sessions (i.e. interleave your revision). This approach is conducive with spotting what makes each topic/concept different and helps you avoid new learning interfering with existing learning.
- Concentrate on orientating your revision environment so that it replicates the most salient features of the exam room. Make sure your study conditions are quiet and undisturbed. Other contextual differences between your revision and exam environments are much less important for your memory and can be easily supressed.
- Although retrieval practice effects translate between different exam formats, it's a good idea to practice your retrieval of information using the same format as your examination, especially when the format of the exam is an essay. This ensures you are practised at both the retrieval of relevant knowledge and demands of the specific exam format on the way you articulate that knowledge.
- You should also incorporate the constraints associated with any exam into your revision. For example, if you have an essay examination of one-hour duration, impose the same time limit on your practice essay attempts. This will avoid you being lulled into a false sense of security by incorporating concessions into your practise that you will not get in the exam itself.

Appropriately enough, this chapter has consolidated a theme that has occurred throughout this book: effective learning requires a premeditated, effortful and evidence-based approach. Revision is often stressful because it illuminates the failings of the methods we've used to study up to that point. All those times we've read our source materials aimlessly, not taken our own notes and not tested ourselves come back to haunt us. Suddenly, we're left with a mountain of material that seems unfamiliar and a short space of time in which to make it familiar. Under these circumstances, it's no wonder that we often end up using methods like cramming, which are easy to implement and seem to get the job done. Of course, this amounts to trying to fix ineffectual study practices with other less than optimal approaches to studying. The central message of the literature on revision is a familiar one. Good practice is defined mainly by the effectiveness, not ease, of its implementation. The advice in this chapter might not be as easy to implement as cramming, but the extra effort you put into its implementation will pay dividends in your grades.

References

Bjork, E. L. & Bjork, R. A. (2011). Making things hard on yourself, but in a good way: Creating desirable difficulties to enhance learning. In M. A. Gernsbacher, R. W. Pew, L. M. Hough & J. R. Pomerantz (Eds.), *Psychology and the real world: Essays illustrating fundamental contributions to society* (pp. 56–64). Worth Publishers.

Carvalho, P. F. & Goldstone, R. L. (2014). Putting category learning in order: Category structure and temporal arrangement affect the benefit of interleaved over blocked study. *Memory & Cognition*, *42*(3), 481–495.

Carvalho, P. F. & Goldstone, R. L. (2015). The benefits of interleaved and blocked study: Different tasks benefit from different schedules of study. *Psychonomic Bulletin & Review*, *22*(1), 281–288.

Cepeda, N. J., Pashler, H., Vul, E., Wixted, J. T. & Rohrer, D. (2006). Distributed practice in verbal recall tasks: A review and quantitative synthesis. *Psychological Bulletin*, *132*(3), 354–380.

Cepeda, N. J., Vul, E., Rohrer, D., Wixted, J. T. & Pashler, H. (2008). Spacing effects in learning: A temporal ridgeline of optimal retention. *Psychological Science*, *19*(11), 1095–1102.

Craik, F. I. & Tulving, E. (1975). Depth of processing and the retention of words in episodic memory. *Journal of Experimental Psychology: General*, *104*(3), 268–294.

Curcio, A. A., Jones, G. T. & Washington, T. M. (2007). Does practice make perfect: An empirical examination of the impact of practice essays on essay exam performance. *Fla. St. UL Rev.*, *35*, 271–313.

Ebbinghaus, H. (1885). *Über das gedächtnis: Untersuchungen zur experimentellen psychologie*. Duncker & Humblot.

Egstrom, G. H., Weltman, G., Baddeley, A. D., Cuccaro, W. J. & Willis, M. A. (1972). Underwater work performance and work tolerance (No. UCLA-ENG-7243). California University, Los Angeles School of Engineering and Applied Science.

Endres, T. & Renkl, A. (2015). Mechanisms behind the testing effect: An empirical investigation of retrieval practice in meaningful learning. *Frontiers in Psychology*, *6*, 1–6.

Godden, D. R. & Baddeley, A. D. (1975). Context-dependent memory in two natural environments: On land and underwater. *British Journal of Psychology*, *66*(3), 325–331.

Grant, H. M., Bredahl, L. C., Clay, J., Ferrie, J., Groves, J. E., McDorman, T. A. & Dark, V. J. (1998). Context-dependent memory for meaningful material: Information for students. *Applied Cognitive Psychology: The Official Journal of the Society for Applied Research in Memory and Cognition*, *12*(6), 617–623.

Gurung, R. A. (2005). How do students really study (and does it matter)? *Education*, *39*, 323–340.

Hyde, T. S. & Jenk ins, J. J. (1969). Differential effects of incidental tasks on the organization of recall of a list of highly associated words. *Journal of Experimental Psychology*, *82*(3), 472–481.

Isarida, T. & Isarida, T. K. (2014). Environmental context-dependent memory. *Advances in Experimental Psychology Research*, 115–151.

Isarida, T., Isarida, T. K. & Sakai, T. (2012). Effects of study time and meaningfulness on environmental context-dependent recognition. *Memory & Cognition*, *40*(8), 1225–1235.

Kang, S. H. & Pashler, H. (2012). Learning painting styles: Spacing is advantageous when it promotes discriminative contrast. *Applied Cognitive Psychology*, *26*(1), 97–103.

Karpicke, J. D. (2017). Retrieval-based learning: A decade of progress. In J. T. Wixted (Ed.), *Cognitive psychology of memory, Vol. 2 of Learning and memory: A comprehensive reference* (J. H. Byrne, Series Ed.) (pp. 487–514). Academic Press.

Karpicke, J. D. & Roediger III, H. L. (2007). Expanding retrieval practice promotes short-term retention, but equally spaced retrieval enhances long-term retention. *Journal of Experimental Psychology: Learning, Memory, and Cognition*, *33*(4), 704.

Karpicke, J. D. & Roediger III, H. L. (2010). Is expanding retrieval a superior method for learning text materials? *Memory & Cognition*, *38*(1), 116–124.

Kornell, N. & Bjork, R. A. (2008). Learning concepts and categories: Is spacing the "enemy of induction"? *Psychological Science*, *19*(6), 585–592.

Küpper-Tetzel, C. E. (2014). Strong effects on weak theoretical grounds: Understanding the distributed practice effect. *Zeitschrift für Psychologie*, *222*, 71–81.

Landauer, T. K. & Bjork, R. A. (1978). Optimum rehearsal patterns and name learning. In M. M. Gruneberg, P. E. Morris & R. N. Sykes (Eds.), *Practical aspects of memory* (pp. 625–632). Academic Press.

McIntyre, S. H. & Munson, J. M. (2008). Exploring cramming: Student behaviors, beliefs, and learning retention in the principles of marketing course. *Journal of Marketing Education*, *30*(3), 226–243.

Rohrer, D. & Taylor, K. (2007). The shuffling of mathematics problems improves learning. *Instructional Science*, *35*(6), 481–498.

Simon, D. A. & Bjork, R. A. (2001). Metacognition in motor learning. *Journal of Experimental Psychology: Learning, Memory, and Cognition*, *27*(4), 907–912.

Smith, S. M. & Vela, E. (2001). Environmental context-dependent memory: A review and meta-analysis. *Psychonomic Bulletin & Review*, *8*(2), 203–220.

Soderstrom, N. C. & Bjork, R. A. (2015). Learning versus performance: An integrative review. *Perspectives on Psychological Science*, 10(2), 176–199.

Storm, B. C., Bjork, R. A. & Storm, J. C. (2010). Optimizing retrieval as a learning event: When and why expanding retrieval practice enhances long-term retention. *Memory & Cognition*, *38*(2), 244–253.

Toppino, T. C. & Cohen, M. S. (2010). Metacognitive control and spaced practice: Clarifying what people do and why. *Journal of Experimental Psychology: Learning, Memory, and Cognition*, *36*(6), 1480–1491.

Index

Made in the USA
Las Vegas, NV
15 February 2023